CONFRONTING POSEIDON

Around the world against the odds

Clive Tully

OFFSHORE
PUBLISHING

Portsmouth ♦ Hayling Island ♦ Mulbarton

First published in the UK 2002 by Offshore Publishing, Suite 11, Portsmouth Enterprise Centre, Quartremaine Road, Portsmouth, PO3 5QT

Copyright © 2002 Clive Tully
All photographs © Clive Tully unless otherwise indicated

Cover design by Sue Miller
Map by Juliet Percival

The right of Clive Tully to be identified as the Author of the Work has been asserted by him in accordance with the Copyright, Designs and Patents Act 1988.

British Library Cataloguing-in-Publication Data.
A CIP record for this book is available from the British Library.

ISBN 0-9544093-0-2

Printed and bound in Great Britain by Holbrooks Printers Ltd., Portsmouth.

All rights reserved.

No part of this publication may be reproduced, stored in a retrieval system, or transmitted in any form or by any means, electronic, mechanical, photocopying, recording or otherwise, without the prior written permission of the publisher.

The contents of this book are believed correct at the time of publication. Whilst every care has been taken to ensure that factual information given is accurate, neither the author nor the publishers can be held responsible for the consequences of any errors or omissions, or for any changes in details given.

CONTENTS

Acknowledgements		6
Frontispiece		7
Prologue		8
1	The Challenge	10
2	Having a Smashing Time	18
3	Communications	30
4	Marlboro Mania	35
5	In the Beginning	50
6	Going Commando	60
7	The Weather	69
8	A Fiery Meal	73
9	Logistics	80
10	The Most Expensive Crisps in the World	84
11	Filming the Documentary	100
12	Betrayal	105
13	Sponsorship	111
14	And Then There Were Three	118
15	Close to Rolling	128
16	Cardiff	136
17	Our New Shipmate	140
18	Windy Japan	146
19	Building the Boat	154
20	The Empty Quarter	162
21	'They Might Shoot You'	167
22	The Great American Dream	173
23	Along the Aleutians	186
24	Perceptions	195
25	A Long Way to Go for a Barbecue	199
26	Night of the Flying Squid	217
27	From one Ocean to Another	233
28	The Ultimate Low	242
29	From the Ridiculous to the Sublime	250
30	The Longest Day	265
Epilogue		272
Appendix I		276
Appendix II		279

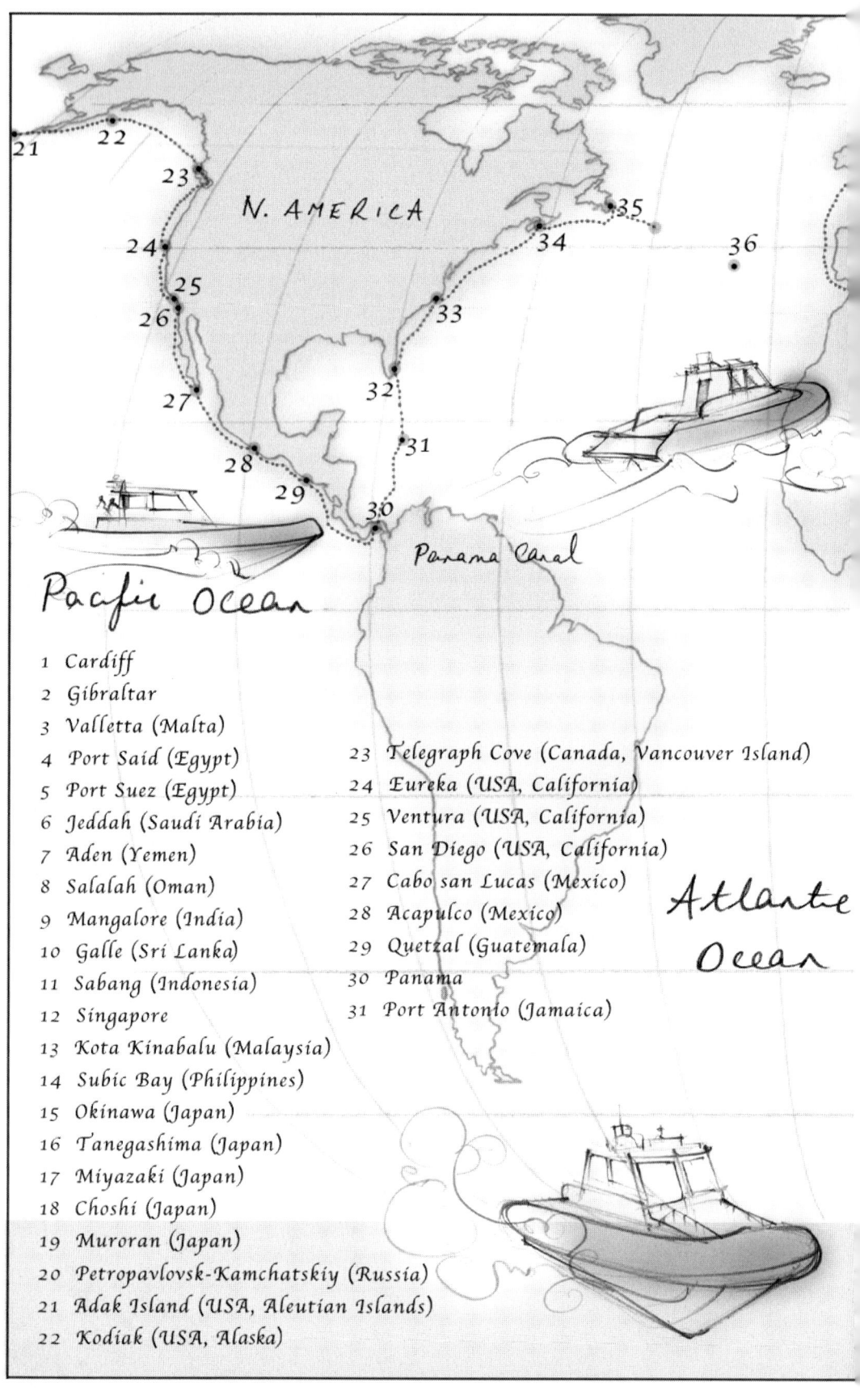

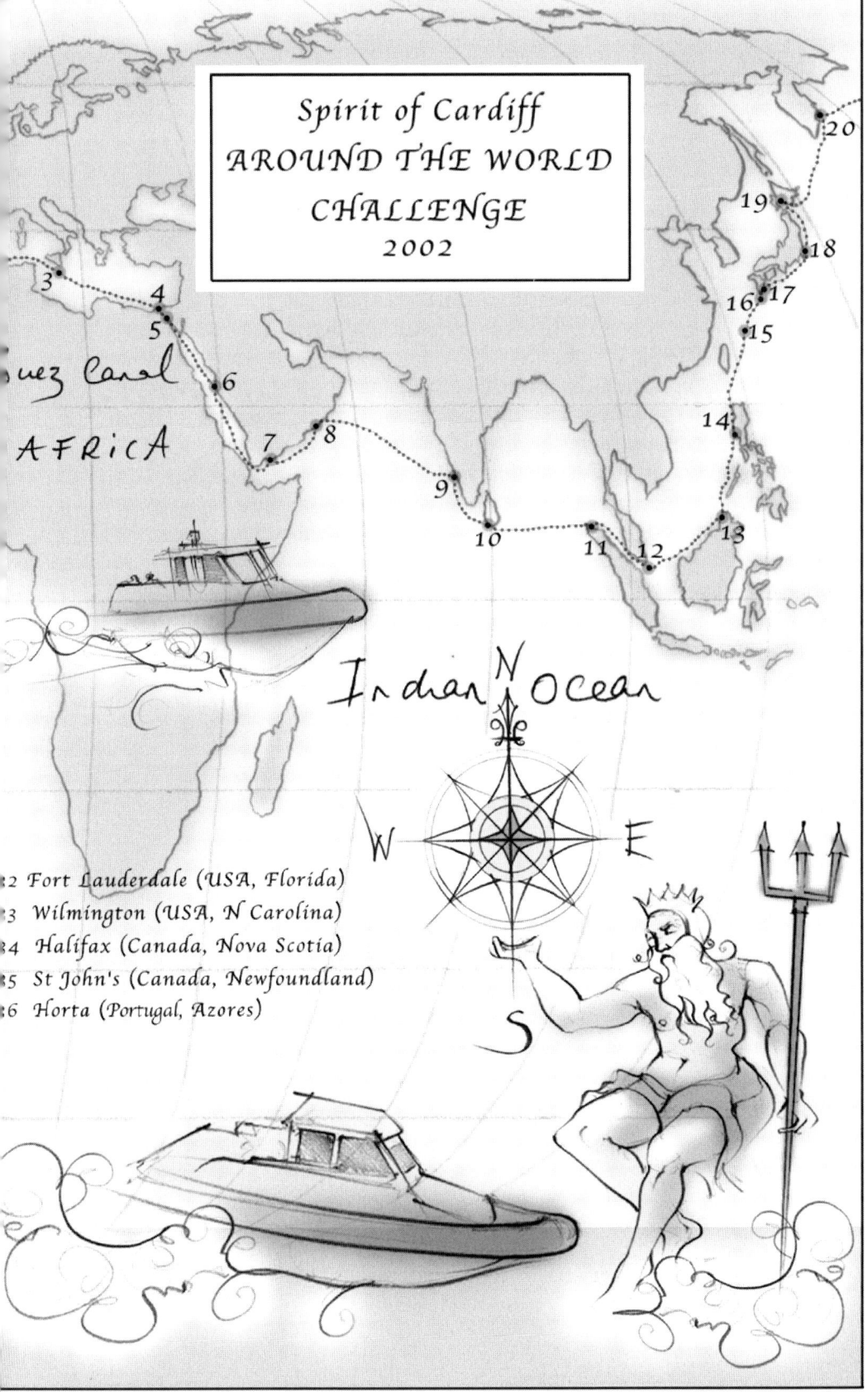

Acknowledgements

IT WAS A pure fluke that led me to Alan Priddy, and I hope a fortuitous one. So first of all my thanks to him and to Steve Lloyd and Jan Falkowski for inviting me to join the crew and providing me with a story. It's been one hell of a ride, both on and off the boat, but I wouldn't have passed it up for anything.

While I normally pride myself on writing scintillating copy which needs no further intervention, in this particular case, my words have definitely benefited from Sue Bryant's editorial skills, not just in tightening things up, but teasing out further explanations where she felt they were necessary.

Thanks too to everyone who posted messages on the Spirit of Cardiff website during the voyage. We couldn't see the website itself while under way, but many of the messages were emailed to us. They lifted our spirits, gave us hope, made us laugh. I've shamelessly plundered the best of them to use as some of my chapter headings.

The events which came together to produce this story have been so numerous, that it was necessary for the sake of relative brevity to leave some out. So I apologise in advance to anyone who doesn't find themselves in these pages when they felt they ought to have been there. To everyone who had a hand in this remarkable story, I extend a heartfelt thanks.

Clive Tully
November 2002

IT IS NOT the critic who counts;
not the man who points out how the strong man stumbles,
or where the doer of deeds could have done them better.
The credit belongs to the man who is actually in the arena,
whose face is marred by dust and sweat and blood,
who strives valiantly; who errs and comes short again and again;
because there is not effort without error and shortcomings;
but who does actually strive to do the deed;
who knows the great enthusiasm,
the great devotion,
who spends himself in a worthy cause,
who at the best knows in the end the triumph of high achievement
and who at the worst, if he fails,
at least he fails while daring greatly.
So that his place shall never be with those cold and timid souls
who know neither victory nor defeat.

Theodore Roosevelt

Prologue

Just heard you've been struck by lightning. Hope you're all OK!
Text message to Alan Priddy from misinformed supporter.

THE SEA IS behind us, the waves short, steep and powerful. The effect on a large boat might not be so pronounced, but for a powerboat just 33 feet (10 metres) long, every movement and change of attitude feels massive. They lift the boat up at the tail, hurling us forward into the wave in front. When the windscreen goes, it isn't so much like driving into a huge wall - more like colliding with a truck. It's a double whammy. The first wave leaves us more or less unscathed, but is immediately followed by a second. It hits with a short, sharp whack which turns the glass frosty. It all happens so quickly, there's no time to shout out or be afraid. But then as the water subsides my reactions catch up, and for a second I'm playing the next possible scenario in my head - the windscreen going completely with the next wave, and half a ton of sea water crashing into the cabin. And maybe, just maybe, we don't make it.

We're in the Atlantic, off Cape St Vincent in Portugal's Algarve, and although over 600 miles away, we're getting the aftermath of a major storm which has devastated the Canaries. Easter in Tenerife has seen the heaviest rain on record, the resulting flash floods killing several people in the capital, Santa Cruz, and making hundreds homeless. It's day three of our passage from Cardiff to Gibraltar, the preliminary to our attempt to make a record circumnavigation of the world, and things aren't going brilliantly. Already we've suffered electrical gremlins which have reduced us to travelling at night with no navigation lights, the autopilot has thrown a wobbler, and the boat's trim tabs - important for keeping the most efficient attitude in the water - aren't working properly. Individually, the problems aren't much more than minor annoyances. Together they add up to less sleep and more stress.

Fortunately the windscreen holds, but both panes are shattered, held together by the internal layer of plastic laminate which has saved us. Glistening in the sunlight, the screens now look like crazy paving, bowed inwards from the force of the impact, and it's virtually impossible to see through them. There are tears here and there in the laminate, and with every subsequent wave, water jets or dribbles through, depending on how hard it hits.

After a brief stop in Lagos to refuel and assess the damage, we're now making the best speed that we can. But here, whipped up by 25 knot winds, the waves once again are short and steep. The result, continuing to drive the boat manually after the autopilot has failed, is that we stuff her snub inflated bow several more times into large waves. Watching the spectacle of huge curtains of spray with a certain degree of amusement - what normally accompanies such an event - is replaced by acute anxiety. With every fresh impact, the cracks in our shattered windscreens become wider and more elongated. Water is jetting in and running over the instrument panel. At one point we have no fewer than four pieces of electronic equipment emitting loud beeping noises to indicate they're malfunctioning. Things are getting decidedly dangerous.

As the sun goes down, we have to be even more careful. Normally on autopilot, the boat essentially drives itself, with one member of the watch as 'throttle jockey' ready to knock the revs back if necessary. But now we have to steer as well, and for a while, it looks as though my handheld GPS receiver is about to be promoted to prime navigation equipment. We limp on towards Gibraltar at reduced speed, taking turns to drive through the night. Luckily for us, as the sun goes down, so does the wind, and the boat's navigation equipment decides to work once more.

We arrive at Sheppards Marina in Gibraltar in the early hours of the 4th April, more than a day behind schedule. We're shattered, suffering from lack of sleep, bruised and aching from the violent motion of the boat in such rough seas, with carpets and belongings soaked from the uninvited sea water. After three and a half days and 1,200 nautical miles, we've brought Spirit of Cardiff through one of her roughest passages ever.

And we haven't even started.

1
THE CHALLENGE

IN 1997, ALAN Priddy, Jan Falkowski and Steve Lloyd crossed the Atlantic Ocean in a 7.5 metre (25 feet) Rigid Inflatable Boat, or RIB, called the Spirit of Portsmouth. No crossing of such a large ocean could ever be dismissed lightly, and particularly not this one. They took a route from Portsmouth, New Hampshire to Portsmouth, England, retracing the Viking burial grounds through Newfoundland, Labrador and Greenland. The crossing took three weeks, during which time the crew encountered icy conditions which afflicted them with frostbite, and violent storms which at one point had them posted by the UK coastguard as missing. Most remarkable was the fact that the boat had no cabin, making them the first completely open vessel to cross the Atlantic at such a high latitude in a thousand years - since the time of the Vikings.

The following year, Alan and crew were nominated for the BT Yachting Journalists' Association's prestigious Yachtsman of the Year award. It was won by Pete Goss for his selfless actions in rescuing fellow competitor Raphael Dinelli during the Vendée Globe round-the-world yacht race, but Alan and his crew came runners-up - no mean feat considering the stiff opposition, and a miracle given that it was the first (and indeed last) time that a powerboater had been considered for the award. The inevitable question afterwards, was: "How do you follow that?"

'It actually didn't take that long to come up with the answer,' admits Alan. 'Once I'd decided I did want to follow it with another boating project, the only logical step after a transatlantic was around the world.'

Alan left school when he was 15, and was indentured as a boat builder. He did that till he was 17, then setting up his own business.

But despite his boat-building qualifications, he started a garage, fixing taxis during the evenings, kicking it off by working during the day as a labourer for three bricklayers. He did that for two years, working virtually 20 hours a day, by which time he'd built up sufficient funds not to have to work on the building site any more.

It also made him enough money to indulge his passion for fast cars. He had a Lotus Seven for fine weather, along with a Triumph Spitfire for less pleasant conditions and other occasional use. By the time he was 20, Alan was driving a Bentley, 'at which point,' he adds jokingly, 'it all started to go downhill.'

In all of Alan's 49 years, there are just eight in which he wasn't messing around with some kind of boat - everything from canoes, dinghies and sailing boats to powerboats. 'I just loved being on the water,' he admits.

But perhaps it was fate taking a hand in 1989 when he spotted a magazine advert looking to set up a group of like-minded people to do some exploring in Rigid Inflatable Boats. It ended up with a group of 40 setting off from Inverness to go for a jolly all the way around Scotland. The rest, as they say, is history. Alan became hooked, and using his boat-building and engineering skills, started to develop RIBs for more extreme cruising, amassing a series of world records along the way.

He was accompanied on all his boating exploits by Steve Lloyd. Steve is married to Alan's younger sister Jenette - not that it needed the pressure of family ties to make Steve want to join in. He has as much salt water coursing through his veins as Alan, and has been sailing since he was a boy. Both he and Alan are Portsmouth lads, but it was Steve who retained the distinctive Pompey accent. His day job as a carpet and floor layer was physically demanding, so he was a good deal fitter and tougher than most, and surprisingly perhaps for such an occupation, incredibly well-travelled.

'The company I worked for had the contract to fit carpets in British embassies all over the world,' he explains. 'We'd fly out business class and stay in four-star hotels.' It also meant bumping into the occasional pieces of privileged information. 'I'd been asked to carpet the floor of the secure communications room of the embassy in Reykjavik,' says Steve with a huge smile on his face, 'when suddenly the telex machine burst into life. I found out the Falklands had been invaded by Argentina long before it made the news headlines.'

And then there's Jan. Dr Jan Falkowski is one of Britain's most eminent psychiatrists, and even though only in his early forties, was in charge of the drugs and alcohol dependency unit of a major London hospital. Those that know him might say he comes across more like one of his patients than the doctor. The classic example is when he drank himself virtually comatose while with Alan one time. When asked later why he did it, Jan explains: 'How can I understand my patients unless I experience what they do?' Such dedication...

Jan is into racing RIBs, a real tough nut, and after crossing the Atlantic with Spirit of Cardiff in 2001, barely had time to draw breath before making the first new record circumnavigation of Britain in nine years - in a small open RIB. But whilst he's qualified as a doctor on the psychiatric side, he's also a trained army medic, which could perhaps prove more useful on long expeditions. Up until two or three years ago, he served as an officer in one of the territorial units of the Special Air Service. When we crossed the Atlantic in Spirit of Cardiff, I asked him why he was reading a fairly dry-looking book about Sarajevo. 'Just wanted to relive a few happy memories,' he replied with a tantalising air of mystery.

When it came to planning the round-the-world trip, it was Jan who had the suggestions for some fairly exotic armaments to take care of any potential issues with pirates - one of our biggest concerns. They included high-powered automatic rifles firing tracer and phosphor-tipped rounds, and a lightweight ceramic rocket launcher. Sadly for us, but fortunately perhaps for the pirates, Jan was forced to drop out from the crew at the beginning of March 2002, just three weeks before departure. With a crisis in the National Health Service and his hospital trust on the verge of bankruptcy, there was no way Jan could contemplate taking two months off.

He was replaced at the last minute by Alan Carter, an outside broadcast TV cameraman, who although English like the rest of us, lived in Penarth, next door to Cardiff. Apart from giving the crew the closest approximation we could hope for to a Welsh flavour, he'd been involved with the project on and off over the past couple of years with the production of promotional videos, so we felt his skills would be invaluable. Now we had a professional TV cameraman to help us produce a classy video of the voyage. Of course, Alan Carter couldn't believe his luck being asked to join the crew at the eleventh hour. If there was any drawback right from the start, it was that we would have two Alans on board. We agreed for the sake of avoiding confusion that Alan Carter would henceforth be known as Al.

And then there's me. After a brief spell chasing stardom as bass player in a rock band in the 1970s, I settled down, if you can call it that, to a life of adventure travel journalism. I was equipment editor of a number of walking magazines, reviewing clothing and equipment for walking and camping, and in my own small way contributing to the way outdoors equipment developed over a number of years. I also spent a good deal of time travelling abroad, researching travel features for national newspapers, and producing a monthly travel programme for local radio stations nationwide. Along the way I managed to build up my own tally of interesting achievements, including becoming the first journalist to fly in a hot air balloon in Russia, descending to the bottom of Windermere in the Lake District in a submersible, and leading a trek in Nepal for British Everest legend Doug Scott.

It was the strangest quirk of fate which led me to meeting Alan Priddy. I injured my ankle on a big trek in Kazakhstan in 1998, badly enough to put paid to my aspirations for serious walks for the next year. In the meantime, I took to writing about activities with a watery flavour. A colleague of mine introduced me to Alan in early 1999 via the Public Relations consultant for Yamaha Motors. Alan had just built his round-the-world boat, complete with shiny new Yamaha engine, and he was looking for someone fool enough to go for a ride in it and conjure up a suitably dramatic story to help publicise the project.

My mistake was to ask him whether I could spend a night on board, so I could get the feel for what it would be like trying to sleep on the high seas in something the size of a small camper van. Before I knew it, I'd agreed to join a record attempt on the British Isles - a feat in itself for someone whose previous experience of large expanses of water was mainly limited to those surrounded by tiles. Somehow along the way I ended up being conned into joining the crew.

While the crew which left Cardiff on Easter Sunday - Alan, Steve, Al and me - were all without doubt four very different people, the one thing we had in common was our age - we were all born in 1953. A great year, of course. The first ascent of Everest, and the Queen's coronation. And if anyone was going to say something stupid like 'You're all too old to be doing this,' I was ready to counter with the fact that Chris Bonington didn't climb Everest until he was 50.

On the face of it, the challenge sounded pretty straightforward. Since the international governing body of powerboating, the Union Internationale Motonautique (UIM), came into being, there had been just one successful record attempt at circumnavigating the world. The 35 metre (115 feet) Cable and Wireless Adventurer went from Gibraltar to Gibraltar in 74 days 20 hours and 58 minutes in 1998, her route through the Suez and Panama Canals taking her on the closest you can get to a great circle route (in other words, the fat bit) around the world. Sailing circumnavigations of the world happen a good deal more regularly, although some would say that whilst the distance is pretty much on a par, those which sail down the Atlantic and circle Antarctica before coming back up again aren't really doing it properly.

The big difference with a powerboat is that you're restricted by its range, and that's dictated by the size of its fuel tanks and the rate at which the engine consumes the fuel. Not only does the force which propels it not come for free, but the wind which sends sailing boats scudding across the waves at 30 knots usually works against a powerboat. Refuelling stops have to be organised - the rules dictate you have to do it from fixed installations, so mid-ocean refuelling is out.

And you have the problems of bureaucracy with every country you visit. Going through the Suez and Panama Canals guarantees not just the closest you can get to a great circle route around the world, but the most aggravation from countries less than imbued with the spirit of competition and fast turn-rounds in port.

1998 saw several attempts at circumnavigating the world under the new UIM rules. All except Cable and Wireless Adventurer, whose attempt was backed by multi-million dollar sponsorship and blessed with near perfect weather, failed, one of them coming unstuck when their boat ran into an 'uncharted reef'. But because they were setting rather than breaking a record, the Cable and Wireless team chose 80 days as their target time, aligning their feat with a little-known but remarkable powered circumnavigation undertaken in 1960 - at the time in conditions of absolute secrecy - by the American nuclear submarine USS Triton, recorded in the Guinness Book of Records as having made the journey in 83 days, nine hours and 54 minutes.

It was the early days of the Cold War, and President Dwight D. Eisenhower wanted to present Soviet premier Nikita Khrushchev with a number of examples of superior American technology and achievement at a forthcoming summit meeting in Paris. One of them was the maiden voyage of the USS Triton. She would circle the world submerged by the Magellan route around Cape Horn and the Cape of Good Hope, and she would do it completely undetected by friend or foe. The voyage was a success, but on the 1st May 1960, five days before Triton was due to return to her base in New London, Connecticut, and just over two weeks before the summit, Gary Powers' U-2 spy plane was shot down over Sverdlovsk in Western Siberia.

The Paris summit collapsed as relations between the USA and Soviet Union descended to a new icy low. The Triton crew's triumphal tickertape parade down Broadway was cancelled, and the whole thing was hushed up. At least until submarine commander Edward L. Beach wrote a book about the voyage two years later.

Unfortunately, the pertinent facts from 'Around the World submerged - the Voyage of the Triton' somehow didn't make it into the Guinness Book of Records, which has the Triton circumnavigating the world in 83 days, nine hours and 54 minutes. But according to Edward Beach, the actual time taken was 60 days 21 hours. I was lucky enough to track down Captain Tom B. Thamm USN, Diving Officer on board the USS Triton during its voyage around the world. He confirmed to me that the circumnavigation was indeed 60 days 21 hours, starting and finishing at St Peter and St Paul's Rocks, a small outcrop of mid-Atlantic rocks belonging to Brazil.

'The Cable and Wireless Adventurer did not beat Triton's record if it took them 75 days to circumnavigate the earth,' he said. 'And if their route was 4,752 statute miles shorter than ours, they simply aren't even close.' Interestingly, the time of 83 days nine hours 54 minutes as quoted by the Guinness Book of Records is actually the total length of the USS Triton's dive (not even the time from dock to dock), which includes all of the route in the North Atlantic before and after the actual circumnavigation.

When a London news agency contacted Guinness World Records about the discrepancy just before we set off from Gibraltar on our circumnavigation attempt, they replied: 'If the US Department of Defense would care to present us with all the facts, we'll look at it again.' Maybe a book written by the submarine commander which has been in the public domain for 40 years and the personal testimony of one of Triton's 18 officers isn't quite enough for them...

Be that as it may, the one undeniable fact was that the Cable and Wireless Adventurer circumnavigated the world in 1998 under UIM rules, and that was the basis upon which we aimed to take them on. Initially the target was to knock over three weeks off their record, but as experience with Spirit of Cardiff grew during her three years of test runs, we modified our aims to what we believed to be a more achievable 60 days. That was still two weeks under their record.

The record attempts from 1999 to 2001 helped us refine our expectations of what the boat could do. We expected to be able to cruise at between 20 and 25 knots, burning around 1.8 to 2 litres of diesel per nautical mile. With fuel tank capacity a colossal 2,850 litres, we knew we had a range of around 1,200 nautical miles. The choice of fuel stops was pretty much based on seeing what places were within range of the preceding stop, and what facilities they had to offer. Every 5,000 miles or so, we would also need to have the boat lifted out of the water to perform the one piece of essential maintenance which couldn't be done afloat - changing the gearbox oil. So it was we built up our route with 31 stops, chosen for the time of year which offered optimum weather conditions.

Unlike a round-the-world sailing race such as the BT Global Challenge, time spent in port on a powered circumnavigation is time that's still ticking away on the clock. Out of their 74 plus days overall, Adventurer spent 62 days at sea. By getting our 'pit stops' out of the way as quickly as possible, we hoped to reduce our time spent in port. The plan was to use teams of ground crews who would meet us at every port to cut through all the red tape and handle all the refuelling and servicing. Our other big advantage was the fact that whilst less than a third of the size of Adventurer, Spirit of Cardiff was the faster boat. We proved that in October 2000 when we bagged the fastest of their port-to-port records from Gibraltar to Monaco, convincing us we could break their record.

But it would take more than a fast boat and will-power to do it.

2
HAVING A SMASHING TIME

Glad you are up and running for a flying, rocky start. Have a good trip but don't get Malta Cross.
Website posting from Tony Lee-Elliott.

It's just after 1800 on March 30th, the day before we're due to set off for Gibraltar, and I'm in my room at the Hanover International hotel in Cardiff. I'm getting ready for our farewell party at the Waterguard pub at Cardiff Bay, when I ring Alan Priddy's mobile.

'Have you seen the news? The Queen Mother's died.'

Not that we'd dream of wishing ill on the grand old lady of the Royal family, but as far as Spirit of Cardiff is concerned, about to set off on the big voyage, this is especially bad news. A nation in mourning seemed unlikely to turn out for what we hoped would be a high-profile departure.

'That's not the half of it,' replies Alan. 'The council has just cancelled all of tomorrow's events. We could end up with no send-off.'

In the end, the repercussions don't affect us that much, and we get a fantastic turn-out as well. The whole weekend has been busy, with people thronging around Cardiff Bay and the Spirit of Cardiff visitor centre on a hot sunny Saturday, and Michael Rees, chaplain of Cardiff Bay holding a short service on board the lightship in Roath Basin to bless the crew. Then it's across to the Norwegian church to bless the boat, moored nearby. Whilst not what you'd call God-fearing folk, we nevertheless very much appreciate the moment, and the sentiment behind it.

Despite Sunday's gloom, both in weather and general mood, there's a considerable crowd gathered at Mermaid Quay to see us off, with short speeches of good wishes from Welsh First Minister Rhodri Morgan, Cardiff South MP Alun Michael and Assembly Member Lorraine Barrett. This isn't the official start of the timed circumnavigation - that takes place in Gibraltar - but leaving the boat's adopted home city was always going to be a big event. The last major maritime expedition to leave Cardiff was Captain Scott, when he set off for the South Pole in 1911. Naturally, we're hoping for better luck than he had. Then we board Spirit and head out across the bay towards the barrage, accompanied by a wonderful flotilla of small craft, some Rigid Inflatable Boats like ours, some sailing yachts, many of them sounding their horns.

I wonder if any of them are puzzled that all four of us are able to appear on the aft deck to pose for the cameras, without anyone apparently driving the boat. The secret is one of Spirit of Cardiff's sophisticated gadgets, a remote control unit which allows us to steer the boat from just about anywhere on board.

And then we're in the lock ready to pass out from Cardiff Bay, and into the Bristol Channel. There are people here, too, gathered around the railings at the top, peering down at us, and giving us a hearty wave. After the mild nerves of all the attention we've had this morning, I'm getting more in my stride now, enjoying the moment.

We've had enough trips out along the Bristol Channel to know that the first part of the journey isn't one to look forward to, and it certainly lives up to its reputation this time. The run down to Land's End is like driving down a cart track strewn with boulders. It's not long before we're down to six or seven knots, battering our way painfully through head seas pushed at us by 25 knot winds. As the bow slams into the oncoming waves, the sea cascades over the windscreen, sometimes just a splattering of spray, sometimes in bathfuls which completely swamp us.

The first mishap, if you can call it that, happens pretty soon. Quite often in head seas you come off the top of a wave and the boat essentially falls into a hole on the other side. Steve's bunk breaks with him on it as we come down particularly heavily. For our record-breaking test runs over the last couple of years, we've been sleeping across the back of the cabin, one on a bunk made up across the two rear seats, one on cushions on the floor between the front and rear seats. Not overly comfortable for the taller members of the crew (me), the arrangement also had the major drawback of putting two sleeping bodies in the way of the cabin's doorway at the back. The new arrangement has bunks on each side of the cabin, with the sleeper's feet going into the box upon which the seat in front is mounted. It's more comfortable, and it leaves the gangway clear for those on watch to use the cabin doorway without having to disturb those sleeping. But the bunks clearly need some reinforcement if they're to stand up to treatment as rough as this. Alan and Steve start to make a shopping list of all the bits and pieces they'll need to get in Gibraltar.

Monday 1st April

Today is April Fool's Day. Given that we're still bashing head seas, and it's cold and wet, nothing could be more apt. After eating virtually nothing yesterday, today I've been having a few more nibbles, as well as a lunch of tinned tuna fish. It's not that I'm feeling seasick at all. It's just a question of getting used to being on the water again after nearly a year.

The wind has dropped by around 10 knots, and we've managed to increase our speed to 15 knots, so we're making much better progress. Our weather man, Bertie, with whom we make contact by satellite phone once a day, reckons we're through the worst of it, and if we head further west into the Atlantic, we'll pick up a northerly which will be just the job for Spain and Portugal. Alan reckons about Monday lunchtime for Spain. As my eyes raise in eager anticipation of sunshine and warmth, he adds: 'northern Spain.'

Our electrical problems seem to continue. Having discovered on Saturday that the trim tab electrics didn't work (and hot-wiring them to correct the problem) we find shortly after we set off yesterday that we can have either navigation equipment or navigation lights, but not both. We opt for the former, hence our interesting close encounter with a fishing boat off Land's End last night.

I'm still not sufficiently acclimatised to the motion of the boat to be able to pee with confidence. Last night's various attempts are only marginally successful, with a lot of it catching in the wind and going down my trousers. Later on in the morning, we have an official poo stop. Rather than put the door on and provide a little privacy, prospective pooers make their way to the well in the bow between the tube and the front of the forward cabin, where a large plastic bucket awaits. In order to get round the washing problem, pooers are equipped with thin plastic gloves with which to wield their toilet paper, so the whole operation takes on a vaguely surgical quality.

Next drama to crop up will be fuel, but at this stage, it will be merely a pumping operation from one tank to another. The boat has four fuel tanks, but the engine takes its feed only from the main tank, so as it empties, we transfer fuel from the forward or side tanks. We're obviously in a main shipping lane as we begin our crossing of Biscay, with lots of large cargo ships in sight.

Tuesday 2nd April

As day dawns, somehow I expect it to fulfil the promise of last night, and better weather. It doesn't. Although we're making good speed at around 19 knots, we're heading straight for a patch of ominously dark clouds. It's actually right over the point where we make contact (not quite) with the Spanish coast at Cap Finisterre, a wild and beautiful coastline, but marred somewhat by a wind farm next to the lighthouse.

After a reasonable crossing of Biscay, we're punching big head seas once more. A powerboat going into the wind not only wastes a lot of fuel without making much headway, it can be excruciatingly painful as the boat drops off the tops of the waves, sometimes several feet into the troughs on the other side. At the very least it can mean cuts and bruises from being thrown about, to internal injuries brought on by the severe shaking. When it's like this, all you can do is wish you were somewhere else. Al admits he's suffering from the runs, which must be quite an achievement, given that we're nowhere near Egypt. Mind you, the diet of instant convenience foods is a far cry from the vegetarian dishes he's used to. He seems to be taking it all quite stoically, but something inside me tells me he's not that happy with it. We shall see.

We spot a sailing yacht heading straight out to sea, and I wonder out loud whether he's sailing to America. 'He can do anything he likes,' replies Alan, 'he's got the wind up his arse. Come to think of it, that's what Al's got.'

Today seems to have been about changing plans. At one point, we're taking such a hammering that Alan decides to head for Porto.

'We're in danger of breaking both us and the boat,' he says.

'And you always said you'd put out a sea anchor rather than take a beating,' adds Steve.

Spirit of Cardiff is probably the most seaworthy boat afloat for its size, and with the engine cut back, she just bobs about happily in the worst conditions. But if we found ourselves in mountainous seas, we have the added safety feature of a sea anchor, essentially a large parachute deployed in the water beneath the boat to keep it stable even in impossibly heavy seas.

But half an hour later, the plan changes again. We decide that whilst it would be good getting into Porto, it would be a fight to get back out again, so better to stay out and just reduce our speed.

Wednesday 3rd April

The last 24 hours have seen conditions that would make going 10 rounds with Mike Tyson seem a much safer option. We've had big head seas with everybody getting battered and bruised to some extent. My personal contribution to the injury catalogue is a bruised head where I nutted the cabin wall several times.

But true to our weather forecaster's form, the wind does turn, and for a while we have a large rolling beam sea, big Atlantic rollers with several thousand miles of momentum behind them. And then gradually the seas came round behind us.

Following seas are always exciting. The boat seems to take forever to claw its way to the top of a wave, as the crest tries to race ahead of us. Then there's a moment as the boat reaches the top of the wave, the bow lifts up into the air, and for several seconds it wallows around aimlessly. Then the bow slams down into the water, and something akin to a runaway train ride begins as we surf down the wave.

It's in these conditions somewhere north of Lisbon that the autopilot decides to pack up, emitting a loud beeping to inform us it's no longer in control. Not the kind of thing you can repair on the move, we're now driving the boat manually, and have arranged with manufacturers Raymarine to have a new unit flown out to Gibraltar tomorrow. Driving without autopilot demands more concentration, not only because you need to ensure you keep the right heading, but also driving around rather than through the waves.

But that's not the end of the drama. During mid-morning, in continuing heavy following seas, Alan manages to stuff the bow of the boat into a large wave, shattering both front windscreens. The location couldn't be more symbolic. Barren and windswept Cape St Vincent in Portugal's Algarve is where the most south-westerly cliffs of Europe jut out into the Atlantic Ocean. Even before Roman times, the area was considered sacred. In the middle ages, Prince Henry the Navigator came here to establish his Vila do Infante, or Town of the Prince. On the southern edge of the peninsula, he set up a school for navigators - the explorers who subsequently founded the Portuguese empire. Until the Americas were discovered, the Cape was widely held to be the end of the world. It could very well have been for us.

Over 300 years after Prince Henry, and this was the place that my fellow Norfolkman Horatio Nelson saw the beginnings of his rise to fame. Vastly outnumbered, a Royal Navy squadron of 15 ships won a resounding victory against the Spanish fleet at the Battle of Cape St Vincent on 14th February 1797. Admiral of the Fleet Sir John Jervis subsequently became Earl St Vincent, whilst Commodore Nelson, whose daring rearguard action won the day, was knighted.

For us, the historical significance of the place which nearly ends our round the world record attempt before it has begun is rather lost. Our priority is to make sure we don't get shoved into any more large waves, and that our already severely weakened windscreens don't cave in completely. The past two or three days of fighting heavy seas have used more fuel than expected, so we call in to Lagos to refuel, taking the opportunity to inspect the damage more closely. The windscreens aren't just shattered, but completely bowed in. It's fortunate that both laminate and the glue which secures the screens to the frames have held. Hopefully, with some reinforcing tape round the more badly damaged port screen, they should hold out till we can effect a proper repair in Gibraltar.

'This is what the trip should have been like,' says Alan as we set off again from Lagos in bright sunshine. He's mindful of the fact that Al has had something of a baptism of fire.

It's a relief when we finally arrive in Gibraltar, a day later than expected, and make arrangements to replace the broken windscreens. We've come here at a significant moment in Gibraltar's history. That famous lump of limestone at the entrance to the Mediterranean, for centuries a symbol of strength and reliability, is now under threat.

Although British since 1704, and a member of the European Union under the British Treaty of Accession, moves are afoot to come to an accommodation with the Spanish Government over the sovereignty of Gibraltar. Less than two weeks before we set off from Cardiff, a massive demonstration takes place, with practically all of Gibraltar's 28,000 population taking to the streets to protest at what they see as the British Government selling them down the river, denying them the right to determine their own future.

Having just passed the 20th anniversary of the Argentine invasion of the Falklands whilst we were crossing the Bay of Biscay, I can't help but draw a parallel. The Argentineans fought for the islands. We fought for the people who lived there who wanted to remain British. Spain wants Gibraltar, and the people who live there don't want to be Spanish. They want to stay British. Unlike the Falklands, Gibraltar doesn't cost the British taxpayer anything. So where's the difference that makes trampling on the Gibraltarians' rights of self-determination worthwhile?

With repairs to the boat under way, we have time to attend a reception generously thrown for us in the City Hall by the Mayor of Gibraltar, Judge John Alcantara, who tells us that he is in fact visiting Cardiff next week. Alan presents him with a plaque and letter of greeting from Cardiff's mayor Russell Goodway, and he reciprocates with a Gibraltar plaque. Over the course of the round the world voyage, our gifts from Cardiff prove increasingly embarassing. Apart from the plaques, we have some unbelievably tacky mouse mats, and some CD-Roms about Cardiff. By contrast, we receive gifts which say much more about the people who gave them.

Sunday 7th April

The wind whistles through the masts in the marina, and the sky is heavy and grey. Not a good day to set off on a world record attempt, but for us, it's THE day, whatever the weather. It's Alan's birthday as well. The second of our merry throng to turn 49, with Alan Carter's in three days time. Some journalists from the specialist boating press along with a camera crew from HTV Wales have flown out to see us off, which if nothing else, helps make the goodbyes a little fuller. Not quite what we had from Cardiff, for sure. What happened to the chief minister and the Royal Gibraltar Artillery Regiment gun that had been mooted as part of the send-off? We really are second-class record-breakers.

Even so, I'm feeling a pang of excitement that the record attempt is about to start, tempered with misgivings about the weather. Just before we left Cardiff, someone asked Steve and me what was in our heads at that point. Steve's reply was: 'If we had anything in our heads, we wouldn't be doing this at all.' If I felt anything in Cardiff, it was all about butterflies for the big occasion. Now I'm starting to think more about the daunting task ahead.

With smashed windscreens repaired, broken autopilot replaced, and everything prepared for the first leg of the voyage, we set out from Sheppards Marina, and make our way to the harbour entrance. Waiting there is Gibraltar's Customs launch, with RYA official timer Wayne Warwick, along with a pilot vessel for the media. We pass the harbour entrance at just a few seconds past midday local time (1000 GMT), starting off on an epic voyage which will hopefully see us arriving back in Gibraltar in substantially less than the 74 days 20 hours 58 minutes taken by the Cable and Wireless Adventurer in 1998.

Two hours later and we're in the thick of a storm, reduced to seven knots. Worse still is the fact that the replacement autopilot has blown, so once again we're back to driving the boat manually. Alan thinks the gears may have stripped.

Suddenly a cargo ship appears from behind us. He's supposed to have given us a wide berth, but he cuts us up as he comes past. At least we decide to put him to some good use as he's heading roughly in the direction of Algiers. We trail him east for a while before deciding he's actually heading further north than we'd like.

Before it gets dark, I manage to fire up my notebook computer, transfer copy to it from the Psion handheld and a digital photograph from my Nikon, and send them all out via the satphone to update the Spirit of Cardiff website. Trying to get my ideal choice - the Psion - talking to the satphone just a day before we set off from Cardiff proved fruitless. Getting a computer and modem talking to each other is something of a black art, particularly when neither manufacturer acknowledges the possibility that you might try to use the two together. So far I've been sending emails with my Psion and mobile phone when there's network coverage, but it's hellishly expensive abroad. Getting the Psion working with the satphone with its sponsored airtime is a top priority, particularly as the notebook is unusable in most conditions.

During the worst of the weather, the boat proves particularly hard to control. One second we're on our correct course heading east, the next we're spun round in almost the opposite direction. It's a good job the position tracking kit (which we assume has started working even though we can't easily check) sends out a fix every hour. Otherwise the web site would show us tracing a drunken squiggle as a course.

The one consolation we have is that we know the worst of the weather experienced by Cable and Wireless Adventurer was in the Mediterranean. It'll be calm seas and sunshine after we get to Suez. That at least is the hope. On a personal note, the toilet situation is marginally improved, with the risk to my trouser legs somewhat reduced. There now seems to be an abundant supply of buckets, so I can stand in the deck well, brace my hands on the side of the boat, and pee into a bucket resting on the side fuel tank.

Monday 8th April

This morning sees the weather much improved. After yesterday's horrendous squalls and heavy seas, the sun has showed its face, and the seas have calmed considerably. It certainly feels much warmer, and the sea has flattened off. We're making around 16 knots, steering a course of 80°, which will have us missing Algiers by 15 miles.

'That way we won't get any interest shown in us by Algerian immigration,' says Alan. 'Provided we stay outside the 12 mile international limit.' He's suffering from a bad cold at the moment.

In the meantime, we're taking the opportunity to enjoy our first glimpse of real sunshine. New boy Al, sporting a ferociously short haircut gained in Gibraltar, proves he's not only a dab-hand with a video camera, but the chopping board as well. Unimpressed with the fare so far, he's volunteered himself into the role of cook. Lunch is tuna with crispy green salad and tomatoes, served in dog bowls. Whilst not particularly elegant, they're functional none the less, particularly when the sea's a little ruff!

But there's a slight moment of tension this morning when Al stows the cabin door into its place in the front cabin the wrong way round.

'Why do you have a go at me every thing I do?' snaps Al.

'We've been running this boat for three years,' says Alan, 'and everything has its place.'

The fact is that unless stowed 'the right way up' the door's hinges will damage the cabin wall. But it seems to me that Al is given to a rather more lax attitude towards tidiness, whereas Alan expects everything to be in its proper place. Even I, who can justly claim a PhD in untidiness, can appreciate that a small boat with four people can't afford to have any clutter.

One vital acquisition from Gibraltar is a cassette radio player. At last, with a number of tapes donated by some of our loyal supporters, life on board is taking on a rather less stressful tone. We're even starting to enjoy it!

Later in the afternoon, and Alan takes a look at the drive from the autopilot. It transpires that something has come loose, and after tightening the offending bit, it all works properly again. Huge sighs of relief all round - it means that we won't have to drive manually the whole time. The evening weather forecast from Bertie bodes well, with reasonably good conditions all the way to Malta. We're looking to arrive some time early evening, which won't be too much behind what we were expecting.

Tuesday 9th April

Today they bury the Queen Mother. It's grim even to have to think it, but hopefully now she won't dominate the headlines, and maybe we'll get a look in. We've been in a following sea during the night, making speeds over 20 knots, and also generating some almighty curtains of spray as the bow ploughs into the waves. The actual height of the waves is probably only three feet or so, but once you get picked up by one, it's like the proverbial runaway train ride.

Strangely, now, as I type on my Psion, and another wave smashes into the windscreen, I pull it back. I never would have done that before the big smash on the way to Gibraltar. An instinctive reaction in the light of what happened, but utterly pointless. If the screen went again, and the sea really did come gushing in, trying to protect my Psion would be the least of my concerns.

With 300 miles to go to Malta, it now looks as though it won't be until at least midnight before we arrive. Just because we're a powered vessel, many people assume we can keep to a tight schedule. But nothing could be further from the truth. As the weather changes, either with us or against us, so we're constantly revising our estimated arrival times.

The only occasional excitement this morning comes with avoiding lobster pot floats. Getting tangled up with floats and the line which attaches them to the lobster pot below is not what we want at all, as it could damage our prop. Instead of brightly coloured purpose-made floats that are easy to spot, the ones off the Tunisian coast are black plastic oil containers - and they don't exactly stand out against a murky sea.

The sun comes out during the afternoon, and after doing battle with the emails, I sample the shower. Simply a tube which picks up water driven by the forward motion of the boat, it's a refreshing if salty way to cool off and get sort of clean. One of this year's improvements to the boat is the dive platform at the back. It's a lot better being able to sit on the back of the boat with feet on the dive platform, taking a bracing shower in the knowledge that you're not likely to fall off the back and take a bath as well. It's also the perfect opportunity for a pee without having to brace myself. No problem at all. But today I discover that of the many plastic buckets which appeared after our arrival in Gibraltar, the one I've been peeing into is the washing up bowl. Still, if anybody noticed they didn't say. Must remember to use the other bucket. Or perhaps take more showers...

As the evening draws in, Bertie tells Alan that we're going to need a fairly tight turnround in Malta. The reason is that another big storm is coming up behind us, so the strategy is to get out of Malta and head south as quickly as possible. We call up our contact there, and learn that a reception with 100 people in the Casino at Grand Harbour Marina is under way, and they're waiting for us with eager anticipation. We can't wait to get there, either, although maybe once the champagne starts to flow, it'll be a bit more difficult to drag ourselves away.

The final run into Malta in the dark has us doing 23 knots, but as we approach the lights of Valletta, some six miles away in St Paul's

Bay, suddenly something like a fence looms out of the darkness. We hit it and ride over something, and there's a sickening clunk. As we gather our wits, it becomes apparent that we've ended up in something resembling a large circular corral, and we now have no power to the outdrive. We're in a tuna fish farm, and the huge bang was our outdrive being ripped off as we shot over the two booms which support the nets.

How could we possibly have run into it? Our electronic charts are bang up to date, and the fish farms aren't marked on them. As we gather our wits, we see others around us with dim flashing lights. This one was invisible until we hit it - its light only came on after the impact. It's an ignominious end to the first leg of our round the world challenge, and possibly an end to the attempt altogether. Just miles from port, at the dead of night, and we're stranded.

3
COMMUNICATIONS

ALAN PRIDDY'S PLAN to take Spirit of Cardiff around the world in something akin to a smooth military operation could only ever work with ultra-reliable communications. Of course, like most boats, we had a VHF radio for short-range communications with harbours, coastguards and other vessels, but the nature of the mission - with over 30 refuelling stops which had to be executed as quickly as possible - demanded something a bit more flexible and wide-reaching. For the first few trips after the boat was built, we simply used our mobile phones. Network coverage would come and go, depending on whether we were sticking close to a coastline, or further offshore.

On our third (successful) attempt to circumnavigate the British Isles in June 2000, we took an Inmarsat mini-M telephone. Roughly the size of a small laptop computer, the top hinged section was the antenna, which had to be lined up fairly precisely to work. The satellite is geostationary, in a high orbit, travelling at the same speed as the earth's rotation, so its footprint - the area it covers on the ground - remains the same. Alan managed to make one or two calls on it when conditions were good, but they were more novelty value than any real use. Sitting outside on the engine box cover in sunny calm conditions is one thing, but in the real world, it would need to be usable in stormy rain-lashed seas, night or day.

The problem was that the phone's antenna needed to remain steady in order to keep pointing at the satellite and maintaining the link. That proved impossible in anything other than glassy smooth conditions, and even then we'd have to stop. But it was just an experiment, so for the Gibraltar to Monaco record run in October 2000 we tried an Inmarsat phone equipped with a proper marine gimballed antenna. The idea of this is that with the antenna on gimbals, hinged and counterbalanced inside a weather-proof dome, it would always point to the same position in the sky, no matter how the boat may move about on the sea.

It proved unsuccessful for a couple of reasons. That particular model had a serial port to which one could attach a computer. I was keen to see how it would work for sending emails with text and photographs to update the Spirit of Cardiff website as we went along. Unfortunately I could get neither my Psion handheld nor my notebook computer talking to the phone, despite having downloaded the correct software from the phone manufacturer's website, and spent hours tinkering with different combinations of settings.

But the biggest problem was that Spirit proved too much for the antenna. Whilst it undoubtedly worked fine on boats taking it more leisurely over the waves, Spirit's motion was just too violent for it. The antenna couldn't maintain a stable lock on the satellite, so consequently we weren't able to use the phone for voice calls either.

So it was back to using mobile phones. I'd bought an Ericsson SH888 just before the first attempt at the British Isles in 1999 - one of the first mobile phones to use infra-red communication. The idea was to use it in conjunction with my Psion handheld computer, where the two units simply had to be 'looking' at each other to allow wireless communication. It worked well, although I did have to cobble together a rather Heath-Robinson arrangement of heavy duty rubber bands to keep both Psion and SH888 anchored to the Psion's protective case to avoid running out of hands while using it in bumpier conditions.

When we took the boat over to the United States in spring 2001, we were full of hope that at last we'd found a system we could work with. Unlike traditional satellite communications, the Iridium network is based on 66 satellites criss-crossing the world in low earth orbit, so that wherever you are, you'll always find coverage. With an antenna which didn't need anything more precise than a clear view of the sky, it seemed ideal, and as the network had only just been rescued from bankruptcy, the prices had come down enough for us to consider viable even without sponsorship.

Alan had also bought an Ericsson T28 Worldphone to give us mobile phone communications, since our normal dual-band phones wouldn't work, but there were a couple of snags. My Psion didn't want to communicate via infra-red with the T28. It was another of those little problems easily ironed out back home, when I found the Psion simply needed a software update. And despite what we'd been led to believe, data capability on the Iridium network wouldn't be available until July 2001 - over a month after we'd finished the Atlantic crossing.

So we used the Iridium phone for voice calls offshore, and all of my website updates and other emails were sent from ashore, either from my notebook computer or Psion plugged into whatever land lines we could blag. Whilst we were based in Lower Manhattan, that included one in the storeroom at the back of McMenamin's pub in Pier 17, which became our combined office and local.

Wherever we went on our promotional tour of the US eastern seaboard before the Atlantic crossing, it became something of a challenge to find places where I could plug into a phone line. It did rather help having an Internet Service Provider with local dial-ups available in most major cities, so I could at least point out I was merely making a free local call.

By the time we set off around the world in 2002, we had new Iridium phones, with sponsored airtime. One of them was for Alan to use as a voice phone for weather forecasts, making arrangements for port stops and staying in touch with base, while mine was for media use - both voice and data communications. But in the days prior to departure from Cardiff, joining phone and Psion with a serial cable wasn't enough, and I just couldn't get the combination to work. I did manage to get it all working fine with my notebook computer, but I was very well aware that this was a far from perfect solution.

There was also a possibility at one stage that we were going to be equipped with a videophone, the kind of which had seen increasing use by TV news teams reporting from the world's more remote hotspots. Not very high quality video, which jerked along behind the audio, but it would have provided some immediacy. The chances are it would only have been usable at the port stops, since it was another piece of equipment which required precise aiming. In the end, we weren't able to get our hands on one, so it was down to voice and data only.

I was also aware that even with satellite communications working properly, I was going to have to ration myself on the number of photographs I could email back to base. With the satellite data connection speed just a quarter of that of a mobile phone - itself extremely slow - a 60kb picture file which would transmit from a normal desktop PC in a matter of seconds could take six to seven minutes to crawl into cyberspace. Neither did I realise how much stress I was letting myself in for trying to stay connected that long. Whilst the satphones worked reasonably well, they were subject to frequent disconnections, more so with data calls. On average I would spend an hour a day trying to send or receive emails. Not that I should complain too bitterly. Ultimately, our Iridium phones contributed to saving Steve Lloyd's life.

Whilst most expeditions in ocean-going yachts will use a laptop computer for emailing, keeping diaries and running navigation software, it's difficult to use on Spirit when she's bouncing about. The mouse pointer is totally uncontrollable, and in bright sunlight, the backlit LCD screen is impossible to read. Which is why the Psion Series 5mx handheld made such a lot of sense, and I'd proved it over previous trips. The mono display is legible in the brightest sunlight (although it does gradually go very dark when it gets too hot), and the touch-sensitive screen uses a stylus for control functions. It's easy to use, even in quite rough conditions. Whatever happened with the communications, I intended to use the Psion to do all my daily writing on, but it would prove a real bind if I was going to have to transfer everything to the notebook computer every time I wanted to email an update back to base.

I tinkered with it some more while we were in Gibraltar before we set off, but still I couldn't get Psion and satphone working together. It was while in Malta on our enforced stopover waiting first for spare parts and then for good weather that it all came together. First, I had an inkling that my dedicated serial cable which I needed to plug into the satphone might have a duff connection. So, with the help of our Grand Harbour Marina host Tony Demajo, I tracked down the only Psion serial cable in Malta.

The icing on the cake came when Spirit of Cardiff supporter Sue Bryant emailed me details of the settings I needed to get my Psion talking to the satphone. She'd spent several days trawling various newsgroups on the internet and posting messages asking if anyone had any experience of using an Iridium phone with a Psion. Someone called Dominic had sent her comprehensive details about how to do it, and after some trial and error, I finally managed to get Psion and satphone working together. At last I was in business!

4
MARLBORO MANIA

I'm really happy for you all that the boat is finally back in the water. At least I guess you won't be short of fish dinners after your unscheduled visit to the farm!
James Williams, organiser of Spirit of Cardiff's refuelling stop in the Philippines.

Wednesday 10th April

'IF WE TAKE a line from another boat, aren't we in danger of being disqualified?'

We're all slightly shocked from the accident, but as we come to our wits and try to determine the best course of action, I'm most concerned that we don't do anything that might result in our losing our record attempt because we accepted assistance from another vessel. So we struggle to attach our diesel outboard engine. Stowed in the starboard side of the engine box, it's essentially the engine from one of those upright machines used by road-menders for tamping down tarmac, but fitted with a leg and propeller. It's not light, and it's awkward to manhandle, lifted in short steps to the back of the boat. Just to play safe, we attach a rope from the engine to one of the lifting eyes so we can retrieve it if our first attempt at locking it over the mounting plate results in it going overboard.

It takes Alan a while to sort out all the cables, and to attach fuel lines, and then he fires it up. It's noisy, but at last we have some hope, even though it's only capable of giving the boat around five knots. The trouble is, five knots isn't enough speed to get the hull to mount the two substantial booms that encircle us, and there's a breeze blowing as well. All that happens is that the boat strikes the boom a glancing blow, then follows it around. We rig up some ropes to keep her nose on to the boom, but that proves fruitless too.

Tired and frustrated, we admit defeat. Alan gets in touch with Grand Harbour Marina to ask if they can tow us out with their launch. By the time they're with us, it's gone midnight. They attach a line to the boat, and drag us out over the twin booms of the fish farm. For a moment I think the spare engine is going to come off as the leg skates over the boom, but it holds.

We arrive in Valletta harbour at about 0400, the party long over. After completing the customs and immigration formalities, we're whisked off to a four-star hotel, the Victoria, in Sliema. It's about 0500 by the time I get to bed. I wake up again just before 1000. My room mate Al is in the bathroom, and some member of the hotel staff has just come in, presumably to clean. I feel really landsick and wobbly, a result of several hours bobbing around in the tuna farm.

We whizz down to get some breakfast, and then meet the others to take a taxi to the marina in Vittoriosa. There we find the boat is already out of the water, standing on blocks on the quayside. The outdrive is basically all right, but the housing is broken. One of the trim tabs has been broken as well, not to mention the pick-up tube for the all-important shower. The towing eye has sheared off the bow, and there are one or two black marks, but thankfully no actual damage to the hull.

Amazingly, the new outdrive is already on its way, thanks to swift action from Yamaha, shipping agents Peters and May, and Air Malta. Alan and Steve remove the broken outdrive, and crane out the engine, while Al and I shoot some video, and field a steady flow of journalists, TV people and others who'd missed us at the party. We're also visited by someone from the fish farm wanting to charge us $1,800 for the damage we've done. Alan suggests he might like to consider the $9,000 worth of damage his fish farm has done to our boat. The fish farm man leaves without anything, but it's all been very friendly - the hallmark of everyone we've met here.

Back in Sliema, we wander along to a restaurant for a meal. Malta is like walking back in time. It's not enough to come to a place where rust-free Mark 2 Ford Cortinas, Anglias and Morris Marinas are commonplace, we're enjoying our evening meal to the strains of Max Bygraves' greatest hits.

The next day, bleary-eyed and still slightly wobbly, we're at the marina by 0730. The outdrive is there waiting for us, together with a customs man waiting patiently for someone to sign his papers. So it's straight into fitting it and getting the boat ready. By 1030 the engine is back in, and the boat itself afloat once more by 1300. We'd leave now, except we're not refuelled, and we know there's bad weather on the way.

Tony Demajo drives us into town, making a detour to get me a new serial lead for my Psion. It transpires I've bought the only one in Malta. Then we're dropped off in Valletta. Not so much sightseeing, we have a bite to eat in a McDonald's, then wander around looking for a drink, ending up in a rather seedy bar - the hallmark of a Spirit of Cardiff drinking expedition. After realising it would be too far to walk back, we take a bus instead. It proves to be a highlight - one Maltese Lire for the four of us, about £1.50 in total. The bus itself was probably built in the 1950s, with two cords running to a bell at the front to indicate when you want the driver to stop.

Back at the boat, I attach my new cable to Psion and satphone, but whilst it works sometimes, the connection seems rather random. The others go off for a drink while I persevere, and eventually I suss it. All the settings are as advised by Dominic, except I lower the baud rate. That does the trick. I download my first emails from satphone onto Psion, and send myself a test message.

Friday 12th April

This morning it's really windy, the aftermath of an incredible electrical storm last night. There's absolutely no chance of setting off today - this is the worst weather they've had here for 17 years. The rain has brought an awful lot of muck down with it, apparently sand from the Sahara.

Just along the quayside is the Alevok, a beautiful traditional sailing boat where Clive (an Aussie) and Lyn (from Llangollen) invite us to use their cabins tonight. Later we stage a short presentation, with Alan giving Tony one of our fabulous Cardiff plaques, letter and mouse mat. More to the point, we thank everyone for the fantastic level of support here, bending the rules to ensure we got the boat fixed as soon as possible.

I'm feeling rather rough today, with a sore throat, slightly spaced out, weak and wobbly. Presumably I'm going down with what Alan had. I take the opportunity for a lie down while the others go off for a walk. I'm just dozing off when the boat is thrown about wildly. I look out to see a fishing boat steaming past at full throttle, his wash throwing all the boats in the marina about. I settle back down again, only to be alerted by a shout from one of the security men from the adjacent casino. The stern line has broken, and the rear of the boat has drifted out. He throws me the line and I manage to tie on just in time.

The others come back, and while we're talking to Joseph, another of the casino security men, I ask if he knows anywhere reasonable to eat. We think he's going off to get us the courtesy bus to give us a lift, when back comes someone else from the casino saying they'd like us to eat there tonight. We enjoy a splendid meal, along with a couple of bottles of wine. The building itself is 500 years old, and was once used by Napoleon's officers.

Then we head back to the Alevok. Clive is asleep, but we have a chat with Lyn before turning in. Alan and Steve stay with Spirit so they can tend to her bilge pumps which keep the engine box free of water during the night (the automatic switch isn't working), so Al and I pick our cabins on the Alevok. I settle in for a good sleep, heartened by the generous hospitality we've received in Malta, but frustrated that we've hit snags so early on.

Saturday 13th April

After a quick cup of coffee, we're off at around 0800. Former powerboat champion Eric Braithwaite - now with a home in Malta - has turned up with his RIB to time us off, and we set off for the fish farm. We have to resume our journey to Valletta harbour from there to complete the leg. Out there we see several fish farms, including ours with the mangled top rail. There's one forlorn cardinal marker. Alan isn't keen on getting too close, so we then head back to Valletta harbour breakwater, arriving at 0914 local.

And then we're off. We don't tell anyone other than the RYA, but it's at this point that we set a second clock running. Mindful of the lengthy delay in Malta, we reckon that if we arrive in Gibraltar missing the Cable and Wireless record by just a day or so, we can continue to Malta instead and still beat it. Good insurance.

I'm not feeling on top form today. Eventually I have to have a poo, but even then Alan wants me to do it with the cabin door off. Ventilation seems to take precedence over comfort or dignity, although with what I'm about to do, maybe some interference in the flow of air from outside might be a good idea. As I'm sitting outside thinking there can't be any more indignities, Al starts moving around. Fortunately there's a Thermarest inflatable sleeping mat outside, so I jam that in the doorway.

Al redeems himself by making a splendid early evening meal of potatoes, sausage, beans and ham. By the evening, the sea has really flattened off, and we're making around 18 knots. We've done 160 miles in 10 hours. That would extrapolate to a total journey time of 56 hours, but given that we'll speed up naturally as fuel burns off, we're looking at some time Monday morning to arrive in Port Said.

Al and I start a watch at around eight in the evening. But it's not long after when the radar alarm goes off. There's something big at around one o'clock. The alarm continues as we close on it, and by the time we're a mile and a half off, there's the suggestion there might be another contact at 11 o'clock. Alan, by now up to see what the commotion is about, thinks perhaps it's a boat under tow, which would mean we might be heading in between for a tow line.

But Al is freaking out because he can't see through the film of salt on the windscreen. 'You're panicking because it's dark,' says Alan. 'The range of visibility hasn't changed since it was light, and you could see then.'

'We need to clean the screen,' insists Al, leaping outside with a cloth. We're doing 19 knots at night, and suddenly he's outside clambering along the side of the cabin. Last week he would have been worrying about wearing a life jacket to do that.

'Al, get back inside,' yells Alan. If he fell off in the dark without a life jacket, we'd never find him again. And besides, trying to clean off the salt with a rag will only make things worse. It transpires that what we're passing is an oil or gas platform, and we're no closer than a mile.

At this point, Alan, who feels his authority being usurped, says: 'We've done thousands of miles at night in this boat. You're panicking because you can't see anything, but that's because there's nothing to see.' He says we'll discuss it all tomorrow, but in the meantime, both Al and I (who wasn't at all panicked) are sent off watch. It's the only way Alan can reassert the fact that there can only be one skipper, and that's him. So he and Steve go through the night, one on, one off.

Sunday 14th April

It's two weeks since we set out from Cardiff, and one week since Gibraltar. No doubt we thought we would have been a lot further on by now - hopefully another 3,500 miles or so down the line, near Mangalore - but here we are, still in the Mediterranean.

I slept very badly, but presumably I had some kind of sleep, as I remember some very vivid and weird dreams. Real anxiety jobs, though for the life of me I can't think why. Al and I are on watch again about an hour before sunrise. I get up unable to find my socks. I vaguely remember removing them whilst in my sleeping bag, so I search the bottom several times in the same disbelieving way when something doesn't turn up where it ought. Alan, now prone in the bunk, is waiting patiently for the light to go out.

'They're hanging out of your arse, mate,' he ventures helpfully. Somewhat perplexed, I discover one sock hanging from the back of my trousers, whilst the other is inside.

On watch, Al is playing his cassette player on headphones, and dozing off. Why does he think it's safer to close his eyes on watch when it's light? And yet in the dark he's paranoid about being able to see instead of trusting the instruments.

At 0714 GMT, we've covered 422 nautical miles from Malta, with just over 500 to go for Port Said. It's looking pretty good. The speed has crept upwards steadily, so I'm sure we'll knock this last bit off by this time tomorrow. And then the highlight of the Suez Canal. I just hope we can get through quickly, though.

The sun comes out, and for a while it's quite warm. We all take our turn to use the ensuite shower facilities - the dive platform. I still haven't quite summoned the nerve to stand up on it, so I sit on the rear edge of the engine box with my feet braced against the frame.

The sea is a lot calmer, often that sort of oily smoothness which makes our speed, now approaching 23 knots, seem quite deceptive. Whilst we're on course to make Port Said by tomorrow morning, we've been warned that we're being chased by a further depression.

In the meantime, the boat is positively caked, not just with salt but sand. It must be in the air, brought across from the desert, but the boat looks really muddy. It gets rather chilly quite early in the afternoon, so the door goes back on - a lot sooner than expected.

Monday 15th April

We arrive in Port Said just after 0700 GMT, having done the passage from Malta in just over 48 hours. It's the fastest leg so far, and little are we to know it will remain the fastest for the rest of the trip. There was a bit of a scene this morning when I called an end to the watch after four hours, when apparently it should have been five. Alan and Steve seem deeply miffed that I've deprived them of an hour's sleep. Nobody told me the watch was supposed to be an hour longer, but instead of arguing the toss, I keep quiet. We've had enough tension already, but we're about to get some more.

Later, once we're ensconced in the marina at Port Said, and we've exchanged gifts with the marina management and local tourist board, we have what could be termed a full and frank discussion to air the problems with Alan Carter. We'd been talking about going off into town when I mentioned I didn't have any dollars. Al and I were both the last to contribute hard cash to the expedition for fuel and provisions, and whilst he'd brought his in US dollars and kept it with him, I'd transferred mine to Alan's bank before leaving home. So immediately Al thinks he's somehow been deceived into coming up with the cash and I hadn't. Much more comes out in the discussion.

'I'm not confident in Clive's abilities, either,' he adds after his dangerous night time excursion to the outside of the cabin is aired in full. While I readily admit I don't have Alan or Steve's huge experience, I do have many thousands of Spirit miles under my belt, many of them at night doing watches on my own. But in the interests of harmony we agree that Al will instead do night watches with either Alan or Steve.

With the air cleared, Al and I wander off for a look round Port Said and to do some shopping. The moment we're outside the secure area around the marina, there's no doubt we're in North Africa. We're overlooked by the impressive spires of a huge mosque, and the whole place is absolutely buzzing. Market stalls are set up along one side of the area where cars queue to drive onto the ferries which run continuously 24 hours a day from one side of the canal to the other.

Amazingly the ferries are absolutely free. I'm amused to walk past a shop with an intriguing display of infant food and rat poison on the same shelf.

Unfortunately it's not too long before we're accosted by a young man, all smiles, and whilst I keep my distance, Al responds to him. It's not unusual to have people like this try and get you to hire them to be your guide, but this chap is unusually persistent. He wants to take us to various shops, coffee bars and so on, and eventually we're led down some dingy back alley to a place that looks decidedly dodgy. At this point I decide enough is enough and walk away, encouraging Al to do the same. I'm not too keen on getting knifed - an extreme reaction, perhaps, but I was getting a bad feeling about the situation.

It's a strange night out, too. We thought we were going out with Nagib Latif, the boss of Felix Maritime, the agency who's made all our canal arrangements. He also arranged the Cable and Wireless Adventurer transit in 1998, and comes highly recommended for the professionalism of his service, and the way in which he cuts through unnecessary bureaucracy.

We're whisked off to Port Said's best seafood restaurant in a Series 5 BMW. 'So is this it?' remarks Alan, noticing just four places around the table. We eat alone. The soup is absolutely crammed with big crunchy lumps - crab pincers, mussels and other bits of shell. A bit daunting, but the soup itself is OK. The meal as a whole appears not to have any terrible effect on my insides, and afterwards we walk to Nagib's office. It's weird, 11 o'clock at night and everyone is in there beavering away.

In the normal run of things, a ship transiting the Suez Canal does it in two days, overnighting in Ismailia. Nagib has arranged for us to go all the way through, but changing pilots at Ismailia, all covered, so we assume, within his fee. Apparently the record for a single day transit of the canal is nine and a half hours, so we're out to break it. Which means we'll arrive in Jeddah probably lunchtime Thursday.

Interestingly, Nagib is also from the class of 1953. We spend a long time discussing his business, world politics, and, inevitably, the consequences of September 11th and the war in Afghanistan which followed. Since then, he tells us, the leisure traffic side of business in the canal has completely dried up, with only commercial and military ships going through. Which makes us something of an unusual event.

'I've seen three wars in my lifetime,' he says. 'I'm worried that soon I'm going to see a fourth.'

It's the first time we speak to someone quite obviously very intelligent and a successful businessman, who gives an indication of just how disliked the Americans are in this part of the world. From the perspective of the majority of people in the Middle East, Uncle Sam only cares about his own interests, and he's not bothered whose toes he treads on to further or protect them.

Tuesday 16th April

Our pilot arrives just after 0700, and by 0730, we're into the canal. It's a slow start first of all, around five knots, but later we're up to 10. The first few miles could in no way be described as pretty, a slightly warmer version of the Manchester ship canal. There's a railway line alongside it, and we spot a train going past - typical dusty carriages with barred windows and people hanging out everywhere.

The canal itself has embankments on either side, and we're too low in the water to see the surrounding countryside, so it gets a bit monotonous after a while. We pass other vessels, tankers and container ships mainly. Further south, at El-Qantara, the embankments have shallowed out, so we can see more. As we come up to a massive suspension bridge, Al suggests it might be a good idea to get some shots of it.

'There's a canal station over there,' says Alan. 'If I get arrested I'll tell them my name is Alan Carter.'

Of course, in places like these, things like bridges are rather more sensitive, which is why it's forbidden to photograph them. If yesterday's incident with the 'guide' in Port Said didn't demonstrate Al's naïvety, this surely does. We also spot many places along the bank with Bailey Bridges - floating kit bridges originally designed by British Army engineers - set up on ramps ready for immediate launching. It's quite clear that what we're passing through is a potential war zone. Indeed, the Sinai Peninsula was occupied by Israel from the Six Day War in 1967 until 1982, when the Israelis agreed to pull out after the Camp David Agreement. From what we've seen, the Egyptians aren't too keen on it being invaded again.

At Ismailia we swap pilots, and this new one is a bit more proactive. Unlike the first, who simply sat unsmilingly in the navigator's seat and waved his hand when he wanted Alan to change course or slow down, this guy takes the helm of the boat, and is rather more interested in cranking up the throttle 'to see what she can do.' Except he cranks it up to the point where Alan is concerned he may be using up rather more fuel than desired, so he asks him to go a little slower.

The southern half of the canal is definitely more interesting from a scenic point of view, the timeless shifting sands of the Sinai Desert to our left. At one point, the artificial canal opens up into a wide waterway with channel markers called Great Bitter Lake. The final narrow stretch sees a little contretemps with the checkpoints. Every so many miles, we've been pulling in to them on instruction from our pilot, and tossing a couple of packs of cigarettes onto the quayside to smooth our passage through the next section of canal. The Suez is known as the Marlboro Canal - it's an organised scam with which our pilot co-operates shamelessly, relying on our lack of knowledge of Arabic as he communicates with the guys on the land. Unfortunately, we've run out of cigarettes. We only gave the last checkpoint a single pack, and they've obviously phoned ahead to this one to organise some grief.

'There's something wrong with your radio,' explains our pilot. Yeah, right. He jumps ashore and goes up the steps to an office. He's gone for over half an hour while we wait anxiously. He returns later with the sad but predictable news that he's had to hand over $40 to authorise our onward passage, and therefore he requires reimbursement.

We arrive at Port Suez at 1345 GMT (1545 local), having transited the canal system in eight and a quarter hours. So if nothing else we've set a new unofficial record for the fastest passage through the 90 miles or so of the Suez Canal. But even here, at the Port Suez yacht club, the manager completing the RYA paperwork recording our time out wants a little extra 'paperwork' before we leave. We've been tied up here for less than five minutes.

'This is the last one,' smiles Alan through gritted teeth, as he holds up a $20 bill to my video camera before handing it over. In all, apart from the standard charges for the transit, we've forked out $200 in bribes and 'tips', along with several packs of cigarettes. *Baksheesh* may be a way of life here, but to us, the people working the Suez Canal appear corrupt beyond belief.

It's good to get out to sea again, even though the weather has turned decidedly dull, and a tinge chilly. Can this really be the baking hot Red Sea I've always heard about? By early evening, we've had a nice meal of tortellini with tuna, and we're looking forward to a mug of tea. Al puts one or two plastic mugs of water in the microwave. Then there's a smell of burning. Something in the microwave is on fire.

Smoke gushes out as Alan opens the door, and suddenly it's panic stations. A major conflagration would spoil our otherwise perfect day. Once the molten mugs are ejected, it transpires that although they'd jammed in the microwave, the wiring for my three 12 volt sockets mounted directly above was the problem. By accidentally pushing the back of one out when I plugged something in, it had shorted out and melted the wiring. But it could have been dodgy. The microwave also shared the rear seat box with a number of cartridges for the gas stove. Al is all for ditching the gas altogether, but we move it to a different location. It's just as well, as the gas stove now takes over from the wrecked microwave.

Al and I are on watch as we make our way from the Gulf of Suez into the Red Sea. It's dark, and the lights and gas flares of numerous oil rigs fill the night sky. It seems rather odd that we should be on a watch together anyway, given what was agreed in Port Said. Cynically, I suspect that what's behind it is that Alan and Steve prefer to stick together because, unlike us, they take turns on watch and therefore get more sleep.

Wednesday 17th April

All this time I'd thought the Red Sea was going to be calm and flat. Instead, we're in a nasty and uncomfortable head sea, and making very little progress. At this rate it's going to be a lot more beyond Thursday lunchtime when we get into Jeddah. Earlier in the day we'd tried to forge on, but it was just too painful. Eventually the boat is in near shutdown mode, making just three knots.

But we've had some elements of relaxation, the others doing a spot of sunbathing, while I try to send emails, and take a few photographs. If there's any good news, it's that Alan reckons it's blowing down slowly.

Late in the afternoon, while the others are languishing in a stupor brought on by our frustrating inaction, I realise we're actually in shallow water, which undoubtedly contributes to the predicament. I've noticed large cargo ships a couple of miles further offshore, and indeed what looks like a guided missile destroyer, so deduce there must be deeper and therefore less choppy water there. So we head over, and lo and behold, the depth reading leaps from nine feet to over 100. Not that it seems to make much difference to the waves. They're still horrendous. We attempt to drive them manually until it gets dark, which is faster than staying on autopilot, after which we have to put the boat back on autopilot. I turn in at 2200 and get a good four hours sleep. I'm just too tired to let anything keep me awake any more.

Thursday 18th April

We wake up to the same horribly punishing seas, making just six knots. 200 miles from Jeddah, and at this rate, it could well be another 24 hours or more before we arrive. The sun rises early, and it's hot long before eight o'clock. My watch ends at 0600, so I catch three hours of kip, then get up for a shower. The trouble is, there's not much pressure in the shower hose at just six knots (there are no pumps - it's simply fed by the forward motion of the boat through the water). I manage a refreshing wash of sorts, and also rinse out my T shirt and pants, which by now are smelling horribly.

Then it's into office mode. I decide to make today's update about the problems of communicating from the boat. It seems like a good idea, especially as today is an 'at sea' day with nothing special going on. So I get Al to take some photographs of me tapping away on the Psion, and then I write my piece. Fittingly, it takes over an hour to connect up in order to send it.

When I do, I receive an email from the Royal Yachting Association to say they're following our progress with interest, and they've linked from their website to Spirit of Cardiff's. Motor Boat and Yachting magazine is also following us after covering our departure from Gibraltar, and they think the Indian Ocean leg will be the decider, although I'm not sure why. It's only fractionally longer than last year's transatlantic leg from St John's to Horta.

Late afternoon, and I retire for my second comfort stop of the day. The Egyptian cuisine may well have taken its toll on my insides after all. Alan and Steve remain in their seats at the front, but Al decides to start getting his meal ready. He can see I'm in need of a little privacy, but appears to carry on regardless. I end up with the bucket on top of one of the side tanks up against the rear of the cabin in order to stay out of view. It's most uncomfortable, but I do manage to perform none the less. The only problem is that I seem to want to go yet again shortly afterwards. Alan admits he has a similar problem - he reckons it might have been the water.

During the day, the wind dies down, and we manage to increase our speed. By the afternoon, we're whistling along, albeit painfully at times, at over 20 knots. As we close on Jeddah in darkness, Al seems to be organising his belongings rather more than usual, which seems unnatural given his general lack of tidyness. He's also been making furtive calls outside on my satphone. His last call, as we approach the port, prompts Steve to wonder what's going on.

'Probably checking his flight's on time,' remarks Alan. Never a truer word spoken in jest.

As we arrive at the harbour breakwater, it takes a while to clear some confusion with Jeddah Port Control. When we call them up on the radio to ask for directions to our berth, they're expecting a large ship to be lying offshore waiting to be piloted in. The conversation goes something like this:

JPC: What is your position?

AP: We're at the harbour entrance.

JPC: And what is your ETA?

AP: We're already here.

There's further silence as it's clear that whilst we're right below their control tower, they can't see us. They ask the same questions over and over again. They're mystified, and we're not making ourselves understood. Eventually a pilot boat appears and leads us into the harbour.

After tying up, two smartly uniformed Saudi policemen board the boat and spend some time going through it with a fine tooth comb. They're on the lookout for banned items such as pork, alcohol and girly magazines.

'You want to watch they don't pinch anything,' warns Steve. 'They will, given half a chance.'

Once they've finished, I try to chat with one. 'Perhaps you can teach me a few words of Arabic,' I ask him. 'I only know one.'

'Oh yes, what is it?'

'You promise you won't be offended?'

He shakes his head, then laughs when I tell him it's 'Imshi' (a not terribly polite way of telling someone to go away). Within minutes I've added three polite but no less useful words to my extensive Arabic vocabulary, and I've shown him the rudimentary steps of a Michael Jackson moonwalk.

Meanwhile, our agent from A.C.T. Shipping has arrived. Dressed in a handsome flowing white dishdash robe and red and white kaffiyeh head scarf, Hamed looks cool and comfortable. We, on the other hand, in our shorts and T-shirts, are feeling decidedly hot and sticky.

'Your food and fuel is on its way,' announces Hamed. 'You'll be on your way again in two hours.'

'I don't suppose there's any chance of a cup of tea before then,' I wonder. 'Proper tea.'

'Of course,' he replies, and gets on his mobile phone to organise it.

Shortly after a guy arrives with a tray full of mugs of tea. It's the best cup of tea I've ever had. Then Hamed produces a typical Arab carpet, takes off his sandals, and invites us to join him cross-legged for a relaxing natter. We talk about all sorts of things - his children, world politics, our challenge. The upshot of it all, as we found in Egypt, is that all anyone wants is a quiet life. In the interests of such, I refrain from asking when the last public beheading was held.

Later, some Kentucky Fried Chicken style chicken and chips arrive, along with our provisions for the next two legs, so I knock back a Red Bull, as well as a Coke, while Alan and Steve continue to refuel the boat. I'm still suffering from a slightly gippy tummy, so have to make one or two calls to the toilet in the port office. It's rather basic - typical French footrests astride a hole in the ground, and horribly smelly. Not to mention the fact that there's no toilet paper, because Arabs wash rather than use toilet paper. Which is fine, except there's nothing to dry with.

It's something of a bizarre situation, all on a Saudi picnic rug at midnight on a dockside in Jeddah, eating chicken and chips. And unfortunately, because of the regulations, we're not permitted to film or take any photographs. But we do have a problem, revealed earlier when Hamed takes Alan to one side.

'Your crewman Alan Carter has been asking for an exit visa,' he says. 'It was too short notice, and now it's the weekend. I'm afraid we can't help.'

5
IN THE BEGINNING

The best boat in the world is not much use without a crew of matching calibre.
Dag Pike, distinguished mariner and writer, referring to Alan Priddy and his Spirit of Portsmouth crew.

ALAN, STEVE AND Jan go back years and years. They'd been involved in all sorts of record-breaking exploits in RIBs since the early 1990s, and Alan had built up a reputation as the foremost exponent of offshore RIBbing. When I met them in 1999, they were already held in awe by the boating establishment for their amazing Atlantic crossing two years earlier.

I remember writing about Alan at the time, describing him as the Chris Bonington of powerboating. It wasn't just that he'd notched up a remarkable list of world records. He's one of those people who believes in putting something back. He'd helped to found BIBOA, the British Inflatable Boat Owners' Association, he'd also helped to found his local branch of Rotary, and he'd used his exploits to generate a considerable amount of income for a variety of charities, including Childline, the Cancer Care Society, the Multiple Sclerosis Society, Make a Wish Foundation and Children in Need. Indulging your passion with great success is one thing, but it takes a genuinely big-hearted man to do that little bit extra.

At the beginning of 1999, I was still hobbling around, unable to walk more than a short distance without major discomfort. I'd treated one of my ankle ligaments to a 75 percent tear while on trek in Kazakhstan the previous summer, and it put paid to all walking bar short strolls for the next year. Which, in a very roundabout way, is how I found myself boarding a small powerboat about to set off from

Portsmouth on a 2,000 mile journey around the British Isles.

It wasn't enough simply to go for a short ride in Spirit of Portsmouth and do a story about it. I was taking part in a world record attempt. Whilst powerboats had set records for circumnavigating Britain on its own, and Ireland on its own, no powerboat had ever attempted to circumnavigate the British Isles - Britain, Ireland, and all other islands bar the Channel Islands and Rockall. The only record which existed was for sailing, five days 21 hours and five minutes, set in 1994 by American multi-millionaire Steve Fossett in his superfast racing trimaran 'Lakota'.

When I turned up on 15th July in the early evening at the Bridge Tavern on Portsmouth's historic Camber, I didn't even know which way round we were going. It would all depend on the weather forecast, and Alan would make his decision at the last minute. I'd expected we might head off in daylight, but the game plan was somewhat different. We'd have something to eat, and a few beers, then head off at closing time. This rather appealed to my anarchic anti-formal organisation side, and we had a pleasant dinner in the upstairs room of the pub before we set off. Many of Alan's sponsors and supporters had come as well, one of whom described us as 'Completely barking mad.'

There was only one thing missing as the pub closed its doors on us and our supporters, eager to see us off, but also to get back home to their loved ones - Jan. He'd been late getting away from work in London, but he wouldn't be here for another hour. He arrived on a motorbike, and we set off just before midnight.

Getting out of Portsmouth harbour was interesting, with Alan, Steve and Jan all at the front, either looking intently through the windscreen or at the radar. Once we were properly under way, Jan and I turned in, with me sleeping on the bunk which had been made up across the back of the cabin, and Jan on cushions on the floor between my bunk and the front seats. I'd somehow thought that we might be sleeping in the cabin forward of the wheelhouse, but realised it would be far too bumpy up there. Besides, it was already occupied by two huge flexible containers of fuel.

Even where I was could hardly be described as comfortable. The sea was rough, and we were thudding up and down through the waves. Once or twice I'd feel my body go into freefall, then when I hit the bunk, I felt the air squashed out of my lungs. I didn't sleep much, but it didn't matter. This was an adventure!

It was still rough when we swapped watches at four in the morning, and Jan took the controls. Or rather he sat at the helm and worked the throttle. The autopilot did the rest of the driving. By lunchtime, the sea had calmed down considerably, and we were making good progress.

We were just off Lizard Point making good headway at around 18 knots, when suddenly there was a sickeningly loud metallic bang. The engine stopped instantly. I thought that perhaps it had blown up, but Alan had seen the warning lights flash and he'd killed it straight away. The look of concern on everyone's faces said everything. Alan lifted the engine box cover to find water pouring in. Further inspection revealed that the outdrive, the gearbox and transmission to the propeller (more commonly known as the leg) had been torn off. At this stage we assumed some submerged obstacle - probably a container, although Steve didn't discount the possibility of a submarine.

At this point, I didn't know what to do, and as everyone else was rushing about relatively efficiently, I decided it would be best to keep out of the way until I was told to do something. Only when Alan said that we were taking on water and were sinking (a tinge dramatic, in retrospect) did I decide it might be time to start worrying.

In truth, we couldn't sink, but we could have been flooded. Jan donned a drysuit and jumped overboard to check it out. There was a two inch hole in the transom plate, and the gearbox appeared to have very little to keep it attached to the boat. He rigged up a rope to keep it stable.

Then Alan called the coastguard. We were about 10 miles off Lizard Point in Cornwall, from where the Lizard lifeboat was despatched. As Spirit bobbed about in the swell without power, I rapidly became seasick.

We were lucky in as much as the pumps kept working. We were doubly lucky in that it could have happened somewhere where rescue facilities were not so conveniently to hand - the west coast of Ireland, or somewhere in the Shetlands. That might have been a lot different. Alan later admitted that had we really started shipping water big time, he had the option of dumping fuel - not very environmentally friendly, but then that wouldn't have been the major concern if it had come to that.

The lifeboat arrived, with what seemed like crowds of people lining the safety rails. Again Jan went over the side, this time to attach a tow rope. It took around one and a half to two hours to be pulled round to Falmouth, during which time we'd all made telephone calls to let friends and family know what had happened, and that we were safe. Before too long, Alan was getting calls from his secretary saying that various people were after interviews. We'd made front page of the Portsmouth Evening News and news bulletins on the BBC.

By the time we arrived in Falmouth, the local press and TV were waiting for us. When the boat was lifted out of the water it was rather like Apollo 13. We knew there was a problem, but up till then we couldn't see the real extent of it. The leg had twisted round at right angles, and there were gouge marks in the glass fibre dive platform above where the propeller had hit it.

While we were still on the water, we'd jokingly blamed Jan for being an hour late. 'If we'd left on time, that container would have been somewhere else!' In hindsight, leaving an hour late proved a blessing. If we'd had the same accident one hour further on from the Lizard, we might have ended up being rescued by the St Mary's lifeboat. Getting home from the Scillies would have proved rather more expensive. Either way, my first trip out in Spirit could only be described as a true baptism of fire.

The boat was repaired in a matter of days. With the first attempt having come to an untimely end, it seemed natural to me to want to follow it through, although I can imagine that the experience of hitting unseen obstacles in the water and being towed ashore by lifeboat might have had some deciding that now would be a good time to take up pruning roses. But throughout my first outing in the boat, though at times desperately uncomfortable, I never felt unsafe. The boat felt safe. When doing other slightly dangerous or adventurous activities, I've always worked on the basis that if you don't feel comfortable, you look at the face of the person in charge. If he doesn't look worried, there's no reason why I should be. Unless of course he really is barking mad. But apart from a few winces on the extra-hard landings, I'd seen no signs of concern.

So the next month we set off again, this time in daylight, from Cowes, on the Isle of Wight. Jan was unable to make it, so it was just Alan, Steve and me. That immediately put me in a different position. Not just a passenger charged with the time-keeping, I was going to have to do the watches, and learn to make some kind of sense of the radar and chart plotter.

We were heading west again, which is probably just as well. The day before we set off, a cargo ship had collided with the luxury cruise liner Norwegian Dream at the northern end of the English Channel, and a number of containers had fallen into the sea. Hopefully by the time we passed through, they would have either dispersed or sunk.

This time we made much better progress. We passed Lizard Point a good four hours ahead of our previous attempt. But as we headed out into the Atlantic for the Fastnet Rock, so it became more unsettled. I remember doing a watch from midnight till about four in the morning, when I crashed out, absolutely shattered, and oblivious to the horrendous pounding as the boat nosed into an increasingly heavy head sea.

When I gradually came to at around 0800, I was aware of a difference in the movement of the boat. No violent pounding, we were slopping about in an enormous swell. And the familiar sound of the engine and whining turbo was absent.

'We're in the middle of a force eight gale,' Alan told me. 'We were wasting fuel trying to fight through it, so I switched off. We're drifting.'

I lifted my bleary eyes to the window and wiped away the condensation. We were in a trough, and a steel-grey wave some 25 to 30 feet tall towered over us like an apartment block.

'I don't see what the problem is,' I muttered, still half asleep. 'Why can't we carry on?'

The reason we couldn't carry on was that we simply wouldn't have made it to our refuelling stop at Scrabster, at the northern tip of mainland Scotland. The gale had come up out of nowhere - had it featured in a weather forecast before we set off, we would have postponed our departure. We drifted for another four hours, wallowing in the mountainous swell, during which time the others dozed fitfully. I switched on the radio to see if I could pick up some music. Classic FM obviously knew we were out here. They were playing 'Shipwrecked', from Rimsky-Korsakov's 'Scheherazade'.

By midday, Alan decided our only course of action was to turn tail and head for home. We'd been 'hot-bunking' whilst sleeping under way - there were only two sleeping bags on board - so the first problem when we arrived in Falmouth was to borrow something from a neighbouring boat in the marina which I might use to keep me warm. It was the following evening in Torquay that Alan asked me if I'd like to go around the world with them. I didn't have to consider it for a moment. I simply said: 'Yes.' Even on the first trip out, the idea of going around the world in this tiny boat had captured my imagination in a way that nothing else I'd ever done had.

Even without the world record we'd been striving to set, Spirit of Portsmouth appeared at the Southampton Boat Show in September 1999. There was lots of interest, and I was presented with my official crew T-shirt embroidered with my name, and the word 'Crew'. I was pleased as punch. It was like joining the Beatles.

We took the boat to the Antwerp boat show at the end of the month, and if I thought that the seas off the south coast of Ireland were nasty, they were nothing compared to the crossing to Belgium. We set off from the boat's marina on Hayling Island mid-evening, but never even made it out of Chichester Harbour. The wind simply turned us through 180°. Again and again. After two hours, we'd covered about five miles. We pulled in to Sparkes Yacht Harbour at the seaward end of Hayling Island and decided to moor up and wait until the morning.

We crossed the Channel the next day, and made our way to Nieuwpoort, just along the coast from Ostend, battling through huge seas. By the time we arrived in Antwerp the following day, we were 24 hours late. Other visiting boats had cancelled due to the foul weather, and the organisers were worried about us. It was an interesting show, not least because it was my first experience of people inflicting their scepticism on me, and for the fact that the port area appeared to be run by the Russian mafia, with shifty-looking thickset men in leather jackets lurking suspiciously on street corners. The red light district was here, too, and we created something of a stir on our last day when we gave away a pile of Hogg Robinson T-shirts and other promotional goodies to the various girls in their little glass-fronted cabins. But we'd somehow overlooked one ample-fronted young lady, who ran down the street after us in nothing more than high heels, a thong and a skimpy see-through top. She was clearly in need of support, so we gladly gave her our last T-shirt.

We next set off in the boat for the third attempt at the British Isles record on the 3rd June 2000, by which time a lot had happened. The project was in the process of moving to Wales, and now the boat was called Spirit of Cardiff. She'd been berthed on the quiet in Penarth Marina, so while the local press and others were anxious to get a look at her, our departure from Cardiff was relatively low key. The visitor centre was due to open the following month, and Alan wanted to keep the boat under wraps until then. And apart from anything else, having had two well-publicised attempts fall flat, we didn't want to shout about this one until we were successful.

We headed west once more, this time with the disadvantage of the extra mileage of the Bristol Channel to contend with. After a clear run out to Fastnet, turning right up the west coast of Ireland saw us reduced to half our cruising speed, battling against rough head seas. Every so often, the buffeting proved too much for the autopilot. It emitted a loud beeping noise and the boat veered off to one side as it threw an electronic tantrum. Fortunately each little wobbler was short-lived, and autopilot and boat regained their composure.

By the time we arrived at St Kilda after 36 hours of horrendous punishment at not much more than 10 knots, I'd seen flashing buoys that weren't there, and pink elephants leaping in front of the boat. I was gobsmacked when an Anglia Railways ticket inspector appeared at my shoulder demanding to see my ticket! We all admitted to hearing things - strange voices and distant music out of the boat's two-way radio, all a product of serious sleep deprivation.

From St Kilda we moved east, knocking off more of the outlying islands, including Sula Sgeir and North Rona. We pulled into Scrabster in the north of Scotland for our first refuelling stop, 57 hours after leaving Cardiff. This was the longest I'd been at sea in a small boat, and I was warned to watch my step when I alighted onto dry land.

'Chances are you'll fall over,' Steve told me. It's just as well I didn't, as getting onto the quay involved a 20 feet vertical climb up an iron rung ladder, but I certainly felt pretty wobbly. After refuelling, we nipped into a local bar for a quick drink, but I was so exhausted I couldn't even fight my way through a pint of shandy.

Three hours after arriving, we were off again into the night - what little there was of it this far north - heading for Shetland. By the morning of the 6th June, we'd reached Muckle Flugga, the furthest point north, as close to Norway as we were to mainland Scotland. We turned south into the blessed relief of a following sea, so good we even started to make up time. Not enough to regain the 30 hours we lost at half speed in the Atlantic, but it was something to see us doing over 25 knots. The next day we were off the east coast of England.

'We've clocked up an impressive 550 miles in 24 hours,' Alan informed us.

In that second a huge wave hit us, crashing down on top of the cabin. Water gushed with incredible force through the partially open hatches in the cabin roof. When we recovered from our mini Niagara, we found that the four spare fuel tanks at the back of the boat - no lightweights at 91 litres each - had ripped from their mountings, and the pipe unions between them ruptured, turning the deck into a lethally slippery combination of diesel and seawater. So now we had to pump out the remaining fuel into the main tank, and try to clean the deck so it was safe to walk on.

By contrast, the trip along the south coast of England was smooth and uneventful. We tied up at Sparkes Yacht Harbour on Hayling Island for our second refuelling stop, and headed off towards Land's End. But there was a final sting in the tail. From there to the Scillies, we picked up a south-westerly wind, with the seas every bit as vicious as we'd encountered up north.

We stopped for a short while to take in the view of Bishop Rock lighthouse, huge plumes of spray shooting up as the waves blasted the rocks which surround it. 'OK, let's go home,' said Alan, turning the Spirit's bow towards the Bristol Channel. We arrived back at the entrance to Cardiff Harbour at 1605 on the 8th June, five days six hours and five minutes after setting off, having travelled around 2,200 nautical miles.

Apart from the refuelling stops, and other occasional stops at sea to rectify a variety of problems, we'd been working around the clock. We'd each averaged four hours sleep a night, split into two chunks of two hours, for five nights. But the reward was setting a new world record with the first ever powerboat circumnavigation of the British

Isles, and knocking 15 hours off Steve Fossett's record for the fastest circumnavigation.

The next trip out in Spirit, four months later, was going to start ratcheting up the pressure on Cable and Wireless Adventurer's records. The original intention was to take on her first two port-to-port records, from Gibraltar to Monaco, and Monaco to Port Said. But lack of money forced us to shelve the second leg. But Gibraltar to Monaco would be the most significant. At 773.6 nautical miles, covered in 36 hours 58 minutes at an average speed of 20.91 knots, it was the Adventurer's fastest leg around the world. If we could beat that, we could beat the rest.

Once again, Jan couldn't come with us, so Alan decided to offer the spare place to the South Wales Echo for one of its reporters. So it was that Matt Lloyd found himself on a rather unusual assignment.

He'd thought he was coming on something a bit more comfortable, and it was a rude awakening to find himself sitting outside throwing up into a bucket as we battered our way down the ever-bumpy Bristol Channel. It was rough all the way out, but by the time we were crossing the Bay of Biscay, it was beautifully calm. Even so, we'd burned fuel at a rate of three litres per nautical mile, which was far more than our nominal consumption, so we made an unscheduled refuelling stop in Porto in Portugal.

We arrived in Gibraltar three days after setting off from Cardiff. 'I should point out,' said Alan, 'that technically, RIBs are banned in Gibraltar. We may get arrested.' The reason is that they're ideal for drug-running across the short stretch of sea between Europe and North Africa. Whilst in Gibraltar, at the other end of the harbour from the stricken nuclear submarine HMS Tireless, we met the local police, who were indeed interested in Spirit of Cardiff. They quite fancied the idea of one made from Kevlar reinforced plastic with bullet-proof windows.

Wayne Warwick, our official RYA timekeeper, timed us out from an impressively powerful RIB operated by HM Customs. They did a few high-speed passes and then we were on our own. Almost immediately we spotted the unmistakable dorsal fins of sharks slicing through the water.

After four hours, we were six and half miles behind Cable and Wireless Adventurer. We always knew this was going to be a very tactical run. Fully fuelled, Spirit was slow and sluggish, but after the first ton of fuel had burned off, she became a different boat, more responsive, and faster. As the boat became lighter, so the speed increased.

It was rough during the night as we passed close by Ibiza, and the other Balearic Islands, but by the morning it had flattened off. By now we were making 23½ knots, and we were on course to knock at least two hours off the Cable and Wireless record. But as the speed increased even further, and we closed on Monaco, we had a heart-stopping moment.

The boat revved madly and lost speed, like a car with a slipping clutch. The worst case scenario was that our transmission had packed up. But Alan persevered. 'I'm not losing this record now,' he said, easing the throttle up once more. It took about 10 minutes, but eventually the boat came back up to speed. The short sea conditions and the lightness of the boat had caused the propeller to cavitate, basically losing its grip on the water.

Our final hours whizzing up the Cote d'Azure at up to 27 knots ended with us arriving in Monaco harbour, looking for somewhere to tie up and for our UIM timekeepers. The harbour was totally awesome, packed with huge luxury yachts, including the Lady Moura, the plaything of some Saudi fat cat businessman, and allegedly the largest and most expensive privately owned yacht in the world.

But most importantly, we'd gained yet another world record. We'd knocked one hour 19 minutes off Cable and Wireless Adventurer's fastest around the world port-to-port record. We'd taken on the big boys and won. Next year we'd challenge their last two port-to-port records, from New York to Horta, and Horta to Gibraltar.

And then we'd take their entire around the world record.

6
GOING COMMANDO

If it was easy we would all be doing it. That is why you are only the second attempt at the challenge and making a good job of it against the odds.
Website posting from official Gibraltar timekeeper Wayne Warwick.

Friday 19th April

As we set off from Jeddah just after midnight, I realise that all our earlier suspicions about Alan Carter have been realised. Whilst on the quayside, we'd sat down with him to talk over the problem. Why, we wondered, hadn't he discussed it with us before?

'I didn't want to bother you until I was fairly certain what I was going to do,' he'd told us. Apparently his wife Mary had found his absence difficult to bear, both in personal terms, and from her also having to run his business. We all sympathised with him. He'd been thrown in at the deep end, just three weeks before setting off, and his family hadn't had the same time to prepare for his absence as ours.

'But I don't want to leave you in a mess,' he'd stated adamantly. 'I'll leave all the filming equipment. I'd still like to remain involved with the project and making the documentary.'

Of course it all turns out to be academic, since there was no way he was going to leave us via Saudi Arabia. And so we set off, knowing we have one rather less than willing crew member on board. It's all very unsettling.

The plus side is that today is sublime, apart from the stifling heat, anyway. For a change, we have good sea conditions, so even with a full fuel load, we're making 15 to 17 knots. At the current estimate, we should be in Aden, Yemen by Saturday lunchtime.

For a spot of light relief, we amuse ourselves with a wacky photo shoot. It involves Alan and Steve standing naked on the back of the boat, with the rifles - our main defence against any pirates - held strategically in front of them. I of course have to pose for one too, but as I'm unable to maintain my balance standing up, I crouch down on one knee on the engine box, the rifle propped at a rakish angle to maintain some sense of decorum. The photo of Alan and Steve is hilarious, and ends up being emailed to a small circle of family and friends who will appreciate the joke. I'm far more sensible with mine, and keep it tucked away in the inner recesses of my Psion. Although the offer of very large sums of money may possibly coax it out.

Late in the afternoon, and what has been like a millpond all day has started to become marginally bumpy. We're just hoping the wind doesn't get up too much. It'll be a southerly if it does - which is not what we want at all. We also find that although the radar alarm has been on, one ship gets to within a mile of us without tripping it. Just the job when we're all lying down, stupefied in the sweltering heat, with no one looking out.

Saturday 20th April

During the night, we see a lot of ships, some of which look decidedly dubious, including one with a speedboat mounted ominously from davits at its stern. Whilst a lot of pirate activity comes from opportunist fishermen out to make a bit on the side when richer pickings present themselves, the professionals use speedboats, and quite often operate in packs. Those are the ones we have to keep our eyes peeled for.

We're approaching Bab-el-Mendeb, the strait at the southern end of the Red Sea, where it narrows to around 17 miles before it opens out into the Gulf of Aden. To our left is Yemen, to our right, Eritrea and Djibouti. The name means 'Gate of Tears', which according to Arabic legend, comes from an earthquake which drowned many people, although it's also ascribed to the dangers of navigating the strait with its strong currents. But I guess it could also have a modern day meaning, given that it's here where most of the reported pirate activity happens - shallow waters in a narrow channel, where the victims, and that includes large cargo ships, have nowhere to go.

According to the International Chamber of Commerce's Maritime

Bureau, there were 13 attempted boardings of ships in the southern part of the Red Sea in 2000, where previously there had been none. That of course doesn't take account of the many incidents which go unreported. The sudden increase in criminal activity is obviously a sign of the times. The biggest potential danger is just after we've passed through the strait, where we're at our closest to the Somali coast. Here warring factions attack passing ships on a regular basis, taking crews hostage for ransom. Official advice for the area is that anywhere within 100 miles of the north Somali coast is unsafe - splendid news given that our route around the coast of Yemen has us within 80 miles at one point.

In the main, we're hoping that the boat's speed and mean police/military profile will stand us in good stead against any pirates. Jan's original suggestion for a more pro-active remedy was for a high-powered automatic rifle with a mixture of tracer and phosphor-tipped rounds to show we meant business with any potential aggressor. Possibly even a hand-portable ceramic rocket launcher. We have a couple of basic rifles, although it's debatable how effective they'd be in bumpier conditions, given that they need to be aimed. Just as an afterthought, I've brought a high-powered laser pointer with me. Made for presentations and slide shows, it has a range of several hundred metres, and the red dot which it throws out could possibly be construed as a laser gun sight. If nothing else, a laser pointer is capable of temporarily blinding someone if it flashes in their eyes, and giving them a splitting headache. Maybe just enough to put off anyone who tries chasing us.

A Singapore registered container ship comes up behind us and overtakes. We're in bumpy head seas at the moment, and Alan tries his usual ploy of nipping round behind to gain some shelter in the ship's wash. He tries to call them up on the radio, but they don't respond.

'They're not looking happy, Al,' says Steve, noticing a flurry of activity on the ship's bridge. We're in the heart of pirate country, and it's common practice for ships not to respond to any radio calls, particularly from small speedboats like ours getting uncomfortably close. Alan decides to draw abreast of the ship so they can get a clearer look at the logos along our side. Before we know it, they're returning our call.

'What are your intentions? Over.'

Alan explains that we're a round-the-world powerboat, and it transpires the ship, the Kota Wajar, is also heading for Aden. So we can take shelter behind her, providing we can keep up. As we continue in her wake, we spot a speedboat off our starboard bow, around a mile off. These are most definitely not pleasure boating waters, and there can be only one assumption as to what it must be. Fortunately for us, he's having much bigger problems than we are in these head seas, and whilst it's almost unbearably uncomfortable tail-gating the Kota Wajar, we're making 19 knots.

So in the space of around 20 minutes, we've been mistaken for pirates, and we've seen them (probably) ourselves. Fortunately we've shown what could well have been the real thing a clean pair of heels.

The problem now is that we simply aren't able to keep up with the Kota Wajar. There's so much air in the water, our prop isn't biting efficiently - a phenomenon called cavitation. We can't get the boat to perform, and we're injuring ourselves in the process. Reluctantly we fall back to a more comfortable speed of around 10 knots. Bang goes our chance of arriving in Aden today - unless the weather changes again. And for once our fairy godmother is working to her job description. As the sea opens out from the strait, it flattens off, and we're up to 21 knots. Maybe we might do Aden today after all.

The coastline looks rugged and mountainous, quite dramatic. Suddenly, we spot a small fishing boat in the distance. There are three or four people aboard, and they appear to be trying to signal us - standing up and waving their arms above their heads. It's an internationally accepted form of distress signal. Do we go over and see what the problem is? The answer comes as another and then another fishing boat comes into view, strangely all with their occupants waving. It's an unusual epidemic of boats in distress, without a doubt. Those that have been taken in by this kind of activity in the past have pulled alongside to have guns levelled at them - not what we're planning on! Needless to say, we leave them all to their fate, which is to go back to fishing until a slower boat crewed by more gullible people comes along.

We'd been hoping to make Aden harbour before nightfall, not least because having only seen Jeddah in darkness, it would be nice to see

Aden - supposedly very beautiful with its surrounding mountains - in daylight. We don't quite make it, though, with dusk gathering while we're still around 10 miles out.

'Fishing boat dead ahead!'

In the half-light, Steve spots the shadowy shape of a slender boat with outboard motor. The guy on board is clearly rattled to see a powerboat bearing down on him at high speed, and after scrabbling about, he flashes a torch at us wildly. Luckily, we've already seen him and taken avoiding action. But it's a salutary reminder that there will be many such incidents of small boats out at night without proper lights.

Located inside the crater of a dead volcano, and protected by a bay, its natural harbour made Aden an important maritime staging post for years. It was a British protectorate up until 1967, when it became the capital of South Yemen. North and South Yemen unified in 1990, with the capital in Sana'a, but dissatisfaction with the government lead to a short-lived civil war in 1994. Aden is now very much the commercial capital of the Republic of Yemen.

We have a few communications problems as we arrive in Aden harbour, where we're not quite sure where to go. It doesn't help that the lighting at various installations isn't particularly bright. Eventually we find the right place to go, although not before attempting to tie up at a secure fuelling berth, where a guy promptly unslings his AK47 and points it at Steve, standing in the well at the front with the bow line. Welcome to Yemen.

After an hour bobbing around in the harbour, a small motorboat comes out to meet us. Alan Priddy, Alan Carter and I hop aboard, to be taken ashore to the harbour administration office. Here we meet Gamal Saddiq, our agent in Aden, who helps us complete the paperwork. When I ask the official in charge whether it's OK to film some of the proceedings, I'm surprised when he nips out and returns shortly, dressed up in a splendid green uniform with epaulettes. He's obviously out to create a good impression. In fact everyone here is extremely warm and friendly.

Also here to meet us is a journalist from a newspaper in Aden. He interviews each of us in turn, with translations from Gamal recorded on cassette. He wonders what we think of Aden. We tell him we're pleased to be here, and that we're looking forward to coming back

Alan Priddy, Clive Tully and Steve Lloyd, about to set off from St John's harbour, across the Atlantic on the final leg of the round the world voyage.
Photograph: Egbert Walters

'What's that big bumper all about?' The down-to-earth fishermen of Gloucester, Massachusetts didn't know quite what to make of Spirit.

South Wales Echo journalist Matt Lloyd on the record-breaking run from Gibraltar to Monaco, October 2000.

Jan Falkowski can't believe what he's eating

End of a record-breaking run. Spirit in Monaco harbour, jam-packed with luxury yachts.

Most of the skyscrapers in lower Manhattan would make Canary Wharf look tiny. But even they were dwarfed by the twin towers of the World Trade Center.

Spirit of Cardiff at South Street Seaport Museum, lower Manhattan, New York, with an impressive backdrop of skyscrapers.

Floating movie star. The Lady Grace, aka Andrea Gail, moored up next to Cape Pond Ice, Gloucester, Massachusetts.

Boston, USA: Spirit of Cardiff poses next to 'Old Ironsides', the USS Constitution, the US Navy's oldest commissioned warship.

The departure from Cardiff on March 31st 2002 was marked by dull and overcast skies. But crowds of people turned out to see us off from both Mermaid Quay and Cardiff Bay Barrage, and we were escorted out by a flotilla of RIBs and other vessels.

After the first windscreen smash off Cape St Vincent, Portugal. Fortunately, the laminate held, but subsequent waves crashing over the front did give rise to leaks over the instrument panel.

Spirit looking sorry for herself at a quick extra refuelling stop in Lagos before carrying on to Gibraltar.

RYA timekeeper Wayne Warwick aboard HM Customs RIB, timing us off on the run from Gibraltar to Monaco, October 2000.

Alan presents Cardiff's plaque and letter of greeting to Gibraltar's mayor, Judge John Alcantara.

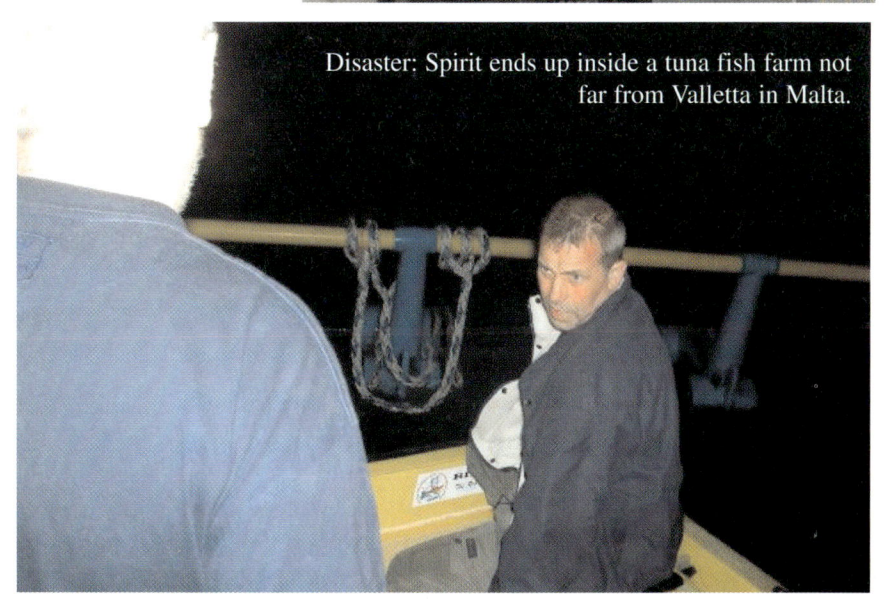

Disaster: Spirit ends up inside a tuna fish farm not far from Valletta in Malta.

Steve Lloyd inspects Spirit's damaged outdrive. The 35hp wing engine is still in place.

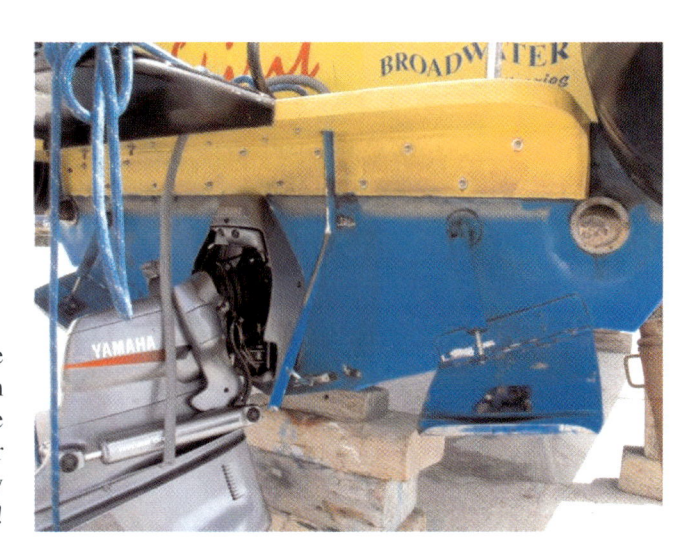

Damaged outdrive and broken trim tab. More to the point, the shower pipe is seriously bent!

Alan in contemplative mood as Spirit heads for Egypt.

Nice thought. Perhaps it should have been bigger!

This splendid mosque overlooked the marina where we were berthed for the best part of a day, waiting to go through the Suez Canal.

Cargo ships on the Suez Canal. We have to wait nearly a day before making our passage through, but when we do, we set a new unofficial record for the fastest transit of the canal.

Tailgating the Kota Wajar at the southern end of the Red Sea. These guys initially thought we were pirates.

Aden, Yemen: Our agent Gamal Saddiq acts as translator for a local journalist interviewing Alan.

Gulf of Aden. Steve bashes some potatoes ready for our evening meal.

An impressive welcome to Salalah in Oman. This is one of two tugs firing its water cannons in salute.

Blue skies and smooth seas, all the way across the Indian Ocean.

After Alan Carter's mishap with the stove, Alan and Steve come up with this temporary remedy until we can get a new pan support welded on in Mangalore.

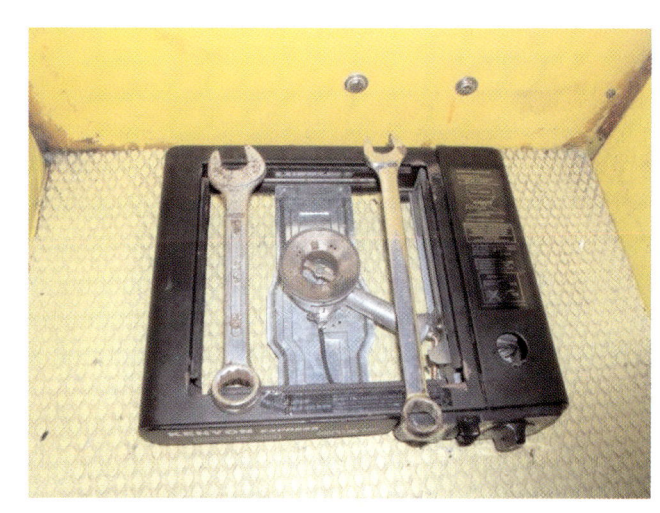

Rows of fishing boats in Mangalore old port. It's early morning, and already the heat is oppressive.

A traditional welcome with garlands in Mangalore. But it has to look right for the camera.

Gently does it! Spirit is lifted out of the water in Mangalore ready for her gearbox oil change. The rope looks as though it has seen better days, but at least it's better than the previous one, which broke, dropping the boat from around two feet into the water.

Refuelling in Galle, Sri Lanka. We needed a navy escort to enter the harbour at night - then we had to listen to the noise of explosives being let off at intervals.

This boat in Sabang looks like something out of a Terry Gilliam film.

When the propeller shed its blades in the Malacca Strait, Alan and Steve tried to remove the remains in order to fit the spare. But it wasn't possible to do the job until we were at Raffles Marina in Singapore. There was virtually nothing left of the old prop barring the sleeve which locates on the prop shaft.

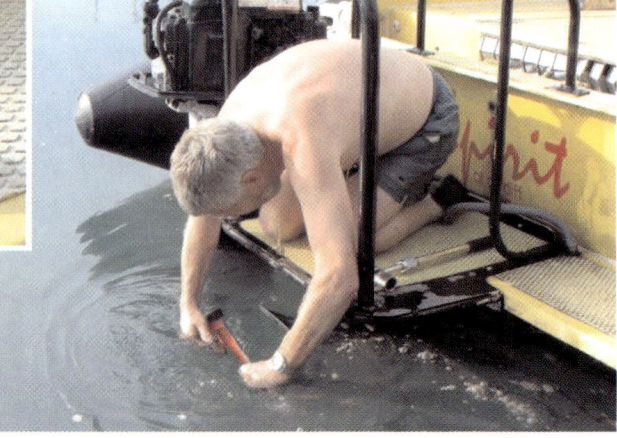

some time to explore the place properly, preferably with the benefit of daylight.

Given that our boat is in the harbour where the guided missile destroyer USS Cole was bombed by al-Qaeda terrorists in October 2000, with the loss of 17 lives, we're interested to hear the locals' version of events. We're told that after the bombing, the Americans threatened to blow out of the water any boat of any nationality which came within what they deemed too close. What seems to annoy most Yemenis - and none of those that I speak to condone the attack in any way - was the heavy-handed manner in which the Americans over-rode the rule of law in their host nation. Which they think simply reinforces the reason why the terrorists - aggrieved over the continuing US presence in Saudi Arabia - felt the need to attack them in the first place.

With formalities and interviews over, we're whisked back to the Spirit, still moored up to another boat out in the harbour - accompanied by a large posse. Steve probably wonders what's going on for a minute as the boat is boarded by at least a dozen people, some in the cabin, some on the engine box, others clinging to the railings along the sides of the cabin. Then it's off to the fuel bunker to get our diesel, before heading out into the night, crew back down to four, and our next stop in Oman.

Sunday 21st April

There's excitement during the night while Al and Steve are on watch. I wake up to hear Steve telling Al with more than a sense of urgency to go plus 10 - using the push-button steering on the autopilot to make it hang a right. They come into a gaggle of fishing boats, but apparently while they have lights, they don't all have conventional ones, and we nearly run into one of them. Then Alan wakens, takes over, and all is resolved safely.

It's now three weeks since setting off from Cardiff, and two since setting off from Gibraltar. It seems like a lifetime away. But we've started to move now with much better conditions.

With the front hatch up, there's a strong breeze blowing through the cabin, so it's quite pleasant. But the sun outside is ferocious, so while the others are soaking it up avidly, I don't venture out too much. In any event, I'm finding that the amount of writing and emailing I have to do each day dictates that I'm chained to my bunk/office for most of the daylight hours.

We spot a group of fishermen in their long thin boats with outboards. They actually appear to be fishing as opposed to waving their arms about pretending to be in distress. In places the sea is absolutely alive with fish.

From the emails we're receiving from Nadia, our one-woman whirlwind pit-stop organiser back in Cardiff, tomorrow's stop in Salalah sounds as though it'll be quite good. We're going to be fed, and there are rumours the British Ambassador may show his face. Perhaps the most heartening news is that Al has decided to stay with us after all, so presumably has resolved the problems his wife was having. It means we won't be short-handed, which is reassuring. I was rather dreading the consequences of our being reduced to a three-man crew.

Alan receives the weather forecast from Bertie. What's classed as head seas for the first day - actually what we're motoring through very smoothly at 21 knots - will be followed by flat seas all the way across to India and round to Sri Lanka. So although we'd expected slow progress on account of the extra fuel weight, we should in theory do much better.

I spend the whole day from about 1000 till 1800 working, but with time off for a shower. The water coming out of the hose at the back of the boat is no longer what you'd call bracing. More like pretty warm.

Al and Steve put together a fine evening meal of boiled potatoes, baked beans and tuna with tomato. It seems as though the gas stove is doing just fine at 21 knots, with no sharp bumps to dislodge the pot. It's a nice friendly occasion with all four of us together, enjoying something substantial to eat as the sun goes down. Certainly everyone's a lot more relaxed together now the issue of Al's possible departure is resolved.

'Come on Steve. Give us a smile.'

Alan has noticed that as it gets darker, Steve's now deeply tanned face blends into the night sky. But as he obliges, his big filmstar grin appears as an almost disembodied glowing set of teeth, rather like the Cheshire cat.

Monday 22nd April

We're making good time, and will arrive in Salalah in Oman ahead of schedule. In fact, we're offshore before 0800, and the sun is already getting unbearably hot. Because the arrangements for this stop are rather more elaborate, and everything is paid for, Alan decides we must bide our time until they're ready for us, calling them later to see how soon we can come in.

That's all very well, but without the boat zipping along at 20 knots, there's no cooling breeze coming through the open front hatch. It rapidly becomes unbearable. The sweat runs off our foreheads, stinging our eyes. I'm tempted to jump in the water for a swim, but after I see a couple of jellyfish close by, it doesn't seem like such a good idea. Eventually, as we're visibly wilting in the oppressive heat and humidity, we put the boat into a holding pattern, driving around in circles at slow speed - just enough to provide a little draught.

It's late morning when we head in to Salalah, Oman's second city and the only port between Europe and Singapore capable of accommodating the biggest container ships, to a welcome which matches the weather. Two tugboats escort us in, water cannons shooting huge jets of water on each side, and we pass the Sultan of Oman's impressive Royal Yacht. Set up by Mike Garside, an old chum of Alan's and one of our strong supporters, the stop has been organised by Salalah Port Services and BP, and their personnel are here to greet us. Up on the quayside, they've set up tables and parasols, and provided hot and cold buffet meals for us, along with a selection of soft drinks. It's almost overwhelming, and the local press and TV have turned up as well. As port staff refuel the boat, people crowd on board to have their pictures taken.

We're suffering from gippy tummies and salt sores - tiny white blisters on our backs and bums which have appeared as a result of the climate, and excessive sitting or lying down. Bed sores, in fact. Alan mentions it discreetly, but before we know it, they've sent for the port doctor, who brings a large bag of various medications, including antibiotic and hydrocortisone creams for the salt sores, and rehydration fluids for the diarrhoea problems.

'Put this one on first,' he tells us. 'Then this one.' It all sounds a bit too clinical, and just as I'm wondering whether any of this will require the use of rubber gloves, he dispenses his most useful advice.

'Don't wear any pants,' he says. 'Just wear loose shorts.' In fact, not only does it cut down the chances of getting the sores, I find subsequently it's a lot better when you're, er, in a hurry. From then on in the tropics, I 'go commando'.

As I'm suffering the most on the tummy side, I have to ask to go to the loo, which involves a short ride in a Toyota Landcruiser to the port admin block. By the time I'm back, the boat is fuelled up and ready to go, and piles of food and drink have been stowed in the forward cabin. The crew of the Royal Fleet Auxiliary Fort Austin - loading up to resupply British warships in the Indian Ocean for the continuing military operations in Afghanistan - have also donated a great pile of NATO 24-hour ration packs, a gesture we very much appreciate. We set off, accompanied once more by the two tugs with water cannons and a spectacular farewell salute blasted out from the horn of the Sultan's Royal Yacht.

Out of harbour, it's one visit after another to the dive platform. At least I've got used to it, hanging my bum over the back. I've even gone native, dispensing with toilet paper in favour of using the shower hose. So far it's been more inconvenient than debilitating. But we also have to do a bit of pruning. We've got so much extra weight on board, it's going to affect fuel consumption, and for the 1,250 mile run to Mangalore, fuel economy is absolutely vital. So the ratpacks are cannibalised for the more important bits - the boil-in-the-bag meals and the absolutely fantastic chocolate bars - and the rest has to be thrown out.

But as we set off across the Indian Ocean on our longest leg around the world, little do we realise just how critical the fuel consumption will become.

7
THE WEATHER

We are the first to admit that we were unbelievably lucky with our 1998 weather window, and you seemed to get all the rubbish that we missed.
John Walker, Logistics Director, Cable and Wireless Adventurer.

IT COULD RAIN as much as it liked - the one thing which powerboats dislike with a passion is high winds. Sailing boats love it when it's windy, but for us, windy weather spelt discomfort, reduced speed and wasted fuel.

Spirit of Cardiff's route for the circumnavigation, and the time of year we attempted it, was planned to make the best of the weather. We'd had a minor taste of the difficulties involved with a large circumnavigation when we went around the British Isles in June 2000. Taking a 2,146 mile route which encompassed the North Sea, the Scillies, the west coast of Ireland and the most northerly of the Scottish islands, there was no way you could expect good weather all the way along. We waited nearly a year between the second and third attempts before a narrow window presented itself, and even then when we set off, it was in the knowledge that the weather would start off bad, but it would get better.

Similarly, we couldn't expect perfect conditions all the way round the world, but we were aiming for the least worst. Looking at the charts, the theory was that for most of the route, the trade winds would give us following seas (behind us) or beam seas (side on), with very few head seas. We couldn't afford to go any later in the year, because we didn't want to get caught up in the south-west monsoon. While there can be typhoons every month of the year in the South China Sea and all the way up Japan, if we were too late into the autumn in Kamchatka, we'd get ice. Too early, and the wind would be in the wrong direction.

Of course, we ended up with a few surprises on that score. 2002 proved to be a year when the weather worldwide was particularly bad. While Cable and Wireless Adventurer had been immensely lucky with the weather, we were immensely unlucky.

But where we did count our blessings was in having an extremely clever weather forecaster, 82 year-old Bertram Ramsey, or Bertie, as we knew him. Bertie spent World War Two in the Royal Navy, where he did have one small brush with his marginally differently spelt namesake, Admiral Sir Bertram Ramsay - who organised the evacuation of Dunkirk, the invasions of North Africa and Sicily, and who was in overall command of naval operations for the D-Day landings in Normandy in 1944. Bertie gave him a weather briefing at the Royal Naval Air Station at Yeovilton before the Admiral flew off and was shot down over Holland.

Bertie had been a weather forecaster since leaving school. When the war came along in 1939, the 19 year-old went along to the recruiting office for the Royal Navy, which he wanted to join more than anything else.

'There was a great big Sergeant from the Royal Marines,' he remembers, 'and he said: "Well what do you want?" I said I'd like to join the navy to be a meteorologist. He said: "What?"'

'He rang up Newcastle, which was the headquarters for my home town of Middlesbrough, and said: "There's a bloke here who wants to be a me, me, me-something." So that was it, I became a meteorologist.'

Bertie's abiding memory of the war is of being sunk. In 1942, he was on the light cruiser HMS Edinburgh - which the previous year had been one of the key players in the hunt for the Bismarck - doing Arctic convoy protection duties. When they fired the guns, he recalled, it was quite dangerous to be close to them, because in the sub-zero conditions, great shards of ice blew off.

Bertie was pretty used to the high winds and big seas which we experienced. On board Edinburgh, it was a comfort in a way to be east of Iceland in 50 foot waves, because it meant no German submarine could launch its torpedoes.

'The day we were caught out,' he says, 'it was a calm afternoon, and I was at my plot desk. Suddenly I heard this bang and fell on my knees, and the plot desk leapt across the room.'

Edinburgh was attacked twice in the Barents Sea north of Murmansk by German submarines in April and May 1942. Severely damaged and without power, she was finally scuttled by torpedo on 7th May by the British destroyer HMS Foresight to prevent the secret cargo of five tons of Russian gold bullion - about £45 millions' worth, being transported to America to pay for armaments - from falling into German hands.

Bertie was married in Sydney in 1945, carrying on in the navy until 1950. Then he joined the Met Office, where he spent the next 28 years travelling all over the world. 'By the time I'd been married 40 years,' he says, 'my wife and I had had 40 different addresses!'

In 1978, 58 years old, Bertie left the Met Office to join a civil firm working with oil rigs in the Gulf. That lasted for six years, then he took ad hoc assignments in a variety of places until 1990, by which time he was 70 and retired. Since then, he's been amusing himself forecasting the weather for various mariners, ourselves included. For a man in his 80s, he's in pretty good health and very sharp - undoubtedly down to keeping himself so well occupied in his retirement.

'There's never a dull moment,' he says. 'Someone's always ringing me up.'

While the technology of weather forecasting has progressed in leaps and bounds over the years, the basic physics has remained the same. Bertie takes most of his information from the US Naval Research Laboratory in Monterey, California, along with the Deutscher Wetterdienst, the German national weather service. The advent of the internet has been a real boon, too. Needless to say, Bertie is on broadband in order to download his data quicker.

Raw weather information comes from many different sources, including ships and buoys. It's all transmitted via satellite and available from one of these services, at which point, Bertie looks at it and interprets it to give us a weather forecast.

'That's a balloon that went up from Cornwall about three hours ago,' he says, pointing to a graph on his computer screen. 'From that, I can tell how moist the air is.'

The downstairs room in his small house in Gosport, which most might use as a lounge, is jam-packed with radios, computers, teletype printers and all sorts of weather equipment, some of it linked up by wires to sensors outside. In the nicest possible way, this is the home of a boffin.

So what's the secret to the amazing accuracy of Bertie's forecasting? 'Years and years of experience,' he laughs. 'But there's a certain feeling about it as well. My mother said I used to scream in the pram until I saw a tree moving about in the wind. As soon as I got into the sixth form at school, I'd take weather reports from the radio, and chart them up in my own way, so I guess it's gone on from there.'

Alan always phoned Bertie every day at 1000 Zulu. Nothing whatsoever to do with Michael Caine or Rorke's Drift, Zulu time is the navy's way of referring to the time at the prime meridian - Greenwich Mean Time, in other words. Alan would give Bertie our position, and Bertie would try to give him a forecast about six days ahead if possible.

Throughout all of our adventures, Bertie had an uncanny knack of being right. Even to the point where we might be bashed about in rough seas, and Bertie would tell us it would get better in half an hour. He was always right on wind direction and strength. But that wasn't what Bertie called weather. Weather, to Bertie, is rain and sunshine. So Bertie might say: 'You haven't got much weather,' even though the wind was blowing at 30 knots.

There were several times when Bertie looked at the conditions we were going through, and feared for our lives, although he didn't say it in so many words at the time. He was most worried when we were in 50 knots of wind - Storm Force 10 - in the Caribbean.

'It always blows more in the summer in the Caribbean, but not as much as that, and it just wouldn't go,' he sighs. 'That storm stayed there long after you'd gone.'

If there was anyone who understood better than most what we went through with everything the weather threw at us, it was, without a doubt, Bertie.

8
A FIERY MEAL

Be careful you don't get more than you bargained for when letting it all hang out, Clive, what with all those fish flying about!
Website posting from Dave 'POP' Davies.

Tuesday 23rd April

WHILE IT'S EASY to dwell on the hardships aboard Spirit of Cardiff, there are moments of pleasure, too. Sunsets at sea can be very beautiful, but my favourite natural light phenomenon is the phosphorescent plankton which we often see at night. It glows eerily in small balls which can be seen zipping past the cabin on each side like Formula One fairy lights, and in our wash behind the boat. But as I discover on a nocturnal visit to the dive platform, what looks green when it's stirred up in the wash is actually an intense electric blue when squirted out of our shower hose. The really bright ones show through the grey plastic of the hose all the way up, and when splashed onto the deck of the dive platform, they remain there glowing for some time.

Whilst we've all suffered from Delhi Belly to an extent over the last couple of days, my attack has been rather more prolonged and vicious. But at least I've got the hang (sorry) of going off the back of the boat, crouching on the edge of the dive platform. Appropriately enough, I'm told that my horoscope for today in London's free newspaper, Metro, says: 'There is a breeze around Uranus!'

I finish my watch with Al as the sun comes up, and zonk out in bed, exhausted from the frequent toilet visits. I wake up at around 0830, aware that the cabin isn't sweltering quite as much as usual. Using drawing pins which were requested at the last minute at our stop in Salalah, Alan and Steve have suspended their towels across part of the front and side windows, creating a substantial level of shade. Where the front windows are unshaded, our portable electronic weather station is recording a temperature of over 50º C.

The main concern at the moment is fuel consumption. We've burned 700 litres in the first 250 miles, averaging 2.8 litres per mile. At that rate of consumption, we'd run out well before we reach Mangalore. The good news is that as the fuel burns off, the boat becomes lighter and therefore more fuel efficient. So while there shouldn't be any problems, we do need to keep a close watch on it, as this leg of the trip - the longest of them all - will have us stretched to the absolute limit of our range.

There's another heated moment when Al appears to be in something of a bad mood, accusing Alan and Steve of keeping him awake when they were on watch and he was trying to sleep. So another meeting is called when Al is then accused of always trying to overrule Alan. It's all resolved once more, and we go back to the status quo. To my mind, the underlying cause is that Al doesn't like the way Alan runs the boat. He's his own boss at home, and probably finds it hard to accept someone else's authority. I'm my own boss, too, but I don't have a problem. Alan has always said that when it comes to the running of the boat and matters of safety, he's skipper, and what he says goes. But on all other matters pertaining to the expedition, it's a democracy, and he's happy to go along with majority decisions.

We see one ship, but other than that, we've had the ocean to ourselves, although we do experience the amazing spectacle of flying fish. They don't just leap out of the water and plop back, but flap their fins/wings and remain airborne for some time, skimming above the waves. Without doubt a missing link in the evolutionary chain.

While the others divide their off-watch time between snoozing and sun-bathing, I'm glued to my Psion, making notes, writing updates, and struggling to send them. I'm not the world's best sun-bather, and I tend to burn fairly easily, so I sit and swelter inside, venturing out once or twice a day for a shower. The water is lukewarm, but the cooling effect of the wind on wet skin is nice. The only problem with washing self and clothes in sea water is that you end up ingrained with salt, which isn't exactly good for your skin. The clothes don't like it much, either. But it's either that or stinking.

By late afternoon the strength is out of the sun, and we enjoy a fine meal of boiled potatoes and mixed vegetables, seasoned with a little salad cream, followed by cold creamed rice with strawberry jam. The final entertainment for the day comes as Al is sitting outside enjoying a post-dinner cup of tea. He lets out a strangled cry, and there on the deck at his feet is a flying fish about nine inches long, no longer flying but crash-landed, flapping weakly.

'Well, chuck it out then,' says Alan from inside. Both Al and I recoil in squeamish horror at the thought of handling a slippery fish, a smelly one at that, so Alan deals with it instead.

'Careful,' warns Steve, 'it might have poisonous spines.' Alan grabs an old rag and picks up the fish to return it to its natural habitat.

Wednesday 24th April

There are times when it feels almost as though we're in the doldrums, even though we're making a good 15 knots. The sea has a flat, oily smoothness, and both it and the sky are intense blue. It's incredibly hot - 40° in the shade - and it's difficult to rake up the enthusiasm and energy to do anything. We don't even see any ships to break the monotony.

We're still doing alright on fuel consumption, but Alan is convinced that based on what's left and what the fuel flow meter tells us we've already used, we're missing some fuel - around 100 litres. He even checks to see whether there are any leaks anywhere. So whether we go for a fast finish still remains to be seen. At the moment it's uncertain whether we have enough fuel, but provided we keep our speed down, we should be able to guarantee our arrival in Mangalore. At the moment, it looks as though that will be first light Friday morning.

If that's a little area of uncertainty, something rather more dramatic happens as the sun goes down. Al is outside putting together a pasta meal when suddenly there are cries of: 'Help, help!' I poke my head around the doorway to see the stove engulfed by a ball of flame, with Al trying to beat out the flames with a rag. But it only seems to make matters worse. Alan runs out and thrashes the flames into submission with a pillow. It seems the gas cartridge hadn't sealed properly to the cooker when it was attached. Now the only problem is that in the panic, the pan support has gone overboard.

Alan and Steve try to find something else that will do. If it comes to it, we know we'll almost certainly be able to get something made up in India. In the meantime, we make do with the saucepan supported by two flat spanners. Heath Robinson it may be, but it does the job.

Thursday 25th April

Alan and I do the midnight to 0400 shift to knock out a reply to a very long list of bureaucratic claptrap pertaining to the Japanese stops. They want to know how much food we'll be carrying. I've said the purpose of calling into the ports is to re-provision, so we won't be carrying any. It takes around 15 minutes to compose the email, then almost an hour to send it. Good old Iridium.

Later in the morning, and Nadia's on the phone for Alan. It must be around 4am her time!

'What's the matter, Nadia?'

I can tell from Alan's reaction that she's upset about something, but apparently she's not making sense. The dodgy satphone connection doesn't help much.

'Speak slowly, Nadia,' he says. 'I can't understand you.'

Just as he's trying to get to the nub of the matter, the line drops.

'She asked me who the master file would go to if she was run over,' he tells me afterwards as he returns to his bunk. 'I said James [Alan's son], and then she said: "Watch out, there's a bus coming!" What the hell's that all about?'

In the ensuing phone calls, it's apparent that the strain back home has been as bad as it has been on the boat. The aberration is short-lived, and there's no doubt that our valued supporters, particularly Nadia, dealing with all the port arrangements, have their own worries.

Alan and Steve have solved the mystery of the missing 100 litres of fuel. Normally, when the boat is refuelled, the front tank is filled first. That settles the bow in the water, and levels off the main and side tanks. But because we were being fuelled up by BP in Oman, the tanks were filled in the wrong order, and there were quite a few people standing on the back of the boat having their pictures taken. The result is that the boat was tipped back sufficiently to ensure that the tanks weren't quite as full to the brim as they could have been. At least we know now for the future. We have to be strict and refuel without any assistance.

Steve lets out a particularly wet fart and a broad smile spreads across his face. 'Listen to me,' he says. 'I'm talking to the dolphins.'

The day wears on, and it's so hot, I find it impossible to go outside. It's instant frazzle. We've had one ship set the radar alarm off today. I guess as we get closer to land we'll see more traffic, but hopefully not all dodgy wooden boats without lights.

Friday 26th April

We wake up early ready for the run in to Mangalore. It's still dark, and as we approach the coast, not only do we see the lights spread out for quite some distance one side to the other, but the most noticeable thing is the smell. Perhaps it's because we've been out at sea for three days, our senses are enhanced by the ozone rich atmosphere. But even a mile offshore, the smell is unmistakeable - that odour which anyone who's been to India will understand immediately. A heady cocktail of things spicy fused with things unmentionable, and indeed things unimaginable.

Mangalore is best known as India's capital of coffee and cashew nuts, and also an important centre for fishing. As we come into the harbour, scores of quite large fishing boats are on their way out. We tie up in Mangalore's old port, first against a rather dilapidated boat. We're given a traditional Indian greeting - garlanded with flowers, rice sprinkled on our heads, vermilion dabbed on the forehead, and the fumes of a lamp wafted around us to ward off the evil spirits.

Once the warm welcome is over, we bring the boat round to the quayside to be lifted out of the water, the crane organised by Yashwanth Kangen, part-owner of the local boat-building company Maha Mysore Boats. This is the first of our scheduled service stops, which entails lifting the boat out to change the gearbox oil - the one item of routine maintenance which can't be done with the boat in the water. To be precise, it's not so much a quayside, more a rubbish dump. Soft ground covered with coconut husks and other things rather less pleasant. I get the feeling that the crane they've brought to do the job will have its work cut out here, and I'm right. The wheels spin into the soft ground and fail to get any traction.

'We're going to move round to the quay on the other side of the ferry jetty,' says Alan, hopping onto the boat. It seems a much better bet here, as the quayside is rather more solid. The only matter for concern now is what passes for lifting strops - four dubious looking blue nylon ropes. They don't look at all substantial to me, and my fears are confirmed when one of them snaps under tension. Fortunately the boat is only a couple of feet above the water, but as it splashes back stern first, it's a heart-stopping moment. I can tell from the look on Alan's face that the whole three and a half years of the project has just flashed in an instant before his eyes. If the boat had dropped like that onto the quayside, it really would have been all over.

The next attempt doesn't appear to look very much more promising. It's an old hemp-laid hawser, about one and a half inches thick, which also appears to have seen better days. The entire rope is threaded through the boat's four lifting eyes and looped over the crane's hook. This doesn't allow any easy way of ensuring the rope is evened up over the four lifting points, with the consequence that the boat comes out of the water bow down. As two and three quarter tons of RIB swings over the quayside, the hull is about an inch off the ground, the stern up in the air. Anyway, it seems to be enough for Alan to do the gearbox oil change, surrounded by a huge crowd of onlookers. I'm sure I'm not the only one to breathe a huge sigh of relief once the boat is safely back in the water.

Al and I are whisked off to the nearby Hotel Taj Manjarun by AbdulRehman Kunil, one of Alan's Rotary contacts, for a wash and brush up and breakfast. It transpires his niece is getting married, and he's booked the entire hotel - all 96 rooms and five suites - for the guests who are coming. A three day event, it's got to be some party! It's wonderful having a shower in fresh water for the first time since Port Said, but a shame I didn't have time to sort out clean clothes too, otherwise I would have done some laundry.

Refreshed, I'm then presented with the choices for breakfast. I decide on papaya, followed by my usual comfort food, a cheese omelette. Plus tea, of course. Not as fantastic as my late night cuppa in Jeddah, but good none the less. The only oddity is the toast, more like a biscuit, which comes in a paper bag.

Then it's back to the boat. After the air-conditioned comfort of the hotel, it's absolutely sweltering, and a stark reminder of the incredible contrasts of India. In the space of a few minutes, we've witnessed extreme poverty around the port area, and the five-star opulence of a luxury hotel.

Someone brings back the gas stove with a couple of steel bars welded on top to replace the pan support. The only thing is they couldn't weld one side where it's plastic, so it has a slightly molten look about it. A couple of guys also come to look at the microwave cooker. They can't unbolt it from within the rear seat box, but determine that something has indeed gone wrong with it. Anyway, at least our gas stove is usable again.

While Alan is at the hotel, he's taken aside to be told the British Ambassador has been in touch to say they can sort a visa for Al if required. Despite his assurance that he was committed to carrying on with us, it seems he still wants to jump ship. When confronted with it, Al admits that he may still go at some point because of some big contract that's coming up, but for the meantime he'll stay with us. So much for the 100% commitment. Now I just wish he'd go. He's nice enough, but he no longer has anyone's confidence, and the uncertainty is bad for morale.

Before we leave, we have a presentation ceremony, with Alan being given a small beautifully carved sandalwood box, representative of the area. It makes our Cardiff plaque and mouse mat look a bit lame. With all the wonderful gifts one could have presented which might be truly representative of Wales, I feel somewhat embarrassed every time we hand out these plaques. Nevertheless, so far, they've still been gracefully accepted.

Then we're on our way, but not before a final 30 minutes delay at the hands of the local police, who keep us waiting for the harbour clearance. While we've had to pay bribes elsewhere, this time we're well and truly mugged. We'd sent a crate of supplies - engineering spares, oil, dried food and toiletries - to Mangalore for us to pick up. It costs us an astonishing $700 to take charge of it, and when we open it up, we find that someone else has been there already. All the toiletries and snack foods have been stolen.

9
LOGISTICS

Someone asked about what food you were eating. I'd like to know, having been both impressed and shocked by the small mountain of tinned and dried groceries at the Spirit of Cardiff exhibition in Cardiff.
Website posting from Catherine McAulay.

WHEN YOU LOOK at round the world sailing races such as the Vendée Globe, the logistical side is relatively easy. You pack a boat with provisions for three months, and head for the horizon. OK, maybe I've over-simplified, but that's the essence of it. A powerboat, on the other hand, has to refuel. To refuel means it has to enter foreign ports, and the moment you do that, you have the delight of dealing with the local bureaucracy, who, on the most part, couldn't give a fig about record attempts, and how much of a hurry you're in.

And whilst ounces weren't critical on Spirit of Cardiff, pounds certainly were. We had limited storage space and no fridge, so there was no way we could pack provisions for four men to take them all the way round the world. In any event, that would create further problems with eagle-eyed customs officials on the look-out for banned food items. So each of Spirit's 'pit-stops' meant not just fuel, but food and drinking water.

Had we achieved our original budgets, the concept was to have three road crews of three leap-frogging around the world ahead of us. They would sort out the political and corruption problems, so we could pick up our provisions and leave, with the minimum of delay. They would also analyse the fuel we'd take on. If it was low grade, they would decant it into a holding tank and then add Cetane booster to improve the quality. That would have been infinitely more preferable than what actually happened, where all we could do was identify a problem after the fuel was in our tanks. We would have been able to run a lot faster, instead of belching black smoke and causing mechanical damage. The road crews would also organise a lot of PR and publicity, ensuring maximum coverage of our short time in port - the plan was to turn the boat round in no more than an hour.

Hogg Robinson, our travel organisers, had costed out the road crew element of the project in detail, and concluded that it could cost up to £200,000. That included airfares and hotels, but didn't cover other expenses or remuneration for road crew members' lost salaries. Even so, it was a drop in the ocean, compared with some high-profile events.

And in tune with our notion of making the Spirit of Cardiff project accessible to as many people as possible, we would throw open road crew places to anyone who was interested. They would have to undertake the same training as the crew to condition them for the stress, the sleepless nights, the tropical conditions. In a perfect world, those volunteers would have sought a certain level of their own sponsorship, so creating another layer of people interested.

It would need to have been run like a military operation, but the service crews could probably have saved us anything up to 30 days. But sadly, without the budgets, they had to be axed.

Once Alan accepted that the road crews were out of the frame, he set about organising our stops on the basis of doing everything ourselves. He'd already had several offers of help from various parts of the world, and he eagerly followed those up, at the same time researching other stops. Many people that came into the visitor centre in Cardiff had offered to help, including James Williams in the Philippines, Dennis and Wendy Cullum in San Diego, and Egbert Walters in St John's, and Alan also used his connections in Rotary.

'When we didn't get the budgets, and we were faced with aborting the whole project, we went down to basic nuts and bolts,' says Alan. 'I sat down for hours, emailing complete strangers who'd offered their support and help, and they actually became our service crews. Arguably, had the project run according to plan, we wouldn't have met more than a small fraction of the people that we actually did.'

Ultimately, it was the internet which proved the biggest asset in researching pit stops. Using a search engine, Alan would type in the name of a port or area - chosen at approximately 1,000 mile intervals - along with keywords such as 'harbour' or 'marina'. If those drew blanks, he looked for 'Port Authority', and if that failed, he'd look for 'diving schools'.

'They always use boats,' he says, 'and if they have boats, they must have fuel.'

If that failed, he'd look for 'marine engineers', and if even that didn't produce any joy, he'd simply find a home page for an area and say 'Help!' That was how the stop in Okinawa came about, and our contact with John Perez, who did a brilliant job of organising everything.

Alan's history in Rotary goes back to the mid-1980s. He's a founder member and past president of his club.

'It's an excellent movement,' he says. 'It's a charitable organisation, and it's world-wide. If someone contacted me saying they wanted some help, I'd give it to them, and so they did with me.'

A typical stop with a Rotary connection was Port Said in Egypt, where they put Alan in touch with the shipping agent for the Suez Canal, contacted the local tourist board and organised the PR. It was pretty much the same with Mangalore in India, but even with other stops which weren't primarily arranged through Rotary connections, some Rotary element would come out through people who turned up and introduced themselves with the offer to help.

Even so, we took things to the limit - not only was Alan skipper, navigator and project leader, he was also the engineer, keeping it all going. He and Steve basically had to do everything as far as refuelling and maintaining the boat was concerned. The only exception to that was when Yamaha's engineers gave the engine and drive a thorough service in Japan. If we'd had the road crews, everything would have been a lot tighter and more efficient. We were down to necessary maintenance rather than the more preferable option of preventive maintenance.

When it came to food, we looked at high-protein, high carbohydrate diets - pasta-based, fish-based, that sort of thing.

'And then,' says Alan, 'we had an introduction to a French food company that offered to supply all our food. At the eleventh hour they said "Oh, by the way. You've got to pay us X amount of Euros."

Needless to say we had to part company with them. I think our dietary requirements were pretty much constant as the trip went on. What we were eating was reasonably OK.'

Alan and Steve lost weight during the voyage - I actually put some on, which may have been down to those foraging sorties for snacks in the middle of the night while on watch. We always aimed to have at least one meal during the day, whatever the conditions. When it was really rough, we'd have to stop the boat while the stove was in use, and while we were eating.

Our staple diet was pasta, noodles, and a variety of tinned and other convenience foods. Keeping fresh food in an edible condition was a major problem on board. We started out with a small 12 volt cool box, but it was no proper fridge. It failed to cope with the demanding conditions, and we ended up dumping it. Whilst we'd always try to take on fresh fruit at each stop, it had to be eaten quickly, particularly in tropical and sub-tropical climes. And even UHT longlife milk would have a very limited lifespan. It was irksome at times to see food go to waste, but Alan was ruthless at throwing anything that looked even marginally iffy, and he was absolutely right. Food poisoning was something we simply couldn't afford.

Drinking water was an easier option. We had no holding tanks for water, and in any event, we couldn't trust tap water in many of the ports we were calling at, so we opted for bottled water instead, each bottle marked with a felt-tipped pen so we drank only from our own bottles. It worked well, and the only times it got a little out of hand was when trying to take a swig as the boat crashed through big seas. You'd have to time a gulp right in order to avoid getting water all down your front.

10
THE MOST EXPENSIVE CRISPS IN THE WORLD

That lightning storm was just a rehearsal for the firework display you should get when you return home.
Website posting from Susan and John Evans.

Saturday 27th April
  'I'M GOING TO bear off round it some more.'
  As I lay in my bunk, I can hear Alan's voice, and I assume he's simply talking about a ship or some other obstacle. Then he says: 'We're 50° off course now!'
  I come to my senses, gradually aware of what's going on. It's the early hours of Saturday morning, we're off the west coast of India, heading south, and it's as though we're inside a wonky neon tube. The clouds which cover the sky are flashing with the diffused blue-white glow of sheet lightning. Then every so often an orange bolt of forked lightning sparks from the base of the cloud to the sea. It's an intense flash, blindingly bright, a bit like World War Three, but with a complete absence of sound.
  Alan has been using the radar to try and steer around the worst of it. It shows up as huge splodges, miles across, and even though we're trying to skirt around the edge of the storm, it still seems frighteningly close, with massive flashes going off all around us. Even on the radar, there's no escaping the power and the beauty of it. Every time a bolt of forked lightning cracks across the sky, it shows up on the radar as a thin blue line arcing from one side of the screen to the other.
  It's at this point I begin to wish there'd been a Trivial Pursuit question which goes something along the lines of: 'What happens when a stainless steel tank containing hundreds of litres of diesel is

hit by several million volts of lightning?' I'd really rather not find out the hard way.

As we move further away from the storm, we hear one or two rumbles of thunder for the first time, and then, as with any decent fireworks display, the best comes last. The cloud ahead of us seems to explode, its entire surface covered with a crazy paving network of thousands of orange glowing electrical pathways. For a moment, it looks like some alien electronic brain from a sci-fi movie.

Eventually it all dies down, but not before me being short-changed on the watches. Alan and Steve had done 2000 till midnight, then it was just me with Alan as he decided the conditions were bad enough that he needed to stay up. So Steve goes to bed. After the worst of the storm is over, Alan goes to bed at 0130.

'What time do you want to be woken?' I ask.

'Well I want my four hours sleep, so it had better be 0600,' he replies. 0600 it is, so I end up doing a six hour watch. No wonder I'm tired during the day.

I wonder whether we'll arrive at Galle only to sit outside the harbour all night. We're told the entrance is blocked during the night, security measures as a result of the civil war which has raged in Sri Lanka for 20 years. It seems a bit drastic, especially as the separatist Tamil Tigers have recently signed a ceasefire with the Sri Lankan government. Later we hear the Sri Lankan navy will nevertheless allow us into the harbour, although we won't be able to complete immigration formalities till the morning.

The day has been the first in a long while when it's not unbearably hot. There's heavy cloud cover at times, and the odd rain squall. The approach to Galle after dark sees us skirting more electrical storms. This time the lightning is more like giant strobe lights going off. We complete the run to the pilot station, and then make our way slowly towards the port. We make telephone contact with our shore man, who tells us the navy are making the arrangements. But we're not sure.

When we arrive at the harbour entrance, it's the usual uncertainty, and then we see a boat. The men on board are calling out to us, but the communication isn't good, and one of them points a rather menacing automatic rifle at me as I try to determine what they want. Eventually Alan loses his rag.

'I want to speak to your commanding officer,' he shouts at them. Never mind the language difficulty, his indignant ranting gets the message across. It transpires that they're the harbour patrol and we have to wait with them until we're cleared to enter. Eventually we're told to follow them, at which point two smaller open boats with outboards come up behind us.

'It's their Navy SEALS,' I joke.

Actually it's not that far from the truth. We're boarded, and the guys guide us to the right spot. The barrier is a string of oil drums floating across the harbour entrance, but one end of it is open, just big enough for Spirit to get through.

Inside the modern well-constructed harbour, we tie up next to a wooden sailing ship. Customs officials descend upon us, and while the paperwork is being done, they're after anything they can lay their hands on. Steve ends up having to hand over the rest of his cigarettes. The trouble is, people like this have us over a barrel. If they don't sign our port clearance papers, we get problems in the next port.

Whilst we're dealing with them, Dan and Mark arrive. They have an old sailing ship across the harbour which they're taking to Singapore to renovate. They tell us about the strange bangs we've been hearing. Actually not so much bangs, more like someone hitting an empty oil drum - the navy throw sticks of gelignite into the harbour at random intervals and locations throughout the night to deter Tamil Tiger frogmen. I imagine all it does is kill a few fish.

They invite us to a bar nearby, but we have to decline. Not having cleared immigration, we'd be arrested if we leave the port area. So we brew up a cup of tea, and enjoy a meal of pasta with pesto. Alan and Steve turn in, while Al and I look at the sailing ship berthed next to us. As I climb aboard, I manage to break one of their railings. Run by some Sri Lankan guys, the boat looks rather dilapidated, and I'm not surprised to hear that their engine is broken. I make my excuses and wander back to our boat.

Sunday 28th April

It was a strange sort of night - the muffled thuds of explosives in the water, the overpowering boom of the generators on some Panamanian cargo ship across the harbour, the bright lights, strange squawking birds at the dead of night. It was warm enough to sleep without a sleeping bag, but eventually I came to a point where a T-shirt draped over me wasn't quite enough, and I ended up foraging for my fleece jacket. Then I had the luxury of putting some of the T-shirt over my eyes to block out the light.

We have a brew up, but by now the sun is hot enough to drive me into the shade of a dockside building. I sit there for quite a while, slowly sipping my tea, then I wander along to the toilet and shower block. I decide to have a shower, even though I haven't brought my towel. Al is there too.

'I wouldn't clean your teeth with that water,' I tell him as he gets his toothbrush and paste out. 'You'll be shitting all the way from here to Sabang.'

Our port agent arrives in a small pickup truck with our fuel on the back in 205 litre drums. So it's just a case of connecting up a pipe and letting gravity take its course, aided by a little breather valve which can speed up or slow down the rate of delivery.

All the papers are signed and we're ready to go. It's three minutes to nine, and we decide on nine as our departure time for the purposes of recording the next leg to Sabang. At this point Al asks Alan if he'd like to do a piece to camera. Alan tells him he should have thought of that earlier. Later he's incredulous.

'He's had two hours this morning when he could have done that. Why does he pick the moment we're setting off? Doesn't he realise this is a record attempt, not a joyride?'

Just at the harbour entrance, we're boarded by a couple of young Sri Lankan navy guys, on the pretext of searching the boat. In fact, they're simply on the scrounge. Have we got any wine? No, we don't have any alcohol. How about a T-shirt? We only have what we're wearing - the Egyptians nabbed the rest. Cigarettes? Gave them away last night to the thieving customs official. What about camera film, then? No, we shoot digital. No film at all.

As they become more desperate, they start rooting around in boxes and lockers. Their eyes alight on the special waterproof matches in the survival kit. Somehow they think they're detonators.

'No', insists Alan. 'They're matches. Look.'

He attempts to strike one, but after several attempts it fails to ignite. Our men are not impressed, but by the same token decide that they're probably not detonators, either. They leave the boat with nothing more than a can of Red Bull each, wishing us luck with our record. I'm tempted to say we'd have done better without having them waste 20 minutes of it seeing what they can scrounge from us. Bastards.

The sea is smooth with an oily reflective surface to it, and as I look out, I can see there's a definite pattern with the weather. The clouds are stacking up into typical thunder clouds, so the chances are we'll get some more electrical storms tonight. Having said that, we've seen a lot of fishing boats, quite a long way out.

'That means one of two things,' says Alan. 'Either they know the weather is going to be good for several days, which is why they've chanced coming this far out. Or they're completely f***ing stupid…'

Monday 29th April

There's another electrical storm during the night. Alan has put us on a route slightly south of a direct line from Galle to Sabang in order to miss the worst of it. Strangely, this storm doesn't appear to show up so much on the radar - only the occasional flashes.

Al and I start a five hour watch at 0100, and he's promptly ensconced in the front cabin on Alan's satphone for around an hour and 40 minutes. When he returns, he explains that it's some business deal he has going down, and he asks if I can type a long email for him in the morning. Later Alan tells me he's set his satphone to record the times and numbers of all outgoing calls. He doesn't trust Al now, and still thinks he's planning to jump ship when it suits him.

Al starts to get a bit windy when we appear to be heading straight for the storm. Amusingly, the flash of lightning directly ahead of us proves to be the last of the night. There's absolutely no shipping visible during the watch, and we turn in at 0600, the sun not yet up. Did we adjust our watches to Indonesian time - six hours ahead of BST - too soon?

I wake up at 0930 and try to connect to my email. 45 minutes of continual trying proves fruitless. I do hope Iridium aren't expecting me to say nice things about their system. It might prove difficult.

Alan has said there's been a fair bit of debris in the water, including a 40 foot tree trunk which we narrowly missed. Having said that, he reckons we did hit something last night.

'It's the strangest sea conditions I've ever seen,' he says. 'The water's inky black, there's a lot of debris in it. And occasionally it turns into a head sea from nowhere, with a few ripples on it. You can see where the clouds are, it forms a vortex and changes the wave pattern. The weather around us is really changeable.'

But at least we're picking up on the speed. We've been hitting over 22 knots at times.

I wash my shorts for a treat this afternoon. I thought I might have been able to make them go another day, but they were getting a bit whiffy. The laundry routine is usually best completed at the same time as the shower. So I dunk the clothing in the small plastic bucket (the one I inadvertently used as a pee bucket) with a little washing up liquid. By the time the showering is over, the clothes are well soaked, but it's amazing how much muck comes out of them. How do they get so dirty?

Then a good rinse off. In the Indian Ocean, the nice thing is the water's quite warm. It certainly won't be the same at the top end of the Pacific or Atlantic. In the normal run of things, just spreading clothes out on the Treadmaster deck covering seems pretty good provided the sun's out, even though they finish up with an interesting lozenge pattern on them rather than neatly pressed. Still, it's better than tying them up somewhere and wondering whether they're going to blow away.

I've decided that I rather like the dive platform toilet, so much so that I want one at home. The appeal of it is for a variety of reasons. First, it's odour free. You don't have to flush it, and there's something aesthetically pleasing about doing your business into the spray churned up by the propeller. It's rather like dropping bombs from 40,000 feet, watching them sail down almost in slow motion through the clouds until they disappear. And to top it all, I've dispensed with toilet paper, using the shower tube instead. So, that's what I want at home - complete with random swaying, buffeting, and spray in the face, of course.

Tuesday 30th April

My Psion palmtop computer has packed up, a screen fault. I'm annoyed that it's given up the ghost after being given a complete service only months previously. On the other hand, it has received a fair amount of abuse, what with spray coming through the doorway, and the rooftop hatch leaking on it. Fortunately I have a backup machine, and I manage to get the most important files transferred to the new Psion. I hope it holds out for the rest of the trip. If it doesn't, the daily updates will come to a sudden end. The only thing I can't transfer is all the emails.

We arrive mid-morning at Pulau Weh, an island off the northern tip of Sumatra. There in Sabang harbour is a navy vessel, plus a couple of odd-looking sailing ships. One looks distinctly like something out of a Terry Gilliam film, while the other appears to be a replica of the Golden Hind as assembled by a discount furniture warehouse.

The fuel arrives quickly, and shortly after, a boat with Ton, the Dutchman who owns Lumba Lumba Diving Centre, and some of his clients. They've sponsored some bottled water for us. I mention to a young German couple that I'm disappointed not to have seen any sharks at all. 'You only have to go diving here,' they tell me. 'You'd see lots.'

I also have to fill in a few forms in the harbour master's office, including crew list, medical forms and quarantine form. As I fill these in, dripping with sweat, I'm told there's a fee of $25 for the quarantine form. Yeah, right. I try to get it from Al, but he tells me he doesn't have the right change. In the meantime Alan has been whisked off in a van to complete immigration formalities.

When he returns an hour later, he tells me he was driven to a secure compound, and interrogated by three or four different people. In between sessions, people come and laugh at him, and prod him with their fingers. One of them wants his cap, but he tells them they're not having it. Ditto the T-shirt and watch. The whole process is quite intimidating. Eventually he's taken to the officer in charge, who decides how much he should pay to leave - $75, communicated to him by writing on a napkin. Astonishingly, the 75 bucks is justified as the purchase of three bags of home-made potato crisps.

He's returned to the boat on the back of a motorbike, where he finds yet more with their palms outstretched. In the end, our two hour stay in Sabang ends up costing quite a bit more than budgeted.

'Our fuel bill was $437, which is OK,' says Alan. 'But then there was a $25 quarantine bill, a $75 immigration bill, $30 harbour bill, $15 for something else and $25 just for tying the rope to the bloody pier. Countries like this have no future until they come into the real world. This is daylight robbery, and I've had enough of it.'

There's a guy in uniform who turns out to be from the Ministry of Information. He has a video camcorder, and asks me to speak on camera about how wonderful Sabang is. I oblige in order not to provide any excuse for further delay or expense, but I cringe inwardly as I'm doing it.

It seems so beautiful, with jungle-clad hills and wonderful clear water - some of the best diving in the world, apparently - but it does prove irksome when you get these thieving officials all on the take. The average wage here is about $15 a month, so they're coining it bigtime.

Now we're on our way to Singapore. The latest is that Raffles Marina won't stay open beyond 1900 tomorrow, so the chances are we can't make it in time. The weather's certainly cooler and more cloudy, and as night draws in, we're making 18 knots. Certainly not the continuing sunshine and glorious weather you might think for south-east Asia.

Wednesday 1st May

My watch from midnight to 0500 sees absolutely masses of boats and ships. We've progressed from the vast emptiness of the Indian Ocean to the Strait of Malacca - one of the busiest shipping lanes in the world, and another piracy hotspot.

Perhaps more intriguing is the variety of lights used by these different vessels. In the normal run of things, one expects a ship or boat to have white mast lights, and red and green lights for port and starboard. That way you can tell whether they're heading for you or away from you, coming across your bow, or passing you to one side. It's a system that's simple and effective. Some of them carry the internationally recognised night running lights, but a lot of them have some very weird assortments, including orange sodium lights. The fishing boats, none of which show up on radar, have great banks of floodlights along their sides, presumably to attract the fish, where they're probably dynamited.

Then there are other vessels of vaguely junk-like appearance absolutely festooned with lights. I'm nearly caught out by one when I spot a red light amidst the numerous whites, and assume he's crossing our bow from right to left. So I ask Al to go plus 10 to give a little extra clearance. But when we get to his other side, I'm somewhat perplexed to see the starboard side showing red as well.

All the time there's a good display of lightning going on, with sheet flashes lighting the sky from one side to another, and the occasional forked lightning strike to the sea.

During the night, I pick up a pile of emails. Basically, the problem with the next stop at Raffles Marina in Singapore is that they close at 1900, and they can't stay open later for us because the fuel pumps are on a computer system which automatically shuts off then. We're pushing as hard as we can, but the chances are we won't arrive until later.

We've also been advised of stringent new immigration regulations taking effect from today, a result of increased security following September 11th. Basically we have to make our way to a holding area offshore, wait to be boarded and complete all the procedures on the boat. Only then are we allowed to land.

The alternative is to go into Raffles Marina on the quiet, fuel up and get the hell out. It would mean no media attention, and having to deny knowledge of the new regulations if challenged.

Nadia phones later, announcing 'Eight hours, all right?'

'Eh, what do you mean?' As usual it's a bad connection, which doesn't help.

'Eight hours,' she repeats.

'What does the eight hours refer to?' I ask, completely mystified.

'Eight hours till I can get you an update on Singapore,' she replies.

'Ah. So you'll call back in the morning...?' The penny drops, and so does the connection.

As dawn breaks, it's overcast and rainy. It could be the North Sea, or somewhere else in British waters. You'd never think we were close to the Equator. Every now and then it brightens up. We pass the pilot point for Port Kelang, the harbour which serves Kuala Lumpur, and can see the shadows of tall objects in the distance. There are cranes in the foreground, but maybe, just maybe the twin Petronas towers beyond. It's an idle dream. They're too far inland, and anyway, it's too misty to be certain.

Alan decides to do a spot of maintenance, and takes apart the wiper motor on the starboard windscreen. It hasn't worked for ages, and once the cover is off, it's not difficult to see why. Corrosion abounds. After digging about, he manages to get it working, albeit rather noisily, and with a fairly limited stroke.

'Still an improvement on what it was before,' he points out.

The people at Raffles Marina appear to be rather unhelpful, although we don't realise how much their hands are tied by new regulations. We've been forbidden to enter after 1900, even just to tie up. If we fail to make it by then, we'll be sent to an anchorage some 30 miles away to wait until the morning. So now Nadia is investigating the possibility of other marinas in Singapore, while Alan is considering going over the strait to Malaysia and forgetting Singapore altogether. We have the fuel to do it.

There's a lot of debris in the water here - we've seen entire tree trunks, presumably swept down rivers in floods. And we've already had a few clonks on the hull. Early afternoon there's one sickening collision which bounces under the hull and hits the stern drive. Alan kills the throttle, then slowly brings it back up. Everything seems OK.

'Better keep your eyes peeled,' he tells Steve.

It's a precursor for the main event in the early evening. Suddenly we lose power, the engine revs increasing, but with no forward movement. It's as though the propeller is cavitating, where air in the water causes the prop to lose its grip. But then Alan realises it's something more serious.

'I'm going over,' he says, after killing the engine. He jumps into the water, and comes back up again with an expression as grim as death.

'The propeller's lost all its blades.'

We carry a spare prop in the engine compartment, so it's hurriedly brought out. Steve goes into the water to try and help Alan remove the remains of the damaged prop. The problem is there's no way of getting a grip on it, and because the drive between engine and gearbox is fluid, there's no way to lock the transmission. Alan cuts his finger quite deeply in the process, and is bleeding profusely. Now I'm starting to worry. We've not seen any, but we know there are sharks in these waters.

In the meantime, we're sitting ducks in the busiest shipping lane in the world, with a cargo ship bearing down on us. Can Alan and Steve fix the prop before it gets too close? As it looms larger, I try to call it up on the radio.

'This is Spirit of Cardiff, Spirit of Cardiff, calling ship bearing down on yellow powerboat. Do you receive? Over.'

There's no reply. I try again. And again. The ship is getting closer. Are they just going to plough into us? Should we stick with the boat or swim for it? Why aren't they answering their radio? When it's really close, I conclude it won't hit us, but that's not much consolation.

'It's going to miss,' I tell Alan and Steve. 'Just watch out for the wash.'

The ship is Arab, and it passes within 100 feet, its wash rocking the boat crazily as Alan and Steve, still in the water, hang on to the dive platform rails. The reason they didn't answer their radio is apparent as the ship passes. There's no one on the bridge.

'It's on autopilot,' says Steve. 'The crew are probably watching telly!'

Eventually they give up trying to undo the propeller nut, and we go through the rigmarole of getting the wing engine out for the second time in three weeks. And so we slowly putter along at three knots (two and a half to begin with), at first just trying to get out of the main shipping lane to reduce our chances of being mown down. We're about 40 miles out of Singapore, with limited speed, and very little manoeuvrability.

Alan is busy putting plasters on the gashes inflicted by the remains of the prop, none of us is saying much. Partly because we're in a state of mild shock at what's happened, but also because it's not that easy to speak over the deafening row produced by the wing engine.

After a while, Al comes up with an idea for locking the propeller shaft by wrapping rope around it. It's a game try, but it doesn't work. As Alan says 'When I put a nut on, I don't intend it to come off.' But he reckons it'll be a five minute job to get it off and the replacement on when we're in port, and now there's no choice - we have to go to Raffles Marina.

Thursday 2nd May

We'd originally agreed to do just two hour shifts, but when Al and I come on at 2300, we carry on past our stop time at 0100. I reckon that Alan and Steve would probably be knackered after their bout in the sea with the propeller.

As we clear one island, I get the impression that the charting might not be that accurate. There appears to be an island out here which isn't on the chart. Lots of brightly lit boats including ones with obvious Chinese shapes - very high prows. It's a beautifully clear night, and it's a lot easier to make out the lie of the land from outside rather than in the cabin, where the windows are misted up.

We get to the waypoint marked on the chart plotter before we have to turn the corner to go across the harbour, and that's the point I turn in, between 0330 and 0400. I'm awake again at just after half six, clocking our arrival in the harbour as 0641, about 10 hours late. Then we make our way up the channel, passing an interesting collection of houses on stilts. It's incredibly scenic, but Al doesn't seem inclined to want to film any of it, just lying in his bunk. Is he tired and apathetic, or has he other things on his mind?

We arrive at Raffles Marina, and there to meet us is Choy Cheok Wing, a RIB enthusiast who's been following our progress on the web not just over this trip, but several years. He photographs our entrance, which isn't particularly elegant, as we have no slow speed steerage, and the engine has no reverse. After fending off the breakwater, we manage to get Spirit round to the fuel berth.

Choy has organised our provisions, and a little buggy brings them all down. Apart from the food and water, he's brought a few little extras - some cans of Singapore's famed Tiger beer, and a bottle of red and white wine. Best still, he's also brought us a brand new gas stove and some cartridges.

I go up to the chandlers with Choy to get a split pin for the propeller nut, and a new masthead light. So hopefully no more standing outside with a torch when big ships loom too close. Back at the boat, Alan has finished putting on the spare propeller, with the remains of the old one on display. Basically just a sleeve, it's not just the blades which went, but the cylindrical shell through which the exhaust goes as well.

Whilst they're finishing, Al and I go up to the health club to use the showers. While we're waiting several minutes for a laundry token to appear, he's sighing and muttering 'Oh dear.' He appears agitated and impatient.

'Don't you find Alan rude?' he says.

'He can certainly be a bit abrupt some times,' I reply. Clearly it's not just work or family problems at home on his mind. I sense there's more to be said, but he doesn't pursue it.

The shower is fantastic, a chance to get days of salt out of my pores. It's so good I have to linger. I even give my glasses their first wash in soap and water for weeks. Then back to the laundry, where the clothes have finished washing. That's nice too. Clothing with all the salt taken out, and a towel that's no longer evil and stiff enough to be used as a door, let alone a curtain.

After that we head to the restaurant, and take a seat. Al then asks me why I think Alan has a problem with him, adding he's still thinking of going. But at this point Alan appears, so the conversation goes three-way.

'You're always rude to me,' complains Al.

'I'm not,' replies Alan in a matter-of-fact way. 'But you have to realise that it's me who's in charge of running the boat.'

Al says he's thinking of going to the immigration authorities in Singapore in order to be able to fly home.

'That would land the people here up to their necks in it,' says Alan. 'They've gone out on a limb to get us in and out without the usual formalities.'

At this point the conversation is adjourned, as Choy turns up along with Major Tan, who runs the marina. Tan knows Alan's home town of Portsmouth quite well, having been in the navy, and done one or two courses there. Choy is obviously quite well off. He has a home on mainland Malaysia as well as Singapore, and he's been a RIB enthusiast for many years. And we discover that he too was born in 1953.

After breakfast, we go up to Major Tan's office, where he briefs us on the best route to get out of Singapore harbour. There's a lot of reclamation work going on, and he also warns us about the harbour patrols. We set off, still with a full complement of crew.

In fact, we're intercepted by a police boat, and, thinking we're about to be boarded, we hide our new Raffles Marina baseball caps. They come alongside, and want to know where we've come from, where we're going. We say we're just passing through on the way from Sabang to Kota Kinabalu, but I'm not sure they buy it. One of them mentions something about cameras, which ties in with what Choy told me. All of the waterways around Singapore are covered by cameras, daylight and night vision. So the chances are they've already seen where we've been for the last few hours. Anyway, they allow us to carry on.

As the afternoon wears on, the dark clouds which have loomed over us are left behind, and we head into sunlight. It would be nice to think that it was symbolic of the mood on the boat, but we have an unwilling passenger aboard, and I for one find it most disconcerting. Not long after sunset we get that awful slipping clutch feeling once again. It's not as though we've hit anything, but the engine races, and nothing happens. Steve investigates and finds a large plastic bag wrapped around the prop. He removes it and Alan starts up again. Still no joy. It's clearly more serious - this time the gearbox appears to have blown.

For a while we sit quietly, almost in disbelief. How the hell can we have so much bad luck? Alan admits later that he cried - a rare occurrence for him. I just feel numb.

There's nothing for it but to haul the trusty wing engine out once more. We're certainly quicker at it now, and we get the engine on and under way. 100 miles out of Singapore in the South China Sea, we reckon it could take up to two days to get back.

Later on, we find that we can augment the wing engine with very low power from the main engine. The gearbox clutches only fail when the turbo kicks in, so provided we don't give it much throttle, we can get our speed up to 10 knots.

Friday 3rd May

I'm up a couple of times during the night doing emails for Alan to sort out a replacement drive unit from Yamaha - each time takes about an hour to connect, so I don't get to sleep until the early hours of the morning. Choy suggests we go to Natsteel Marine on the eastern end of Singapore Island, near Changi Airport. It'll cut 15 miles off our return, and will be less distance for when we set off once more.

We arrive on the outskirts of Singapore at around 0600, looking out for signs of police boats or harbour patrols. From our conversation with Choy earlier on, we can be sure they're already following our movements, and I'm slightly nervous that we're going to get into trouble for having bucked the system yesterday.

We have to find our way around a vast area delineated by pilings - part of a massive land reclamation scheme, the scale of which only becomes apparent when you see the number of tugs pulling barges with gravel. Clearly it's something which will continue round the clock for several years.

Later a police boat approaches us, but they only want to know if we need any help. We tell them we're fine, and carry on our way. Whilst Natsteel Marine is a part owner of Raffles Marina, there the similarity ends. This is definitely more downmarket, a commercial marina with working boats - no posh restaurant and laundry facilities. The first toilet block we look in is pretty rancid, but later we find one which is somewhat cleaner.

But Jeffrey Ling, the manager, is very nice, and he contacts the local Yamaha agent for us to see whether he has an outdrive. If he did, we could simply do a trade with the unit Yamaha are sending. But it seems the ones he has aren't compatible with our engine, which is so new it's only just coming on the market.

So it's back to the original plan, and getting one shipped from the UK. As luck would have it, Japan has a public holiday this week, so getting one from there isn't possible. But if it goes on a flight tomorrow, it won't arrive until Sunday, more like Monday by the time it clears customs. More delay we can do without. But the important thing now is to sort everything immigration-wise. We've now landed in Singapore twice without following the correct procedure.

Choy turns up and he drives us into Singapore city in his rather nice air-conditioned vehicle. First we visit the Port Authority office, and get legal on that front. Then to another building to clear immigration. Alan is given a slight ticking off because we contravened the new anti-terrorist laws. He apologises, saying we didn't know about them because they were so new. It's not a problem, they say, but don't let it happen again.

They really mean it, too. A computer record is kept, along with a note to say Alan received the warning. The people here are very friendly and helpful, but one can't forget that this is the place where there's a $1,000 fine for littering, and where people caught in the act of spraying graffiti are caned.

But then, as we're sitting in the immigration office, Alan Carter gets up and has a word with one of the officials. He's decided he's going home.

11
FILMING THE DOCUMENTARY

I have just watched the video and I forward my compliments on a job well done, both visually and nautically! It is so true that one picture is worth a thousand words! As we watched in the office, Beverly and I were captivated by the vastness of the ocean, the close quarters of the boat, the physical and mental strain that such a voyage exacts, and the critical role that teamwork and logistics play in the success of the mission!
Rick Kenney, US Coast Guard Battery Park, New York; commenting on Spirit of Cardiff's Transatlantic Challenge TV documentary.

RIGHT FROM THE beginning, we'd always thought that Spirit's epic voyage would make dynamic television. If it's possible that an object as opposed to a person could love the camera, Spirit did. From whatever angle you looked at her, she exuded everything from beauty to ungainliness, mean and moodiness to something which primary school children delighted in drawing pictures of. Whether moored up in 'show-off' conditions, with all her hatches opened up like the air brakes on an aeroplane, or crashing through the waves at speed, Spirit had that indefinable quality of charisma. She turned heads everywhere she went. She was a natural TV star.

More to the point, the story of taking a tiny powerboat around the world would make a fantastic travelogue. I'd always reckoned that whilst the story on board the boat would be compelling, exploring the stresses and tensions of four men living together in close proximity for two months, the fuel stops would add a fascinating new dimension to it.

The ground crews we'd originally planned to have flying around the world ahead of us would each be accompanied by a camera crew.

They would record their experiences as they tried to cut through all the red tape ahead of our arrival, and then film the pit stops, capturing the hectic moments as the boat was refuelled, the crew changed into the next leg's clothing and doing their media interviews. And of course there would be the scenery, the widely varying characters of all the different countries we were planning to stop at around the world. We reckoned it would be a story to rival or surpass one of Michael Palin's epic TV series.

It wasn't long before one TV production company thought so, too. After my first story about Spirit made the whole of the front page of the Independent on Sunday's relaunched travel section in September 1999, Tim Exton of London television production company Tricky Pictures contacted Alan to say he was interested in filming us. He roughed out the synopsis of what would be a six-part documentary series, and came to meet us at the Southampton Boat Show, where I was to be presented with my crew T-shirt at a press call to announce my official induction into the crew. It would depend on which broadcasters took it up, he told us, but if possible, the budget would allow for dramatic helicopter shots of the boat going through the Suez and Panama Canals, along with other important points in the journey.

The time between Spirit's second abortive attempt to circumnavigate the British Isles in 1999 and our successful third attempt in June 2000 saw many changes. The project had migrated from Portsmouth to Cardiff, and I had joined the crew as onboard journalist. Unfortunately the Tricky Pictures connection went cold. Tim Exton had packed his bags in search of new work opportunities in the USA.

But having bought myself a new digital stills camera to photograph our momentous voyage around the British Isles, it suddenly occurred to me that time was passing, and we were missing opportunities to catch events on video. So I bought myself a small MiniDV camcorder, just before we set off from Cardiff on our next adventure, in October 2000. Fresh from our triumph around the British Isles, we'd set ourselves the difficult and challenging task of taking on Cable and Wireless Adventurer's fastest around the world leg - from Gibraltar to Monaco.

Sky News and ITN both did news items about our departure from

Cardiff, and as we were about to set off, ITN's Tim Rogers spotted my camcorder.

'Give me a call when you get back,' he said. 'I'd like to take a look at what you get.'

Given that my experience with moving pictures was absolutely zero, I wasn't confident I'd be able to produce anything that would be up to scratch - I'd simply felt some effort should be made to record our adventures for our own purposes.

We broke the Cable and Wireless Adventurer's Gibraltar to Monaco record, knocking an hour and 19 minutes off their 36 hours 58 minutes record. Leaving Alan and Steve to attempt to bring the boat home by sea, I flew back from Nice to London, stopping off at ITN's offices in Holborn.

The engineers who copied my tape hadn't seen MiniDV before. They were amazed at the technical quality. More to the point, they were extremely complimentary about the standard of my filming. 'A natural flair for it,' they said. I'd done all the right things - maybe could have kept some of the shots running for a few seconds longer - but hadn't fallen for any of the common mistakes made by amateurs. All I'd done was to use my years' experience as a stills photographer, utilising the same rules regarding composition, and trying not to go too wild with unnecessary camera movements. It worked. My first ever footage shot on a video camcorder was broadcast on ITN's 'News at Ten'.

The next year was our last big trip before the circumnavigation in 2002. We were going to cross the Atlantic, taking a northerly route from New York to St John's, Newfoundland, before heading south again to Horta in the Azores, then on to Gibraltar and back to Cardiff; a route which promised great excitement visually - from the skyscrapers of Manhattan and possible icebergs off Newfoundland, to the subtropical lushness of the Azores. Once again I had my camcorder, but it wasn't until we were close to departure from New York, after a one month promotional tour of the US eastern seaboard, that someone showed interest in making a documentary about the crossing.

APP Broadcast, specialists in TV programmes with a watersports slant, and makers of the programme about Ellen MacArthur's solo voyage around the world in a sailing boat, wanted to make a documentary in order to sow the seeds for covering the main event next year. They hoped to take some footage of our departure from a news broadcaster in New York, and they'd film our arrival back in Cardiff themselves. All it needed was someone to fill in the bit in the middle - me!

The Atlantic crossing was anything but a textbook performance, but it did at least make for exciting video. The resulting short documentary - about 18½ minutes - was shown worldwide on Sky Sports' 'Watersports World', to an estimated maximum audience of 555 million. It wasn't bad, although they rushed the recording of the narration, and the soundtrack music wasn't to my liking. But even as the programme was being broadcast in 82 countries, so the world was gripped by the horror and consequences of September 11th.

From our point of view, it was the moment the bottom dropped out of any last hopes for major cash sponsorship, which meant we weren't going to be able to meet APP's price for making a quality documentary of the voyage around the world. We were gutted. It was always a chicken and egg situation. Having achieved enviable news coverage throughout the life of the project, the icing on the cake for any prospective sponsor was going to be high visibility in the documentary and video. Not that we told anyone else that we didn't have the TV production in hand, of course, because we were always confident that something else would come along, even if at the last minute. Surely no broadcaster could pass up the chance for a documentary about a historic and daring voyage around the world.

Whatever happened, I was geared up for the responsibility, not just of all media communications from the boat, but filming as well. The question as to who might be interested in producing the documentary was half answered for us in March 2002, when the last minute change in crew saw Alan Carter taking over Jan Falkowski's place.

Not only was Carter an outside broadcast TV cameraman by profession, and therefore able to concentrate solely on filming our story, he'd also elicited interest in a documentary from HTV Wales. Whether or not it subsequently went nation-wide, it would be a start. During his time on board, he made it clear to Alan that the only reason HTV Wales was interested in making the documentary was because he was involved.

Thankful I'd had a burden taken off my shoulders, I nevertheless decided to bring my camcorder and some ancillary equipment, simply to do some filling in. I was mindful that Al could only be in one place at a time, and that we might appreciate having two different angles on whatever events transpired. Having said that, I saw my role with a camcorder as very much a subsidiary one to Al's. With the amount of writing and emailing work I envisaged, I couldn't see myself doing much more other than filling in. Al's role was pivotal to making a good documentary.

When the possibility of Carter's leaving first arose in Jeddah, he assured us that he was committed to the documentary, even if circumstances prevented him continuing with us on the boat. He'd leave us his filming equipment. His professional camera ran at twice the speed of my domestic camcorder, recording images and audio with vastly superior quality, and his remote boom mike picked up sounds without so much interference from background noises. It would all be vital.

All I'd brought with me were camcorder, spare batteries and charger. No wide-angle lens, and no decent remote microphone to improve on the audio captured by the small on-camera mike. Even if Carter was going, his equipment would be absolutely essential to our achieving the best possible quality TV.

12
BETRAYAL

It is always interesting to see how people perform under pressure. And it seems you have pressure in abundance.
Website posting from Pete Bethune.

I'M NOT EVEN aware first of all that Carter is leaving. It's only when Alan comes back from the counter to speak to Steve and me that he says that's what's happening. I guess by now we'd seen it as pretty likely, and we were all hopeful it could be handled in a friendly manner.

When Choy drops us back to the marina, Al asks him for a lift to the airport to arrange his ticket, so off he goes. We spend the afternoon sorting things out on the boat, somehow expecting to see him return later to collect his things and wish us goodbye. After all, it doesn't take that long to buy an airline ticket, does it?

'He won't come back,' says Alan bitterly. 'Not while we're here. He's spineless.'

The afternoon wears on, and we go to the shower block for a freshen up, then change into our (relatively) smart clothes ready to go out for a quick bite to eat. We've met someone here who's recommended a bar/restaurant called Bernie's. Not far, he said.

As we leave, Steve muses idly that Alan Carter is hiding nearby, waiting for us to go so he can return to the boat for his things. I reckon the idea that he might be lurking in the bushes to be a little far-fetched. As we wander along, I realise just how much it must rain when they get a downpour here. The storm drains are numerous, and the main ones are enormous. You wouldn't want to fall into one of those after a few in the pub.

We wander for what seems like miles past the heavily fenced

perimeter of Changi prison. This of course is the place where allied POWs from the surrender of Singapore ended up, many of whom didn't come home. Eventually we arrive at Bernie's, a small place which seems to have quite a large British expat clientéle. We order our beer by the pitcher, and go for burgers and chips - a simple enough meal, but luxury for us after the rather more rudimentary fare on board.

We hail a taxi to take us back to the marina. It's not late, but when we arrive, we find that Alan Carter has indeed been back, and completely cleared the boat of all his belongings. Despite what he'd told us in Jeddah, he's gone off with all his video kit and tapes, and what's left of his money - £5,000 in US dollar bills. Unlike me, he'd never entrusted Alan with his £10,000 contribution - he'd kept all of it about him the whole time, handing over money piecemeal whenever an expense needed to be met. He could of course have given Alan a call to say he was back at the boat, and whatever his differences with him, it might have been courteous to wish Steve and me goodbye. It's not often that I feel ill of anyone, but at that moment, I can only echo Alan's earlier words. We didn't deserve to be treated like this.

Later, we discuss the implications of Carter's departure. We have enough money to make some further progress, but he's as good as abandoned us on the other side of the world without enough to get home. Apart from what we've just lost, we had a shortfall of around £8,000 when we left Cardiff, so we're definitely up the proverbial creek without a paddle. We're now £13,000 short. While people subsequently rally round and help, at that moment, we feel alone and vulnerable. So far I've had my hands full with writing and emailing. I'm close to tears as the realisation hits me that I now have the added role of video cameraman, and that the documentary will succeed or fail by my efforts.

Saturday 4th May

We grab a cab into Singapore City. First stop is the Funan Centre, a shopping mall devoted to electronics - a place of worship for gadget junkies. The shop Choy recommended has Psions, but they're a lot more expensive than expected, so I decide not to take the plunge and stick with my one backup. Fingers crossed it's up to the rest of the trip. I also need to find a wide-angle lens to give my Sony camcorder a better chance of recording the remainder of the trip now that Carter has removed his more sophisticated equipment. I can't find anywhere that does Sony lenses, but a guy in one shop directs us to Bugis Junction, where there's a dedicated Sony shop.

It has just what I need, so I get the wide-angle lens plus some tapes - S$369, about £160. Help! Whilst there, we look at the Spirit of Cardiff website on one of their flashy computers. The comments we've been getting from followers around the world are amazing. If good will alone was enough to see us through the hardship, we'd breeze our way around the world.

There's a fascinating computer-controlled fountain at Bugis Junction sending jets in short and long bursts arcing over from one side to another. It's mesmerizing to watch, and the kids there love it - getting soaked as the different spurts catch them out.

Whilst sitting at a bar, Alan receives a text message from Carter, now presumably back home. He hasn't been to the press yet, and he'd like the rest of his money back, about £5,000, by Monday. Alan texts him back to say that we've already been to the press, and the question over who owes what to whom will be settled when he consults his lawyer.

It's breathtaking that he should demand a complete refund. He'd been on the boat for a month, incurring the same expense as the rest of us. There was never any question of a money back guarantee, and from Alan's point of view, we are the ones who've been let down - a potential breach of contract situation.

After a few more beers, we pick our way through the crowds along the famed Bugis Street, with its masses of stalls selling branded goods at ridiculous prices. Of course, they're all counterfeit, with 'Rolex' watches going for around $40, 'Gucci' sunglasses for $10.

Eventually we wander off in search of the famous Raffles Hotel. It's one of those things you just have to do when you're in Singapore. As the staff start to twitch at our coming in wearing shorts and T-shirts, I ask for the Duty Manager and flash my press card. Out he comes, and gives us a quick history of the hotel, which oozes colonial tradition. Naturally I'm hopeful he might like to treat us to a drink, but sadly he doesn't bite. We retire to the bar nevertheless for a couple of Singapore Slings - this, after all, is where the drink was invented. They're very lurid, and unbelievably expensive.

As I video Alan and Steve walking smiling along the red carpet at the entrance to Raffles, I'm very mindful that the reason we're here is far from a holiday, even if we have had a pleasant day doing some shopping and more than a little bit of drinking. We're stuck here until our spare parts arrive. And still the clock is ticking.

Sunday 5th May

I spend some time going through all the video I've shot since leaving Cardiff. It's just under an hour's worth of material. Up until now it wasn't my job, other than as second cameraman, and I'd been shooting material simply because I enjoy using a camcorder. It seems I didn't actually miss that much of the story so far, but a lot of what I did get was stuff that Carter seemed not to have shot. Maybe we don't need his video after all.

As we have time to kill, Alan decides to placate Associated British Ports, who lost their sponsor stickers when we smashed the windscreens on the way to Gibraltar, by drawing their logo on the inside at the back of the boat. Felt pens are wonderful things. The finished artwork looks pretty reasonable, and should last until we can get some proper stickers.

Whilst in the shower, I wash both pairs of shorts, thinking one pair will dry on me fairly quickly in the heat. But I didn't count on the massive level of humidity, so several hours later, they're still damp.

We take a cab to try and find Changi Sailing Club. It's something else to pass the time, and Alan sees it as a courtesy call. Unfortunately we've managed to hail the only cab driver in Singapore who doesn't know where it is. He drops us off near the beach, and we wander along the front. But we're out on a peninsula, on the wrong side. So back we walk to find a bridge. It's hot, close, strength-sapping weather.

Eventually we find the sailing club. It's slightly disconcerting to discover that the revered Royal Dorset Yacht Club, of which Alan is a member, isn't recognised here. Even so, they let us in to use the bar and restaurant, but sadly not the swimming pool.

We spend the rest of the afternoon and early evening wandering from one bar to another, then a restaurant, to another bar before taking a taxi back to the marina. There's a real feeling of powerlessness. Not so much a question of drowning our sorrows, but simply that that there's little else we can do. At the moment, our fate lies in the hands of others. It's only 2030 when we turn in, but not before a discussion about how Alan Carter can justify asking for his £5,000 back. Apart from anything else, Alan reckons he's run up around 24 hours worth of calls since the satphone has been recording each call, which at the standard rate of US$1.50 a minute means a total bill of over $2,000.

Monday 6th May

Another unbelievably hot and airless night. Despite plastering myself with insect repellent, it's made no difference. I wake up with masses of new bites. I always react badly to mosquito bites, which come up in angry red lumps, giving me the look of someone who's suffering from some medieval social disease. Please let the drive come today. Whatever the discomforts, at least at sea you can escape the mosquitoes, or so I think at the time.

Alan discovers that we probably won't get the drive till late afternoon. It's arrived, and with the freight forwarding company, but all the paperwork has to be done. The trouble is that the boatyard workers knock off at 1700, so whilst we can get the boat lifted, and Alan and Steve can do the repairs, we may not be able to get Spirit back in the water until tomorrow morning. All this waiting is so wearisome, knowing that the spares which can see us on our way are here.

The theories as to why we're in this mechanical predicament are getting more interesting. It could be down to overheating. The air temperature is higher, the sea temperature is higher. We've also been burning lower grade diesel - in some cases bunkered fuel not much better than paraffin - which is forcing us to operate at higher than normal revs, hence higher operating temperatures. The design of our leg is such that the hot exhaust gases go down it rather than discharged separately. And last but not least, we're running 24 hours a day - day in, day out - which is not what you'd class as normal usage. All of these factors could have combined to cause the gearbox to fail. If it can do it once, it could possibly do it again.

As we're wilting in the heat, there's good news mid-afternoon. The parts have arrived. Apparently the carriers phoned Jeffrey to say they were setting out on their round, and he told them to make sure that Natsteel was their first call.

The boat is driven over to the lift and taken out of the water. The outdrive has seen some very high temperatures, and incomplete combustion. Where once it was yellow glass fibre with blue anti-foul coating below the waterline, now much of the transom, the back of the boat, is jet black. Until then, we were still not discounting the possibility that the gearbox failure was a knock-on effect of the collision which wrecked the prop. Now we have to consider whether the prop became so hot that it de-tempered and simply fell apart. That could account for the clean way it sheared off leaving just the propshaft sleeve behind. Alan removes the top plate of the gearbox to discover the clutches completely burnt out.

So the theory is proved - the poor fuel quality combined with higher than normal air and sea temperatures have made the unit overheat. We're definitely going to have to watch that. We were looking at changing drives in Japan in any event - now Alan's considering taking that as a spare. We're almost certain to get more duff fuel along the way.

The job is finished in just over an hour and the boat put back in the water. We set off without further ado. The plan is to go to the grid reference intended for departing vessels, but we're not going to hang around if they don't spot us and come straight away. It's rather silly that the authorities provide a grid reference, which is only of significance to local vessels. Visiting international vessels need lat/long co-ordinates to know exactly where they should go.

We've already sent the immigration people a five page fax declaring our intention to leave. We're flying the proper flags, and Alan has called them up on the radio, with no response. There's no way we're going to wait, so we leave Singapore as we first arrived, ever so slightly bending the rules. As we're under way, Alan gets a phone call from Choy. After a weekend away, he was on his way to the marina to see us, so we've missed him. It's a great shame - he's been so helpful.

So that's it. We're on our way to Kota Kinabalu, or KK as they call it locally, in Malaysia. Fingers crossed our troubles are over. Now all we have to do is run the boat with just a three-man crew.

13
SPONSORSHIP

Bring your around the world project to Cardiff, and you'll have an open chequebook.
Managing Director of a large Cardiff-based company speaking to Alan Priddy, St David's Hotel, 7th January 2000.

ANYONE WHO HAS ever put together an expedition knows that the expedition part is relatively easy. The legwork beforehand, trying to raise funds to support it, is the really tricky bit. It can involve writing hundreds of letters, having numerous meetings, making presentations - only to be turned down. In fact you're lucky if you're turned down. In most instances, you don't even get a reply.

Whom you ask and how you pitch is pretty important. There was one stage when we were approached by the marketing department of Coca Cola, asking how the Spirit of Cardiff project might appeal to teenagers. Trying to think ourselves into the shoes of teenagers, evoking the 'Gee Fizz' factor, we came up with our unofficial checklist: 1) it doesn't involve proper work; 2) it uses up all your cash; 3) the boat is full of artificial colourings; 4) you could die at any time. In the end, we had to conclude that a bunch of late 40-somethings in a funny boat probably wouldn't appeal to teenagers anyway, so we waved farewell to the Coca Cola millions.

The boat itself was paid for mainly by Alan personally. As owner of his company, Express Gearboxes, he was able to fund the building by a substantial amount. Yamaha, which had previously supported other Alan Priddy ventures, came up with a deal to supply three engines and outdrives, which hopefully would see the boat through the life of the project. And similarly, Raymarine kitted the boat out with thousands of pounds worth of electronic navigation equipment and other instrumentation - much of it still in the prototype stage. Part of the deal there was that Spirit would be a floating testbed for them to develop new products.

When it comes to it, it's a lot easier asking a manufacturer to supply you with products, if they happen to be useful to you. The really difficult bit is finding someone who can come up with hard cash. That was what we needed more than anything, and we needed lots if the project was going to work properly. The whole thing was very carefully costed out, arriving at our original budget of £1.2 million. That would cover the cost of refits to the boat, the ground crews, the cost of fuel and supplies, and the bribes and sundry other 'under the counter' payments that oil the wheels of business in some third world countries. The budget even allowed for modest wages to be paid to the crew, who would all be leaving their day jobs for up to three months.

Alan's dream all the way along was to take as many people as possible around the world with us, and that extended to his vision of the way the project would be sponsored. In the early days, he shied away from trying to do a single deal with a title sponsor, preferring to retain complete freedom and flexibility to run things the way he wanted. Instead, he envisaged lots more smaller scale sponsorship packages, similar to the way Captain Scott's expedition to the South Pole was funded. That extended to having every section of the voyage sponsored, so each leg would bear the sponsor's name, and the world record for that leg would be presented to them afterwards. If nothing else it would make for an easy way out with the laundry - we'd simply arrive in port, do our media interviews, then go off for a quick shower and change into fresh clothes bearing the logos for the next leg's sponsor.

Getting members of the public involved was important, too, and that's where the visitor centre and website played their parts with the ship's log and buy-a-mile schemes. But even they needed funding to kick-start them, so while they did reasonably well, they could have done much better.

As the money situation became more desperate, and we had to start trimming, then hacking budgets, we were on the lookout for anyone who might help. Whilst much of the problem was simply down to the general economic downturn and consequent cuts in corporate marketing budgets, our lack of result was annoying on two counts. Many expeditions managed to attract big money sponsorship out of virtually thin air. We prided ourselves on our extensive track record. We could prove that we would achieve what we were setting out to do. How many other world record attempts have started out already with a list of records as long as your arm?

Of course, success should always be viewed as a bonus by any potential sponsor. Trying to guarantee something which is in the hands of the weather would be stupid, and possibly put lives at risk. And yet there were many rejections from companies on the grounds that they didn't believe we could do it. What they missed, and what they should have based their sponsorship strategy on, was the amount of publicity we gained. Throughout the life of the project, we always achieved lots of media coverage - in newspapers, magazines, on the radio and on TV. We were often surprised that some events, such as simply re-opening the visitor centre in Cardiff after a refit, would attract coverage from the likes of Sky News. If you took the value of all of the coverage we gained throughout Spirit of Cardiff's life, you'd be talking hundreds of thousands of pounds, probably millions. And yet in the end, we had not much more than £100,000 come into the sponsorship coffers.

But if the money side was shaky, the relationships with Spirit of Cardiff's core providers of equipment and services were solid as a rock. Alan's connection with Yamaha went back to 1990. It was a relationship built on achievement. If he said he was going to do something, he'd do it. Yamaha had been very supportive, but on the engineering side, Alan enjoyed working with a global company which was developing products way beyond what people might imagine.

The relationship with corporate travel organisers Hogg Robinson had been a very close one since 1997. Alan and crew were at the 1998 London Boat Show after doing the transatlantic, when they were approached by Hogg Robinson chief executive David Radcliffe. 'Congratulations,' he said. 'Is there anything we can do for you?' They sponsored the Spirit of Portsmouth London to Monaco world record, and have been firm supporters ever since.

The Raymarine (or Raytheon as it was) relationship goes back to 1994/95. Both they and Alan are based in Portsmouth, and Alan knows all the designers and development team. They trusted him to test and evaluate their products, and give them good reports.

But it came to a point when Alan realised he might need to somehow change tack in order to get the required cash sponsorship. Portsmouth hadn't provided what Alan wanted in terms of facilities, but Cardiff had thrown open its doors to us. We'd moved the project there to open up the visitor centre, and to work closely with a prominent Cardiff company which had promised to find us the money we needed to make it all work.

'It was in July 2000 that alarm bells began to ring,' he says, 'when I'd started to think that the move to Cardiff might not have been the best thing from a commercial point of view. Interest was beginning to drop away, and I felt we were being cast adrift to find our own way. It carried on for the remainder of that year, and came to a head in February 2001, when I came to the conclusion that "Corporate Cardiff", my Captain Scott vision for financing the project, wasn't going to happen.'

'I felt let down and betrayed. People ask why I moved to Cardiff. It wasn't for my health, and it wasn't because we didn't have other options, because we did.'

In the end, we tried all sorts of possible angles to gain sponsorship. The people who were supposed to do the spadework for us in Cardiff had failed to deliver, so we had to look elsewhere. That included trying one of the country's supposedly top sponsorship agencies. They specialised in putting sporting and other projects in front of corporate sponsors, and cementing the deal. The agency we approached sent out some 200 letters and then presented us with a bill for £5,000. Not one letter drew a positive response.

Then there was a group of ex-city traders who came up with lots of suggestions. So we told them 'Fine, do it. We're happy with the commission rates you're asking.' But the relationship with them turned out to be very short, because Alan sacked them.

'All they wanted to do was take,' he says. 'They didn't find any sponsors for the project at all. Their original idea was to place it on the spread betting market. Basically that's the IG Index and Cantor Fitzgerald, companies like that. Each day you can place a bet on anything you like. So the idea was that every day, people would log on to the internet, find out where we were, and bet on how long it would take to get to our next stop. They'd even take odds on whether we'd die during the attempt. I feel it would have been an excellent form of income, because people would have bet on our survival or demise. Unfortunately they didn't have the guts to see it through.'

Alan remembers September 11th 2001 quite vividly. He'd had a very good meeting with Yamaha, and they'd tied up a lot of loose ends. He was driving back home when he heard the news of the terrorist attacks on the radio. Then he had a call on his mobile phone from the city slickers saying 'It's all over. You're never ever going to pull this together. You'll never get down through the Middle East.'

Alan's reply was simply: 'Watch me.'

As far as sponsorship was concerned, September 11th closed all the doors, certainly as far as any major American involvement was concerned. We'd been talking to the communications company Global Crossing, whom we thought were very interested. We'd been talking to NTL as well, and while there was a faint glimmer of hope that they might have come on board at one stage, it was never a realistic hope. We must have had more money than they did!

We'd also been talking for over a year to the Dutch insurance company NCM. With their UK and Ireland headquarters in a graceful polished pink granite and tinted glass building on Cardiff Bay, not far from our visitor centre, it would have been the perfect partnership. We felt we were making progress with them, further cemented by meeting with their North American head office in Baltimore during our US tour in 2001. Unfortunately for NCM, what looked like two good company acquisitions turned horribly sour. They provided the buildings and consequential loss insurance cover for the World Trade Center. NCM subsequently merged with the Gerling Credit Insurance Group in December 2001, and whilst we followed up shortly after with another presentation to them, it came to nothing.

Without the level of sponsorship the project needed, Alan had to consider some drastic budget cuts. 'I never cut any corners on safety,' he says. 'The road crews had to go, and we had to smile a lot more than we wanted to, when it would have been easier to have an argument with someone and pay them money for time. We had to accept that we were in the hands of whoever wanted to keep us on the quayside. The original budget had $50,000 down for 'gifts' which was to be used for bribery.' Interestingly enough, we did well by keeping those payments down to $18,000.

The one major item of equipment which was shelved early on due to lack of sponsorship was that which essentially changed our route from one confined to warmer climes, to one which had us battling the cold and stormy conditions of the north Pacific and north Atlantic.

The fuel drogue was intended to carry 2,000 litres of spare fuel on the long ocean legs, allowing us to go straight from Yokohama to Midway Island, then on to Honolulu and San Diego in the Pacific, and from New York to Horta in the Azores. Built from biodegradable plastic, it would have been shaped like a torpedo with fins at the back, and a swivel assembly on the nose to allow it to rotate. The boat would also have had a swivel assembly and pay line, so it could either be let out up to 300 metres, or pulled in close, depending on the sea conditions. It would have cost around £5,000 to develop, including having the moulds built - not a huge sum of money in the grand scheme of things, but by then we were scratching around for pennies.

We did end up with a title sponsor, but it wasn't for cash. It was the South Wales Echo, the leading newspaper for Cardiff and South Wales, and after they came on board about six weeks before we set off, the voyage became known as the 'South Wales Echo Around the World Challenge'. South Wales Echo editor Alastair Milburn said: 'This is one of the most exciting challenges of the new millennium and demonstrates a fantastic spirit of adventure.' It was a shame no one else saw that.

We set off from Cardiff on Easter Sunday 2002, having propped up the costs of fuel and other expenses with several thousand pounds of our own money, and still some £8,000 short. We just had to work on the basis that media coverage as we progressed would help us make up the shortfall. That of course was exacerbated when Alan Carter left us in Singapore, leaving us to find another £5,000.

There were so many facets to the sponsorship saga, some tied up with Cardiff, others not. We concluded that we were unfortunate in picking a bad time to go after any corporate disposable income. It was possible we could have done without if the numbers we'd been told would go through the doors of the visitor centre in Cardiff actually materialised. They never did. It may be that the reduced number of tourist visits in 2001 due to foot-and-mouth had a part in that.

Arguably, we might have done better sitting in a shop doorway on Oxford Street with a rug over our laps and a begging bowl.

14
AND THEN THERE WERE THREE

In Finland we talk about 'sisu', which means the ultimate perseverance supposed to be typical for Finns. You guys definitely have that!
Tuomo Riihimäki - a Finn living in Cardiff.

Tuesday 7th May

IT'S BREAKFAST TIME. I check my handheld GPS - we're 230 miles from Singapore. This time we're on our way. We've passed the point where the gearbox went before, which feels significant. Let's hope the run of bad luck went home on an aeroplane from Singapore.

I spend the morning writing and logging video clips. Then Alan emerges from the forward cabin with a stern look on his face and a rifle in each hand. He's spotted a couple of suspicious looking fishing boats, and doesn't want to take any chances.

'If they want to mess with me,' he hisses, 'they're going to bloody regret it.'

I rush to grab my laser pointer, on the offchance it might be useful. Of course the boats are perfectly innocent, but there's no harm in a bit of adrenalin to give you an appetite for lunch.

The real problem here, even offshore, is the amount of debris in the water. Large lumps of wood. We've had a few bumps and bangs, but fortunately nothing major. I suspect closer inshore, we'd be getting massive tree trunks coming at us thick and fast.

Otherwise, today is pretty uneventful. I think we're just getting back into the swing of being at sea again after several days' break, and we're getting used to the fact that Alan Carter is no longer with us. There certainly seems to be a lot more space, and it doesn't feel anywhere near so claustrophobic.

News comes through that the Rib.Net internet forum has received £3,500 in pledges for us in 24 hours. It's the best news we've had for ages. There are people out there who care!

We also hear that Alan Carter has appeared on television saying the real reason he left was because of our 'cavalier attitude to safety'. This coming from a man whose only experience of endurance offshore powerboating is dinghy sailing in the Bristol Channel, and who clambered outside the cabin in the dark at over 20 knots without a lifejacket. It would be easy to get angry over something like that, but after a few mutterings of 'Prat!' we carry on with life. Alan does get the chance to rebut the accusations, but doing an interview by satellite phone isn't quite the same as appearing on camera.

Wednesday 8th May

It's quite bumpy during the night, the first head sea we've picked up for quite a while, and our speed cuts down to not much more than around 13 knots. When I come on watch, at around midnight, Alan stays with me for a while, then has a lie down. I end up doing around four hours on my own, turning in at 0530.

But back in Singapore, as we discussed the consequences of Carter's departure, we'd agreed it wouldn't be a good idea to have people doing watches on their own. It's easy enough to nod off, but two people on watch can keep each other awake. So what's happening? Surely if it's OK to leave me on my own for that amount of time, it would be better for everyone to do solo watches of two hours each, giving us all the opportunity to get twice the sleep for the amount of watch time. I decide to raise the matter later. In the meantime, my heart is in my mouth as we run over numerous floating obstacles. With no visibility, picking our way through a minefield would probably be a lot easier.

And then we approach KK. Surrounded by low jungle-clad hills, the town itself (or at least the waterfront) has a modern look to it with a posh resort and marina. As we come in to the harbour area, we're met by a small motor boat, which we follow in to Sutera Harbour. There to meet us are Danny Tan and George Lam, along with a gaggle of local journalists and other interested onlookers.

We're in the province of Sabah, known as 'Land below the wind'. Sutera Harbour is a brand new complex of holiday resort, golf and country club, business hotel, swimming pools and marina, all built in the last two or three years on reclaimed land.

The boat is fuelled up, and then brought round to the marina. We're whisked inside and sat down at a restaurant table, ready for a beer and meal. I order a chicken dish which turns out to be particularly tasty. I'm tempted to try the local food, but know it would probably be a mistake with my constitution. In fact I have to take every opportunity to wolf down the mouthfuls, as one of the journalists keeps bombarding me with questions all the way through the meal. Sitting next to me is someone who's obviously a well-off local businessman. He presents us with a number of bottles of wine to take away.

After the meal, Alan has to go and complete the immigration formalities, so George takes Steve and me to the health club to use the showers. On the way, we ask if it would be possible to get a haircut. My grade three has gone particularly toilet brush-like. So after a shower, we find ourselves in the resort salon.

At least when I ask for grade three on the top, two on the sides and back, my glamorous hairdresser says 'That shouldn't take long.' After the cutting, I'm taken for a rinse by a young girl, before being shepherded back to the lady for the final tidy up. 'You look good,' she tells me as we finish. Steve, on the other hand, is getting his hair teased up with gel by the nice young man attending to him - probably not quite what he expected.

When we meet up later with the chap who sponsored the wine, he wonders why George didn't take us to the 'other' hairdressers. There, apparently, not only do you get a haircut, but other services performed by young ladies at the same time. It would certainly bring a whole new meaning to having a cut and blow dry…

All too soon it's time to leave, although the stop has been rather longer than average. But then they have been amazingly good to us here. So we untie and set off, fresh with haircuts and new shirts, baskets of fruit, bottles of wine - sorry to be leaving, but looking forward to returning some time in the future. I reckon a nice relaxing stay here coupled with a yomp up nearby Mount Kinabalu would be great.

As the sun sets, I mention the watch issue. If it's all right for me to do four hours on my own, why can't we each do two hours on - on our own - and four hours off? We give it a go, and it seems very successful.

Thursday 9th May

I watch the sun rise during my second shift, and video it happening. It's really quite pretty as it turns from a watery pink to yellow. Then of course it starts to get hot. There are one or two interesting moments with boats today - including a large fishing boat that appears to keep altering its course towards us as we alter ours away. It is just a fishing boat, isn't it? Suddenly our VHF radio crackles into life.

'What a day!' says the voice, with a degree of exultation. It's an odd remark to hear on Channel 16, and it certainly doesn't conform to the normal rules of radio traffic. But then again, the fact that he's altered course towards us again suggests that what he's fishing for isn't what's swimming in the water beneath him.

This part of the South China Sea is another piracy hotspot - we're just a couple of hundred miles east of the Spratly Islands, where many of them hide out, and a similar distance west of the Sulu Sea, which Major Tan warned us about. In the main, hostile boardings are all about grabbing people and boats for ransom, but we have no intention of finding out first hand.

Alan gently eases our throttle open, and starts to pull away from him. The fishing boat tries to keep up with us. Within a minute thick black smoke is pouring out of his exhaust stack - he's at full throttle. We've gauged his limit, we've teased him. Now we open our throttle and leave him standing, our whale-tail wash slapping against his bow as the final insult.

At one point Steve says he saw a flying fish sail right over the top of the cabin, which is pretty amazing going for such little fish. Then during the afternoon, Alan sees a big fish breach the water, possibly a marlin.

We've been making good progress, but during the afternoon the wind springs up, and we find ourselves bashing through a head sea. That and the lack of success connecting up through Iridium - or Iridiot as I've affectionately christened it - has me feeling frustrated. Still, we should be in Subic Bay in the Philippines by early tomorrow morning. We can't fuel up till 0800, so if we arrive earlier, we'll just have to hunker down and wait.

Spirit of Cardiff IT Director John Kennett informs us today's update has created some amusement. I've done a quiz based on all of the various items of safety equipment on board. It has a photograph of Steve looking like airline cabin crew, wearing a life jacket, holding a CO^2 fire extinguisher, and pointing to the indicator light for the Seafire automatic halon gas fire extinguisher in the engine compartment. Most would think it's simply another entertaining update. Those in the know realise I've unleashed a sarcastic side-swipe at Alan Carter's on-air allegations that we have a cavalier attitude to safety.

Friday 10th May

It's a truly awful night. Before and after my first watch from 2330 to 0130 I get absolutely no sleep at all. The wind has sprung up out of nowhere, and we're battering through head seas.

'You always want to go faster when others are trying to sleep,' Steve complains to Alan. 'You only want it to be slower when you're trying to sleep.'

He say's he's absolutely pissed off with it, and I agree. Alan recognises the frustration, and decides against trying to blast along quickly. Not that it makes much difference to our sleep. Even on the other bad weather bits I've managed to catnap, but this time it's been just too painful being constantly buffeted. When I'm supposed to start my second watch at 0530, I'm awake, but Alan stays up and makes a cup of tea, so I take the opportunity to do an early email check.

When I go outside, I'm puzzled to see oil all over the engine box and along the port side of the cabin. Alan reckons that the boat we apparently came quite close to last night must have thrown a bagful of oil at us. How odd.

And in recognition of the fact that we're now past the potential threat of pirates, he chucks both rifles over the side. Some might wonder whether it's being a bit premature, but we also have to weigh that against the consequences of entering some ports with illegal firearms.

The sea calms down later, and we end up doing over 20 knots, which is a bit more like it. The approach to Subic is absolutely stunning. Rugged mountains rising from the sea, but not as jungle-clad as I might have thought. In fact, some of it is quite reminiscent of Scotland (although somewhat sunnier).

Subic Bay is a large natural harbour, site of a US naval base for many years. It was fought over in World War Two, and there are sunken American and Japanese warships in the harbour. Later, in the Vietnam War, Subic was a big R&R base.

At Subic Bay Yacht Club we find James Williams waiting for us. He's a computer software expert specialising in banking systems, working in Manila. Apparently he came into the visitor centre in Cardiff not long after it opened in 2000, signed the ship's log, and became a dedicated follower after that.

After breakfast, I'm whizzed upstairs to James's room for a shower, while Alan and Steve take the boat to be refuelled. It turns out that because the marina is so conscious of pollution - the entire harbour is a designated fish wildlife haven - they put a boom around the boat to prevent any possible fuel spills from spreading.

Just before we leave, the local politician bigwig arrives, with national TV channel in tow. It's quite funny, because as we troop down the gangway to the pontoon for the big speech, he looks behind to check the camera is still on him.

And then we're off. James comes out in the marina boat to time us out from Grande Island. Not that he looks terribly comfortable sitting there in his life jacket.

The promise is for more rough seas ahead. But by the time we're under way and I've completed my update, I'm feeling utterly zonked. Alan insists I should stop working - I'm pushing myself too hard. So Steve gets his Walkman out for me to borrow, and I listen to a couple of episodes of Blackadder 3, which cheers me up no end.

One interesting email today, from Jim Leishman, captain of a boat we'd read about in a magazine in Singapore. The American trawler yacht Nordhavn has been circumnavigating the world in the opposite direction to us, from Dana Point in California. They're just arriving in the Caribbean, and Jim has offered to help out with any information we might need for our Pacific crossing. We decide to stay in touch.

Saturday 11th May

Alan has decided that today we should shoot a dedicated tape for BBC Wales, to send back to Sophie Brading, who's handling our public relations, in the hope that it will be used on the national TV news in Wales. Hopefully it will be a further spur to sponsorship. So I've been snatching a few typical moments of life on board - preparing meals, working out the navigation - plus one or two pieces to camera.

Later it gets much rougher - I presume because we're heading out more into the Pacific. We pass shoals and lots of islands as we cross the Luzon Strait, including Batan Island. Very soon we'll be crossing the Tropic of Cancer. The last time we crossed it was in the Red Sea - the next time will be Mexico, followed by the Caribbean.

This evening's meal is ratpack corned beef hash - very nice. Today is Bertie's 82nd birthday, and when Alan rings him up for today's weather forecast, we all give him a hearty round of Happy Birthday. Not often you get such a greeting from the middle of the Pacific. To us, Bertie is very much the unsung hero of the trip. The weather for the next few days seems to be pretty much the same, then a depression setting in, but only 10 knots of wind, with a fair smattering of rain.

Sunday 12th May

We're now in a following sea, making up to 20 knots at times. We crossed the Tropic of Cancer early this morning, somewhere east of Taiwan. Tomorrow might see the depression move through, then we'll get several days of settled weather, hopefully enough to see us all the way up Japan to P-K (Petropavlovsk-Kamchatskiy) in Russia.

I've been doing a few sums, and we can still beat the Cable and Wireless record. Just, provided we don't get any more delays. We can arrive at any time on the 20th June and still get it. At our current average mileage (including normal stops as opposed to delays) we ought to be able to arrive back in Gibraltar on the 19th June. But of course that doesn't allow for further unforeseen problems. Still, at least we know we're still in with a chance, and of course we also have the Malta ace up our sleeve.

It starts off quite cloudy today, but gradually the sun breaks through. It's still very warm, but without the horrific intensity of previous days. We're making our way north fairly quickly, so we'll be back in temperate climes quite soon. Having said that, I wonder about the weather in Russia and the Aleutians. Alan thought it would be cold, but I'm not so sure. Summer in Alaska can be pretty scorching from my recollection, and P-K is also on the end of another large land mass. Maybe it's still to early in the year, but I'm hoping we might be pleasantly surprised.

I spend a bit of time doing some more shooting for the dedicated BBC Wales tape which we're going to post from Okinawa, but I'm not sure the audio quality is going to be that good.

We should be arriving in Okinawa's capital, Naha, at about eight o'clock tonight, though I calculated somewhat later. Unfortunately this is another stop where we have a delay because we can't refuel until the morning. What a pain. And even if we did refuel and set off tonight it would apparently muck up the timing for our next Japanese stop in Choshi, another marina where we can only refuel during the day. We can't win.

We spend an interesting 10 minutes or so talking about the ramifications of coming back to an award of some sort. Powerboat Yachtsman of the Year award is quite likely. Yachtsman of the Year is not so likely, as Alan was told in 1998 that he was the first and last powerboater to be considered. Then there's the prestigious Rolex award. And then of course the possibility of an official gong. Well, Ellen MacArthur got an MBE, and all she did was come second in a race.

In hindsight it might seem brash and over-confident, but at this stage, we feel the world record is still within our grasp, and it's not unreasonable to surmise on the consequences of our moment of resulting fame.

The sun has set by the time we start our run in to Okinawa. We see lots of lights in the distance, and an orange glow in the sky which signifies a big city. Alan and Steve are up front making sense of all the channel markers and harbour lights. We have to be careful of a coral reef, apparently.

But we make it to the safe water mark, and when we phone up, we're told a boat is coming out. When it arrives, we can hear the sound of laughter and ladies' voices. Sounds like a party, which I suppose it is. On board is John Perez, his wife and family, and Tom

Mekuhara, who hops aboard Spirit. It's John's son's birthday, and they've certainly picked an interesting way to celebrate it.

We follow the other boat in to Naha, and tie up at the marina. Once ashore, a cooler box appears, and we each have a bottle of beer. So here we are in Japan. John is actually an American of Mexican descent, married to a Japanese lady. He's lived on Okinawa for around seven years.

'It's very different to the Japanese mainland,' he explains. 'The island was American until 1972, when it reverted to Japan. The Americans still have a big military base here, so the influence continues.'

Naha was completely flattened by the Americans, and at the end of the war, Okinawa saw a grisly period of mass suicides, women and children throwing themselves off cliffs. They believed that the advancing Americans would rape them, and death would be better. Thousands died this way. I discover that Okinawa has always been very much a gateway kind of place for Japan. It's also the birthplace of karate.

We sit at some tables in the marina pool area, finishing off another beer, and then head into the restaurant. John and Tom have some of their friends with them, so we make a fine party. We're presented with Okinawa baseball caps - proper American ones with curved peaks - and some very nice polished wood bowls made of coconut.

We order steaks, and just to complement things, Alan goes back to the boat to grab some of our supply of wine. There's a bit of a problem getting it in, sorted out by Tom. 'He could talk a snake out of his skin,' says John.

After the meal, we end up outside at the pool for a while. Eyebrows are only slightly raised when I go for a quick late night skinny dip, which washes the salt off me, and presumably exchanges it for chlorine.

Back to the boat for some shut-eye, and the sleeping bags come out for the first time in weeks. But it's not really cool enough to warrant them, and I end up lying on top of mine.

Monday 13th May

I wake up with a slight feeling of hangover, but the worst of it is having gippy insides once more. Several visits to the toilet later, and

I'm not much improved. I take a quick look at the Spirit of Cardiff website to see the latest update pages. I'm pleasantly surprised to see a message from Kristen Greenaway, a New Zealander who was on the trek I led in Nepal for Doug Scott in 1996. She now lives in San Diego, which could quite possibly be of some use to us (if we get that far).

First to visit us is a quarantine official, who has a quick poke around the boat, presumably to ensure we have no mad cows on board. Then a couple of customs officers appear. They search the boat fairly thoroughly - asking if we have any weapons. It's a good job they went over the side.

Once we've filled in a couple of forms, that's it. We're legal. A guy comes along to refuel the boat. It's not cheap here - US$1,300 for 2,150 litres. Alan doesn't have quite the right dollar bills, so he tells the driver to keep the change. A broad smile sweeps across his face, and he gives a charming little bow as he says: 'Thank you.'

Once that's done, John and Tom take us off to breakfast. McDonald's is closed, but we find a Japanese equivalent. I have sausage meat and cheese with fried egg in a bap, and a few chips - quite reasonable.

Then back to the boat. John reappears with some final few provisions. He's replaced our wine with some evil drink which apparently is taken diluted. And he's given us a couple of bottles of cold jasmine tea - his favourite drink.

We set off at 1000 local (0100 GMT). But we've already been warned by Bertie - the weather for the next leg is going to be miserable. Utterly miserable.

15
CLOSE TO ROLLING

Just keep your mind on the fact that it's going to pass - by the end of the week you'll be looking back on this bit, marvelling at how well you got through it under such horrible conditions.
Website posting from Paula Gardiner.

BERTIE WAS RIGHT again. We're in big seas, and down to eight knots. If it doesn't let up, we could take four days to get to Choshi, 1,050 nautical miles away. I'm despairing because the skylight above my bunk is still leaking, dripping water incessantly, and because we're in big head seas, we're taking a lot of waves over the top of the boat, which then cascade in a waterfall at the back of the cabin and splashing inside. I'm being attacked by water from two directions, and whilst I can just about cope with the discomfort, I'm most mindful of the potential damage when I'm using my Psion.

'Still,' says Alan. 'It should flatten down when the sun goes down,' echoing with more than a truckload of irony an old saying that Steve comes out with: 'When the sun goes down, the wind goes down.'

'I've got news for you,' adds Steve. 'There isn't any sun!'

Alan rings Bertie early evening. The news is that the horrible conditions we're in at the moment will last at least another 10 hours. There'll still be easterlies, but not so strong, so hopefully we'll be able to get going again.

Steve isn't feeling too well at the moment. Although we've now stopped taking our anti-malaria pills, he's suffered the worst with the side effects, which in his case manifests itself with frequent diarrhoea. So now we're all a bit under the weather.

Tuesday 14th May

We're halfway through May, over six weeks since leaving, and we're still not yet even halfway around the world. It's unbelievably depressing, particularly as the weather is so awful. We're in big seas, reduced to eight knots, and since we left Okinawa yesterday, we've managed to make just over 200 miles. Not exactly record-breaking stuff.

As we pound into big waves, the tube at the bow waggles up and down, and every so often, a wave goes right over the roof, with water cascading onto the aft deck, and inevitably some of it splashing inside. Putting the door on would help counter some of the spray, but then we'd mist up the windows even more than they are now.

The radar has just one massive splodge on the display. If there are any ships out there, they're invisible. The point is rather proven when I glance out of the port window to see a tanker overtaking us. That probably explains a burst of static on the radio a few minutes previously. Not dangerously close, but close enough to be impressive, and to warrant a spot of video. Mind you, the conditions for shooting video without trashing the camera are far from ideal. Later we get another ship coming straight at us. Fortunately the radar shows it, and we're able to get out of its way.

'I wouldn't want that at night in a rainstorm,' admits Alan.

Water is getting everywhere in the cabin. The hatches in the roof are leaking, and there's a lot of splatter coming through the door. Steve rigs up a curtain for the doorway using the piece of material which lined our fruit basket from KK. It fits just fine, keeping the spray at bay, but allowing a reasonable level of ventilation.

Steve somehow manages to put into words what the rest of us merely think. 'I could just do with a nice juicy leg of chicken,' he muses, 'and some roast potatoes.'

'Would you do another long voyage like this?' he asks me.

'I don't think so,' I reply.

Once is definitely enough. And all the time I'm thinking about that Cable and Wireless record slipping out of our hands. We're going to have to do some serious catching up if we want any chance of doing this. At times like this it's very easy to feel despondent and want to give up. But when you're 150 miles from the nearest land and only making 144 miles a day, with the wind coming at you at 30 knots, and the rain horizontal, you realise you just have to stick with it.

'Let's face it,' says Alan, 'it can't last forever, can it?'

'It could last a week,' adds Steve helpfully.

Wednesday 15th May

A boat, like an aeroplane, is capable of moving about three axes. Pitching and yawing are relatively easy to live with, even when the movement is quite violent. But rolling is always sickening, particularly when you're sliding sideways down waves anything from 30 to 60 feet high. The moment of truth comes when Steve is on watch during the night.

'It was when the sea appeared at the side windows,' he says. 'The waves were pushing us right over. I've never experienced anything as bad as this.'

I realise the gravity of the situation when I wake up to find him wearing a life jacket. Nice of him to let us know.

'I thought the boat was going to roll,' he tells me. 'And I thought you were going to fall out of your bunk. You were dead to the world.'

Never a truer word if we really had gone over. It isn't just the fact that the waves are big, but that they're breaking. While a big RIB like Spirit has seaworthiness that's second to none in bad conditions, the fact that the waves are breaking makes a crucial difference in the dynamics of any boat's stability.

What would happen if the boat rolled doesn't bear thinking about. The theory is that with all the weight on the keel side of the tube, she'd flip back. But not before everything inside gets smashed up, including the crew. And if any of the windows popped, that would be it. We'd be dead.

Alan realises the futility of trying to maintain even five knots in these awful, awful seas. It's the point when essentially we put the boat into shut-down mode, the engine ticking over just enough to maintain about a knot. That should keep us stable and pointed in the right direction.

We've been beaten black and blue by this storm for 40 hours. We've had virtually nothing to eat or drink, and we're exhausted, each sporting various injuries. Steve has cut his head, Alan has whacked his knee which has now blown up, and I'm bruised in various places.

Everything is soaking wet as well. Our three American-made hatches - one at the front and two in the cabin roof - all leak badly. I guess we've pushed a lot of the equipment and fittings on the boat well beyond what they were designed for.

The cushions for our bunks are saturated, and the carpet on the floor is soaked. Everything, absolutely everything is wet. Going to sleep with wet underneath you and wet dripping from above might seem horrific, but when you're as exhausted as we are, believe it or not, it's still possible. My various bits of electronics and camera kit have survived purely because they're protected by hard-shelled waterproof camera cases.

Gradually we make our way between two small islands south of the Japanese mainland island of Kyushu, managing to pick up some speed for a short while.

'We've managed to cover more distance in the last 20 minutes than we have all night,' observes Alan.

Once sheltered off Tanegashima, and the town of Nishinoomote, we stop for our first brew up and beans and Spam in two days. Up until now it's been too rough to use the stove even with the boat stopped. The sun even comes out, so we take the cushions outside for a while to dry them off. After our brief respite, we set off again. At the end of the islands we cross a tidal race, then suddenly we're in big seas again.

'I think we should turn back,' says Steve.

'What do you think?' Alan asks me.

'Well, it's not very comfortable,' I admit. 'But I defer to your knowledge as to what's safe or not.'

'OK, we're going back.'

We make our way into the harbour at Nishinoomote, tying up next to a small sailing yacht. The man and his wife on the boat speak absolutely no English, but they're friendly enough, and let us raft up against them.

We take a wander around the town, first of all trying to find a bank to change some US dollars into Yen. We go into about three places, not sure whether we're actually in banks, post offices or social security buildings. It's all very confusing, as the signs give absolutely no clue at all, and just because there are Automated Teller Machines in some doorways doesn't necessarily mean that what's inside includes a foreign exchange desk. Eventually we find somewhere, and have an entertaining half hour changing the money, and trying to convince the bank workers we're not an advance guard of football supporters travelling to Japan for the World Cup. Very few people here speak English, it seems, which may be something to do with the fact that it's a small island.

Once we have some currency, we track down the local pizza parlour for some lunch. Alan and I have a set menu, which is a plate of noodles with bean shoots and mushrooms, along with a delicious side salad. Then we do a little shopping. The toilet bucket made a mysterious disappearance on our short foray out to the north of the islands, so we have to replace that, along with some sealant to try and cure the various places that are leaking.

On our way back to the boat, we pass the Jionji Temple, a charming red and white building with stone torii gate at its entrance. In 1552, Francisco Xavier, the first Christian missionary to Japan came to Tanegashima while on his way to Bungo in China. This is the oldest temple in the Nansei Islands. Over 100 Portuguese and other traders spent six months here, establishing trading contacts. Guns, powder, camphor, and even scissors came into Japan through here. These days, Tanegashima is the centre of Japan's space programme.

I spend some time catching up on writing while Alan and Steve wander off in search of a bucket. Before they went, Steve helped the lady in the boat next door manhandle a large cooler box of provisions from the quayside onto the boat. Now she appears with three large apples for us. Of course, the exchange of gifts is very much a Japanese thing.

The sun's out, so we've spread everything out to dry - I even leave my towel and shorts (wet since Monday) in the engine compartment to dry out. But as the afternoon wears on, the seat cushions and covers are damp again. They're so impregnated with salt, they just suck moisture back in again. They're going to need a good scrub in fresh water to cure that.

The carpet is still very damp, and it stinks horribly. No wonder we've found lots of mosquitoes making their homes in it. So we spray the cabin liberally with insecticide before shutting it up to go out for the evening.

First port of call is a quaint little bar. We're the only ones in it. There's Japanese baseball on the telly, and the landlady tries to make us feel welcome by plying us with various nibbles to accompany our large bottles of Asahi beer. I'm not so keen on the pickled prunes, but things start to look up when she produces some chocolate.

We try to explain why we're here, and I end up drawing a crude representation of the world and a small boat complete with arrow. Perhaps we should have had something like it as part of Spirit's corporate logo. Then we wander off. We find another bar cum restaurant where four women are sitting on little mats at a low table set up on a platform, their shoes on the floor below.

We sit at the bar, gazing into the eyes of fish staring lifelessly at us from a glass cabinet on top. Alan goes outside to phone Bertie, while Steve tells me about his golden years of carpet fitting, when he'd earn hundreds of pounds in a single night's work. When he started doing all the overseas embassies, they'd always fly British Airways First Class, and would be put up either in five-star hotels or in the embassy compound. He told me of the time he carpeted the secure room - a small room with just a table, chair and telephone - of the British embassy in Prague. This is where the ambassador would make sensitive phone calls, in a room guaranteed bug-free. The embassy's head of security was miffed because Steve was allowed to go in, when even he didn't have clearance.

The news from Bertie isn't encouraging. He says this depression will be with us for another 72 hours. So we're not going to risk trying to run all the way to Choshi. Instead, we're going to make a short dash north through what will probably be mountainous seas to Miyazaki, on the mainland. The city was once on Alan's prime list of refuelling stops, and there's the intriguing prospect that it's twinned with Portsmouth. Fed up with the lack of support from the business community in Cardiff, Alan is keen on playing the Portsmouth card to see whether they can give us any assistance.

We finish the evening in a karaoke bar. It's not exactly heaving on a Wednesday night - we're the only ones here. There's no beer, so Alan and Steve have a Jack Daniels, while I sample the saki, which most closely approximates lighter fuel.

And then we start the karaoke. The resulting excruciating sounds make listening to fingernails down a blackboard pleasant by comparison. We do all the old favourites - Crocodile Rock, 20th Century Boy. The lyrics of some of the songs are a bit dodgy, as well. Eventually we get to Bohemian Rhapsody, but something appears to have been lost in the transcription. The bit where it goes: 'Bismillah, no. We will not let him go...' has been replaced by: 'Miss Miller...'

Thursday 16th May

We're up bright and early at 0600, surprisingly headache-free. No cuppa, we just head straight off. Once we're out in it, the waves are positively massive - big rolling waves, but fortunately not breaking. But the size of them comes home as we approach the Japanese mainland island of Kyushu, and we come across a number of fishing boats. It seems as though they're weaving in and out of the hills. One second we can see them, the next, they're out of sight. The wind is still coming in hard from the north-east, which is no use for attempting to get to Choshi. The only consolation is that we're now better lined up for it when the wind does drop.

We make our way into Miyazaki harbour, passing a splendid four-masted tall ship, moored next to the Osaka Express, which appears to be a ferry. But after that, we can't find any sign of pleasure boat moorings at all - it's all fishing boats moored up against concrete harbour walls. We pass under a bridge, which actually appears to be a barrage of some kind, hopeful that we might find a marina. But all we can see is a line of small boats tied up along the river bank, and water quickly diminishing to less than what's safe for us - it is low water as we come in. So we tie up in a part of the harbour which has some pleasure boats, but, it seems, absolutely no facilities. Bang goes the shower and laundry.

Steve cooks up some toast, beans and Spam, followed by a mug of tea. I feel a bit better after that. Today has been one of those days when I've just felt a bit down, and I can't really put my finger on the reason why. A combination of homesickness, the realisation that the record has very nearly fallen from our grasp, and the fact that the weather is denying us a speedy return home. I really don't want to end up having been away from home for three whole months, but that's the way it's starting to look.

Alan and Steve wander off to do a recce - hopeful that they might find a marina further up the river. Meanwhile I stay with boat, writing, and watching a fish eagle circle effortlessly over the harbour. Somehow it looks as though the Portsmouth connection won't be that useful. A couple of hours later, Alan and Steve return to say they walked miles but didn't find anything of use.

We're going to be in Miyazaki for a day, possibly two while the atrocious weather passes through, and there's absolutely nothing here. It's not looking good.

16
CARDIFF

Next year, a boat called Spirit of Cardiff will set a new world record for going around the world, thus illustrating the spirit of a constituency that still has higher male unemployment than any other Welsh constituency. In setting that world record, Spirit of Cardiff will put Cardiff and indeed Wales on the map.
Alun Michael MP, House of Commons, 5th March 2001.

BOATING EVENTS IN the main rely very heavily on associations with host cities, whether it be around the world yacht races, or powerboat races. Born and bred in Portsmouth, Alan had always tried to cultivate a working relationship with Portsmouth. That worked with the transatlantic in 1997, when the boat ran as the Spirit of Portsmouth. The round the world boat was also christened with the same name on 19th May 1999, when she was showed off by being towed on her trailer by a pair of brewery dray horses into the square in front of Portsmouth Guildhall.

But there were problems with Portsmouth. When the around the world project was launched, Portsmouth assumed they had it in the bag. When the local government changed, so all the arrangements for showing off the boat at various high-profile locations were scrapped.

'It was a city in turmoil,' says Alan. 'The council could never agree on anything. Being non-political, I could see that it just wasn't going to work.' They were happy enough to bask in Alan's reflected glory, and weren't forward-looking enough to see that he might take his project elsewhere if his home city didn't provide the support he needed to make it happen.

Alan's plan to bring the project to a wider audience included a visitor centre which would explain the complexities of taking a small powerboat around the world, and would provide people with an easy channel by which to support the project if they wanted.

'We knew exactly what we wanted,' says Alan, 'and although we had premises in Portsmouth, they weren't in a prime location. We needed something that was going to be more accessible to the public. That's when we started looking for another host city.'

Apart from the visitor centre, the host needed to be a vibrant town or city, but it didn't necessarily have to be beside the water. Possibles in the frame included Manchester and Brighton. Then there were the obvious things if the boat was actually going to be based there - dockage for the boat, workshop facilities, and somewhere to show the boat off. Above all, the host city needed to have an enthusiasm about the project, and a willingness to promote it.

'When we went to Cardiff,' explains Alan, 'we saw everything that we needed.'

Alan's original introduction to Cardiff came about when he gave an after-dinner talk to some 800 delegates at a Rotary conference in Llandudno. It was about his transatlantic expedition in 1997, and the strong Rotary connections that helped make it a success. His host was retired Cardiff policeman David Wiltshire, who suggested that he look at Cardiff as a possible base for Alan's proposed around the world record attempt.

'Then I had a phone call from David,' recalls Alan, 'asking whether I'd do another talk for a Rotary club in Cardiff. So I agreed to do that one, and then he asked if I'd like to do one for a company called Symonds Group.' It was their 40th anniversary in business, and they were holding a celebratory dinner in January 2000 in Sir Rocco Forte's new five star hotel, the St David's in Cardiff Bay. The Welsh First Minister and Cardiff MP Alun Michael would be there, along with the mayor of Cardiff, and local captains of industry.

'I asked David if there was an angle on this, and he said that Symonds' project manager felt that he could do something with our project in Cardiff. We investigated a bit more - Symonds was a big management and project consultancy company for the construction industry - and we liked what we saw. We went along to the dinner, told everyone what we'd done already, then told them what we intended to do with the around the world project. I closed it by saying: "Do you want to come with me?" To our amazement, everybody said: "Yes".'

Pledges were made in the room for substantial amounts of money (which never materialised). But Alun Michael was sold on the idea. He could see that it was just what Cardiff needed, something that would demonstrate to the world the 'Hwyl', the spirit of Wales and Cardiff.

Cardiff had a long history of seafaring. It was a major port. Captain Scott's ill-fated expedition to Antarctica and the South Pole started in Cardiff, and it was the Cardiff business community that funded his expedition. In relative terms, the funding he received would be equivalent to £15 million today. He was a pioneer and explorer, and we were about to embark on something pioneering in its own way.

Once the coal capital of the world, and in whose Coal Exchange the first ever million pound cheque was written out, Cardiff is more than just the capital city of Wales. It's Europe's youngest capital. Cardiff's waterfront is Cardiff Bay, formerly the site of large docks and run-down housing. But the last few years has seen the most incredible transformation, at its heart the impoundment of the Ely and Taff river outfalls by the Cardiff Bay Barrage. Running across Cardiff Bay between the Queen Alexandra dock and Penarth, this incredible piece of civil engineering created a 500 acre freshwater lake, made clear and fresh by an aeration system which blows air into the water from submerged pipes. As you gaze out over the bay, you can see the curious tell-tale circles dotted across the surface.

The whole of the waterfront area has seen a massive regeneration, transforming grimy docks into a thriving area of shops, restaurants and bars, and traffic-free walkways enlivened by imaginative works of art. Here too is the Tube, the weirdest looking building you're ever likely to see. Originally built in the early 1990s as a temporary structure, and winner of a RIBA award for its striking architecture, it was still going strong long after it was expected to be dismantled. Cardiff's visitor information centre was here, but the end overlooking Roath Basin was given over to the Spirit of Cardiff visitor and education centre.

And so the around the world project moved lock, stock and barrel to Cardiff. I was tempted at the time to put out a press release entitled: 'Around the world boat springs a leek', but thought better of it. We rented a house for members of the crew and other project staff to stay in while in Cardiff, and we set about producing a visitor centre which Cardiff could be proud of. But the Symonds connection went cold, and the project manager who'd promised to find the sponsors we needed left the company.

'It was a buzz city,' says Alan, 'and the figures were right.' The numbers of people expected to visit Cardiff Bay, and our realistic percentage of them who might come into the visitor centre and support us all stacked up. Our business plan and the loans we took out to create the visitor centre were put together on those figures. Unfortunately they didn't bear any relation to the true numbers.

'I was attracted by history,' concludes Alan wistfully, 'and fooled by current affairs.'

17
OUR NEW SHIPMATE

If you guys fell off a pier you'd land on a lobster. You certainly know where to park a boat.
Website posting from Dom Palmeri.

SOMEONE COMES OVER and invites us on to a large motor cruiser a couple of boats away from us. It's big, and very smart. The owner is Maretoshi Iwamitsu, who appears to be a wealthy businessman who's president of a whole group of companies. His English is virtually non-existent, but we manage to make ourselves understood, even though the process at times is rather tortuous.

We spend some time having coffee, and explaining as best we can what we're doing, and under what circumstances we find ourselves slightly off-track in Miyazaki, waiting for the weather to improve. He invites us to dine with him in the evening. So we change into our smart Rohan trousers and red T-shirts, and he whisks us into town in his car. It's funny, I'd said on Tanegashima that we hadn't seen any imported cars like Mercedes or BMW, and here we are, taking a ride in a smart Mercedes with sumptuous leather seats.

At the restaurant, we have to remove our sandals and step into a small cabin with sliding doors. The table is in the middle, with a bench platform all the way around. So we take our places, sitting on sort of legless chairs. Soon we're enjoying a beer, and then Maretoshi's wife arrives, plus a friend and his wife. The conversation is still a little difficult, but much eased now by a Sony Bookman with Japanese/English dictionary. Maretoshi has two daughters studying in England, one in London and one in Eastbourne. Every time we get really stuck trying to explain something, he rings one of them on his mobile, and gets her to speak to Alan. It's an expensive way to have a conversation, but it does the job, and it's entertaining without doubt.

The phone itself is amazing. A compact folding mobile with fantastic colour graphics, and the ring tones are incredible. You can have one which sounds like a real old-fashioned telephone ringing, or an orchestra playing various themes. Apparently in Japan the phones are provided free, and the calls are just a penny a minute. A far cry from what we have to pay in rip-off Britain.

Everyone is clearly impressed at our endeavour. Then the food arrives. First it's the traditional sashimi - sliccs of raw fish, which are dipped in a sauce and eaten with chopsticks. Steve and I show a bit of willing and eat a couple, but that's enough for us. Alan is clearly more adventurous gastronomically, and carries on with the raw fish. Then some glowing coals are brought in and placed in a tiny sand pit set in the middle of the table. It becomes a mini barbecue, with thin slices of pork and beef sizzling away merrily. That's much more palatable, as are the vegetables - beans, shitake mushrooms, and lettuce. It's certainly a new experience to have cooked lettuce, and it's also something different to experience the traditional Japanese table manners, which encourages noisy eating.

At the end of the evening, we've been getting on famously, finding out in the process that Maretoshi owns the restaurant. When it's time to go, we assume we'll be given a lift back to the docks to sleep on board the boat. But no, Maretoshi produces three plastic keycards for us. It turns out the rest of the building is a hotel called Urban Kit, and he owns that as well. We each have a free room for the night!

We retire for the evening - but not before Alan phones Bertie to discover tomorrow's weather is not good, and there's absolutely no chance of getting away. So we agree to meet up with Maretoshi at 1100, as he's suggested taking us to the spa.

Friday 17th May

It's unbelievably strange to be sleeping in a real bed for the first time in weeks - since Malta, in fact. And it's nice to be on my own, as well. Not that I don't enjoy Alan and Steve's company, but real privacy is the one thing that's lacking on board the boat. You might think I'd sleep like a baby, but I've become so used to crashing out for short stretches on a bunk whose movement encompasses everything from gentle sleep-inducing rocking to violently hurling me at the walls and ceiling, I'm unable to get a decent night's sleep in a proper one which stays still.

After a restless night I go for a short morning wander before heading back to the hotel for a coffee. Alan and Steve show up later, and we go out for another walk. There doesn't appear to be much in the way of breakfast at the hotel, so we end up in a supermarket buying some pastries, tucking into them as we sit on a bench overlooking the river. The flower beds here have loudspeakers playing soothing music. It's an interesting idea, but I'm sure they wouldn't survive the ravages of vandals for long back home. The streets in the city are festooned with flags, ready for the start of the World Cup. The German and Swedish teams will be based here, and they're expecting a lot of visitors.

Back at the hotel, we meet up with Maretoshi and his wife, and head off to a hamburger joint for an early lunch. I order a cheeseburger, which arrives sizzling on a metal plate set in wood, similar to the plates they serve steaks on.

Afterwards, we drive to the dock to go back to the boat. We've already ascertained that the weather will be too bad to allow us to get away today, so we want to rescue the more valuable items just to be sure they're safe, given the lack of security at the docks. I'd quite like to do some laundry, too, so I grab my clothes bag as well as the equipment cases.

Then we drive off to a new marina, just up the coast from where we came into Miyazaki harbour. This is the place we would have gone to if we'd been able to find it, and had we not been tempted to dive into the first inlet available. It looks really nice, and here we meet up with a big sailing boat we passed on the way to Miyazaki. Of course, if we had pitched up in here, we'd never have met Maretoshi.

Having tried and failed to send the daily update from the dock, I ask for Maretoshi's car keys so I can have another go while sitting in his car, the phone charging from the lighter socket. It takes over an hour to connect up. Steve reappears - he's not too good on the tummy front, and has rushed back to the toilet. But then we find the gate to the pontoons has been locked. We sit around for a while, and then he goes off in search of someone who might let us in.

By the time we're at the sailing boat again, the others have clearly been having a good time. We're presented with a bag of 'Japanese chocolate', which turns out to be lumps of brown sugar. 'I wouldn't eat this even if I was dying,' says an unimpressed Alan when he can't be overheard. It doesn't taste that bad, but munching through large lumps of brown sugar doesn't appeal very much, so it gets ditched once back at the hotel.

From the marina we drive to the main harbour to take a look at the Kaiwo Maru (King of the Sea), the 309ft four-masted barque which we passed on our way in on Thursday. It's a nice looking vessel, run as a sail-training ship for the Japanese merchant navy. Apparently she was the overall winner of the Boston to Halifax leg of the Tall Ships 2000 race.

All the while we're here, some old van has a tannoy blaring out the same mournful singing, over and over again: 'Yakimo, yakimo.' I discover that this is the traditional way of selling sweet potatoes, but I get worried when we set off in Maretoshi's car and it appears to follow us out of the car park, still broadcasting its plaintive advertising jingle.

We drive back to the hotel, where we have time for a short break before Maretoshi asks us to meet downstairs at 1700. I take the chance to do my laundry - my towel and shorts in particular turn the water a disgusting colour. But it'll be nice to have a salt-free towel for a while, even if it is only short-lived.

And then we're off to the spa. It's a proper Japanese baths, with various hot pools, a sauna, and area with lots of shower stations. Here you sit on a low plastic stool and wash yourself. You have to be properly rinsed off before entering the baths. The way they do it in Japan is sans cozzie, but apart from your main towel, you're also provided with a smaller flannel, which seems to be used more or less in a strategic capacity to hide your dangly bits as you move from one pool to another. Except that yours truly without his glasses manages to mislay the all-important flannel, and so possibly commits something of a faux pas.

The sauna is hot enough to finish off me and Alan. By the time we wilt out into the changing room, while Steve goes for a bonus extra soak in a hot pool, I'm feeling warm, relaxed, and absolutely squeaky clean. I also take the opportunity to weigh my naked body on some amazingly accurate electronic scales - 69.45 kilos. I guess I must have lost a couple of pounds on the trip.

Then it's back to the hotel for another short break and continuing tending of the laundry before meeting up for dinner. So it's cheers, or rather kampai, to some more beer, and then we're ushered into another separate room to eat. This time it's a low table with no footwell, so after attempting to sit cross-legged for a short while, my knees start to complain, and I end up adopting a variety of ungainly positions.

Some more of Maretoshi's friends are here. They all seem to be rich. We met one this afternoon at the tall ship, a stunning girl on his arm, and a brand new Bentley Mulsanne Turbo in the car park - 250 grand's worth, according to Alan. One chap at dinner in a smart blue suit with casual shirt definitely oozes money. He tells us his brother is an ambassador for UNICEF.

The weather tomorrow isn't going to be perfect, but we have to set off for Choshi anyway. Typhoon Hagibis is forming in the Philippines, and it's coming this way. If we're here when it arrives, we can kiss goodbye to the rest of the trip. We need to be gone a good few days by the time it arrives. So it'll be 15 knot north-easterlies, as opposed to today's near-suicidal 45 knot winds. We agree to meet in the hotel lobby at 0900.

Saturday 18th May

We leave the hotel at around 0930, and get things loaded onto the boat. Not only have our new friends already given us three boxes of beer (12 cans in each - good for bribery in Russia), we're also presented with some water and a few other provisions, including a packet of Kellogg's Frosties.

I spend the usual ages trying to connect to my email, and give up after an hour. We've been waiting for Maretoshi's wife, and she arrives with multiple sets of the photos they've been taking of us over the last couple of days, all mounted in little folders. So we each have a memento of our stay - a lovely gift. It's late morning by the time we cast off. As we head out up the harbour, Maretoshi, his wife and friends are there, waving enthusiastically the whole time, right until the very last moment.

The last couple of days have been almost like a dream. It's hard to

Alan Priddy, the Chris Bonington of powerboating.

Raffles Marina's Major Tan Hua Chiow gives Alan a few welcome tips on navigating out of Singapore. It's a long while since we've looked at a paper chart!

Bugis Street in downtown Singapore is the place to pick up lots of unexpected bargains.

Natsteel Marine, Singapore. Alan and Steve replace Spirit's outdrive.

'Land below the wind.' Sutera Harbour, Kota Kinabalu, in Malaysia.

Breakfast in the Philippines. Spirit of Cardiff supporter James Williams talking to Alan.

Subic Bay, Philippines. Once an R&R base for American servicemen, now an idyllic tourist destination.

Top: Naha Marina, Okinawa; Left: Maretoshi and his wife with Alan; Bottom: Sheltering off Tanegashima.

Fearsome looking statue at the Temple of Maeganji, near Choshi.

A stone torii gate leads you to the steps of the Jionji Temple on Tanegashima.

Built by Englishman Richard Henry Brampton, the lighthouse on Cape Inubo near Choshi looks out over a wild and rugged coastline.

Sunset over the Kamchatka Peninsula - bitterly cold, but unbelievably beautiful.

We have to prepare numerous lists with multiple copies before our arrival in Petropavlovsk-Kamchatskiy - easier said then done when they have to be handwritten on a moving boat.

When eventually we're allowed into port, excursions onto the quayside are restricted to a 20 metre radius from the boat. (OK, so I cheated to take the photograph.)

Top: Part of the abandoned US military base on Adak Island in the Aleutians. Right: So good they named a bear after it - Kodiak.

Hundreds of miles from land - Steve Lloyd enjoys a beautiful sunset as we cross the Gulf of Alaska.

Spirit moored up in beautiful Telegraph Cove, at the northern tip of Vancouver Island. Old timber buildings are joined by a wooden walkway on piles at the water's edge.

This ancient truck blends in with the scenery at Telegraph Cove, British Columbia.

'Alright, officer. It's a fair cop, but society is to blame!' Alan Priddy on board the RCMP boat 'Nadon' after we've been stopped for not showing a mast light.

The new cruise liner 'Radiance of the Seas', heading off from Vancouver on a cruise to Alaska.

Flamboyant, without a doubt, and with a heart of gold. Fred Deo and Alan Priddy with their new friend.

The Founder's Tree, a Californian Redwood which stands nearly as tall as Norwich Cathedral spire.

Fred Deo's 32 feet long stretch limo parked outside the Pacific Lumber Company's museum in Scotia.

The author, doing his daily 'tippy-tappy'. The Psion Series 5mx was the only computer capable of being used in the often violent motion which accompanied Spirit's progress across the waves. It was linked by cable to an Iridium satellite phone to transmit daily updates by email.

Seeing a pod of humpback whales off the California coast is pretty special. You can even hear them squealing as their tail flukes come out of the water.

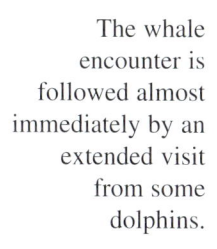

The whale encounter is followed almost immediately by an extended visit from some dolphins.

The wing engine is back on for the fourth time. Now it's just a case of connecting up the fuel line...

...and the electrical cables inside the engine box.

It was just getting dark as we tracked down the Nordhavn, 50 miles off the Baja Peninsula.

The guys on the Nordhavn were amazed we'd met up with them sooner than they'd expected.

While Spirit is let out on a line to trundle on behind us.

Cabo san Lucas, on the southern tip of the Baja Peninsula, was our first stop in Mexico.

But apart from sorting out Alan with a new car, Acapulco proved a frustrating waste of time.

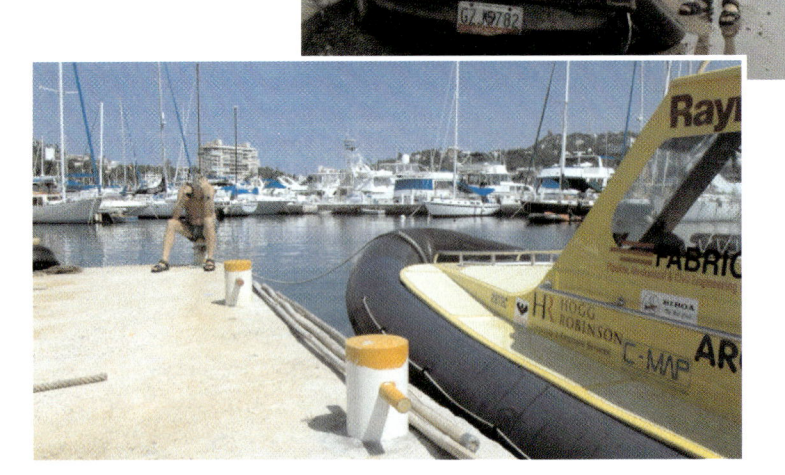

imagine anything like this happening back at home - a stark contrast from the meanness of the businesses in Cardiff who stand to gain from the exposure we're giving Cardiff all over the world, but who haven't coughed up a bean to support us. Three ragtag mariners turn up in a commercial fishing port, get befriended by a complete stranger, and taken under his wing. He wines and dines us, puts us up in his hotel, and gives us that most valuable commodity of any successful businessman - his time. And he wants nothing in return, other than our friendship. We're all speechless.

18
WINDY JAPAN

Have just re-read your journal from page one to get a feel for the overall trend of your voyage. It seems you went from 'OK' to 'bad' to 'very bad' to 'worse' to 'worse still', then to 'bad' to 'good' and now 'better'. Let's hope that 'the best' is yet to come.
Website posting from Steve Evans.

IT SEEMS FAIRLY calm to start with, but further out to sea we start pulling in some big rollers, and a lot on the beam again, which I don't like. The swells are supposed to be eight feet today, dropping to five tomorrow. Roll on tomorrow, is all I can say. The only good thing is that we're making excellent speed, up to 20 knots. In fact, when we stop for a quick brew up, we're still making 10 knots with the engine throttled back to not much more than tickover. There's a big tide behind us, clearly.

Now we're going again, we seem a little quiet. We're all pleased to be on our way again, but the last couple of days has been quite special. Befriended and unable to pay for anything - you just couldn't ever imagine it happening.

Alan has performed a superb running repair to the satphone data pack - the connector which allows me to plug my Psion data cable into the phone - whose clip broke some while ago. I was concerned that the connectors were corroding, so he sorted that out, and then, using a piece of copper strip salvaged from the fuse box in his hotel room (sorry Maretoshi) and a couple of cable ties, he's fixed it so it clips on firmly. But just to be on the safe side, he arranges to have a new data pack sent to Telegraph Cove in British Columbia. All being well, we should be there in around 10 days.

By the time I turn in mid-evening, it's quite rough and bumpy -

uncomfortable to the point of hurting my back. I don't sleep for my first four hours. Apart from the bumping, Alan is getting a lot of phone calls from people at RIBEX, the world's largest annual show of RIBs, held at Ocean Village in Southampton. Nadia, Oli and Kevin are there from the visitor centre, along with Alan's sons James and Wayne, all trying to raise money for us. Basically saying: 'We're out here - this is the cutting edge of RIBbing, everyone is watching what we're doing. Please support us!'

Sunday 19th May

We're on a main shipping route, and there are lots of fishing boats about as well. The swells are quite big, but even so we're still making 19 to 20 knots. So whilst I'm on watch, I'm pretty busy, checking how many boats there are around us. On my night time watch, we pass a headland with lots of lights. There's a tidal race here, so we skirt past it a bit further offshore. While I'm doing my second watch, by now daylight, Alan relieves me. His back is giving him trouble, and he'd rather go back on watch.

'So you can do your tippy-tappy,' he says.

The tippy-tappy includes an email check, with a reply from Tim Exton, a British TV producer now living in Seattle with whom I'd been in touch about making a possible documentary for American consumption. I'd emailed him asking if he'd like to join us for one or two legs from Telegraph Cove, and it seems he may be able to. But he also tells me that Alan Carter has been in touch with him, saying he left us in Singapore on the understanding that he was still involved in the documentary. Strange that he didn't tell us that himself, and if that was really the case, why did he remove all his video kit and money? Or the text message demanding a complete refund of his money?

After a run of over 500 miles from Miyazaki, we arrive in Choshi, about 50 miles east of Tokyo in the early evening. It's still daylight, which is just as well, as we don't have detailed charts for the harbour. As it is, we're intercepted at the entrance by a boat, which leads us to the marina. There we're met by a welcoming party of yacht club members who were told we were on our way in, and who've clearly already been celebrating the fact. If I'd ever held any opinion that the Japanese might be rather formal and reserved, this was the moment when the illusion would have been shattered. Before we know it, cans of beer are thrust into our hands, and my video does a quick tour of various pairs of hands so I appear in some of the shots - assuming they pushed the right buttons.

Had we arrived earlier in the day, we could have been in and out in a matter of hours, but apart from refuelling, Choshi is the second stop where the boat must come out of the water for a 5,000 mile service. Our engine and gearbox manufacturers Yamaha are based in Yokohama, on the other side of Tokyo, and their engineers are going to do the job for us, but we'll have to wait until the morning.

So we're whisked off to a local restaurant, where Alan does the adventurous bit with the sashimi once more, while Steve and I try some more conservative fried fish. We start off outside, but then it begins to rain, so we decamp inside to the traditional low table and little cushions before digging in to a huge pile of noodles.

It's an enjoyable, convivial evening, but even so we're back at the boat by about 2030, and we end up having an early night. I sleep like a log - not surprising, I suppose, as I'd slept very little the night before.

Monday 20th May

The wind is really strong this morning, and the prospects of getting away today are looking remote. One chap we met last night said this bit of the coast is always windy, and that we were extremely lucky to get in when it wasn't.

First visitor this morning, fairly early, is a man from Japanese customs. He's come all the way from Yokohama, a good 70 miles away on the other side of Tokyo. Once all the formalities are completed, the boat is whizzed round to the travelift. It's lifted out and put on a trolley, then wheeled into a shed so a team of Yamaha engineers can work on it under cover.

They don't just change the gearbox oil, they give both engine and gearbox a thorough service, finishing up by steam-cleaning the engine and respraying it. Also the man from Solpower Japan, a sponsor who provides our Soltron fuel additive, gives us a bright yellow Soltron jacket, along with a Japanese good luck charm each. They'd better work.

It's chilly standing around, even in the shed, but we have a minor diversion opening up our second crate of supplies. Unlike the one we sent to India, this one has arrived with all the contents still there. But this time they're in a slightly different order. A packet of soap flakes has burst open, mixing soap with everything else in the crate. The next few pasta meals should be interesting.

Once the boat's back in the water, and as we're still not in a position to depart, we're taken out to lunch by marina manager Taka and the Yamaha man, along with 'Mad Dog' - so called because of the slogan on his baseball cap - Yutaka Furukawa. He's a commodities broker in Tokyo, and also a sailing enthusiast. He has a boat at the marina called Little Mo, named after legendary tennis player Maureen Connolly.

'So why aren't you working today?' Alan asks him.

'If I'm going to lose money,' replies Mad Dog, 'it might as well be here as in Tokyo.'

It's just a fast food place, but each table has an amazing screen on which you can either watch a movie, or colour in a cartoon figure, which then animates on a background, still with your colouring.

After that, we do a short sightseeing tour, first to the dramatic coastline of Cape Inubo, overlooked by a 100 year-old lighthouse built by Richard Henry Brampton, well known English lighthouse builder, then to the temple of Maeganji in Choshi. We take the opportunity to make a few pleas for good luck. Surely by now we deserve it. Both Steve and I toss coins into a wishing well.

'I've wished I was home tomorrow,' he admits. I think the same as I throw my coin in.

Later we're sitting in the lounge back at the marina, watching a programme on BBC World about Afghanistan under the Taliban overdubbed in Japanese, when Alan, whom I don't think was really concentrating on the programme, says suddenly: 'It's depressing, isn't it?'

'What, women being brutalised by an evil theocracy,' I reply, 'or trying to go around the world in a powerboat?'

'Well, I have it on good authority from Kodiak that the wind'll be behind us.'

'At 50 knots?'

There's a washing machine and tumble dryer in the clubhouse, so we get some laundry in there washing. A chance to get the towels nice and soft again, as well as a few fresh clothes. Alan and I have some noodles and tuna for tea, while Steve, still with his gippy tummy, sits it out.

Back at the clubhouse we settle down with a few beers and nibbles to watch a video about gladiators starring Lou Ferrigno (Incredible Hulk) and Mandy Rice Davies. It's truly awful, but entertaining in its own excruciating way - a sort of budget Roman version of the Magnificent Seven.

Then we start watching another film with Rip Torn recommended by Steve, so we're surprised when he's the first to give up and go to bed. Alan and I hang on till 2300 so he can ring Bertie, and then we retire too. But instead of being asleep, Steve is back in the boat as chatty as you like. Instead of drifting off to sleep, I end up wide awake for ages as he presses me to tell him about one of my mountain exploits. I suspect the dull monotone of my voice is just what he needs to get off to sleep.

Tuesday 21st May

The wind has dropped, so we're away from Choshi by around 0630, heading for our last Japanese stop - Muroran, just over 400 miles away on the island of Hokkaido. There's still a slight remnant of yesterday's waves, but not much, and we're making a good 18 knots. Lots of fishing boats are out, surrounded by thousands of seabirds, which if nothing else confirms the good weather. Although the sun comes out occasionally, it's not at all warm. The boat's cabin, being flat at the back just like a box van, tends to suck air through the door, so there's always a draught. Now that the temperature's dropping, it's not so pleasant.

The cabin at the front of the boat is rather differently organised now. We've kept our outdrive from Singapore (now fully serviced) and the one delivered to Choshi is in its box in the front, carried as a spare. Chances are we're going to need it. We'll either run over something else, or burn out the clutch plates again once we return to higher temperatures and lower quality diesel.

The mood on the boat is somewhat restrained. I think we're all a bit apprehensive, feeling the psychological barrier of the journey up to Russia and 'going around the top'. Once we've made our first couple of US landfalls, we'll know we're finally on our way home, with fewer miles remaining than those elapsed.

At the moment, I just wish I was somewhere else. I'm deprived of music, warmth, and decent food. I'm sick of junk food - I want fresh fruit and vegetables, not some rubbish out of a tin or packet. And someone was supposed to be giving us a cassette player at Choshi as well, to replace the communal tape player which somehow found its way into Alan Carter's luggage. But sadly that didn't turn up.

As the afternoon wears on, it gets colder and colder. I go forward to the helm seat for a bit while Alan is lying down, then put on my waterproof jacket. Even so my feet and legs are cold. We haven't had anything to eat of any note today, which doesn't help at all. I see some seals popping their heads up to look around, then diving out rather like dolphins. Another sign, I reckon, that we're moving into colder waters.

Eventually the door goes on, but not before I've managed to get quite cold, wet and miserable. The sea becomes rougher, and it comes in on the beam - 'Your favourite,' as Steve tells me. It proves relatively short-lived as we negotiate a tidal race. We're also closer inshore now, seeking shelter from the land - a beautifully rugged coastline with rolling hills.

But it's not too long before we're up to speed again, and Steve says: 'We're back up to record speeds again. Another 30 days and I could be in the arms of my loved ones.'

'What,' says Alan mischievously, 'in San Diego?'

Later, as we're bumping through another tidal race, the jangling of the Japanese good luck charm, inches from Alan's ear, becomes too much, and he pulls it off the wall.

'We'll get struck by lightning, now,' I suggest.

'A perfect end to the trip.'

It gets dark and more bumpy. We have beef stew for dinner, enhanced somewhat by the addition of water biscuits to help soak up the gravy. Then I try to get some sleep, which proves useless. My first watch from 2200 till midnight sees masses of boats and ships all over the place, enough to keep me on my toes - and awake. Most of the time, the lights show before they appear on the radar. Whilst quite a few come close, I only have to alter course to avoid one - waiting till he's just under a mile before I hit the minus 10 button.

At midnight Alan phones Bertie, and my heart sinks when I hear the conditions will be like this for the next 72 hours - in other words, all the way to Russia.

Wednesday 22nd May

After my watch, I try vainly to sleep for the next four hours, but it's no good. I suppose lying there resting your eyes would be of some benefit under normal conditions, but when you're being buffeted about, there's no hope of any rest. By the time I start my next watch, somewhat later at 0440, the sun is up. The fact that you can feel the warmth of the sun is something, but the air temperature isn't very high, and the sea is whipped up into angry little waves which have cut our speed down to five knots.

But as we turn the corner to head west along the southern shore of Hokkaido, the conditions improve. The wind drops, and we're able to make 20 knots. We end up arriving in Muroran, our last Japanese stop, just before midday, which given the time we lost during the night isn't that bad.

Apart from the Enrum Marina staff and someone from Yamaha, there's a whole gaggle of press and TV waiting for us, or to be more precise, Alan. They're not at all interested in Steve and me - as Steve says later: 'We're just chief cook and bottle washer, and tippy-tappy. No one will remember us afterwards.'

They seem far too polite as well, waiting patiently as the man from Yamaha translates, although several seem quite able to understand English anyway. If it was British press, it would doubtless be a bit more of a scrum than a gaggle. Not that the British press - apart from specialist boating media and regional press - have shown a lot of interest in us.

While Alan is occupied with the usual port formalities, Steve sets about fixing the leak in the Bomar hatch above my bunk. We can see where the water has been coming in, as the wooden roof lining is discoloured. So he squirts a load of sealant all around, which hopefully should sort out the problem. Fingers crossed - I'm fed up with drips falling on me, as well as on the Psion and other expensive equipment.

Once that's over with, we're walked over to the marina office, where they've hung a huge banner welcoming Spirit of Cardiff. 'Go for the record,' it says. As it is, we have the usual red tape with the

Customs people, and then we're taken off to lunch at the nearby ferry terminal restaurant.

Afterwards, we need to get a few supplies, so we go off to one shop, but decide it's not quite up to what we want. We ditch everything we've collected there, and visit the Muroran version of Asda. Here we collect everything we need, including a good supply of fruit, choccie bars, gas cartridges and a small electric kettle to use when it's too rough for the gas stove. Steve is after a card to send to Jen to mark their wedding anniversary which comes up next week, but we can't find anything. Perhaps not something they commemorate?

Then the Yamaha man decides he wants to buy us each a windbreaker jacket. 'It may be useful in Russia,' he says, so off we go in search of a suitable shop. But all we find is a sort of DIY-cum gardening shop, and some other place. Not that any of us really needs another jacket, but they're concerned to see us leave with a gift that will be of real use to us.

Eventually we get away late afternoon, a Japanese national TV news camera rolling as we depart, with the sun going down and an advancing chill in the air. We're making 13 to 14 knots, which isn't bad given that we're fully laden with three tons of diesel for the thousand mile-plus journey to Petropavlovsk. The sea is almost flat at the moment, with barely a breath of wind. But how long will that last? We have no idea. There are two depressions hanging around, and nobody seems to know what they're going to do.

19
BUILDING THE BOAT

You're going around the world in THAT?
Astonished words spoken by just about everyone.

Where's the boat?
American visitor at South Street Seaport Museum, New York, while staring straight at it.

RIGID INFLATABLE BOATS, or RIBs, are often described as the four-wheel drives of the ocean. They have a robustness and sea-keeping quality which other boats can't match. By a strange co-incidence, although it's entirely unrelated, the original concept of a conventional rigid-hulled boat with an inflatable sponson or tube came from South Wales. It was in the 1960s that Rear Admiral Desmond Hoare at Atlantic College pioneered a design of boat for the RNLI (Royal National Lifeboat Institution) to use as an inshore rescue boat.

Spirit occupies a unique place in the history of RIBs. Whilst an overall length of 33 feet (10 metres) might not sound much for a boat, when she was built in 1999, she had an advanced construction, and she was the biggest RIB in the world. With the benefit of hindsight, she wasn't big enough.

Alan's transatlantic boat Still Never Enough, named Spirit of Portsmouth for the trip, proved that you could go anywhere in the right kind of boat, even though it was only 23 feet long - provided you had enough fuel. He knew that if you could expand upon that and create something with sufficient fuel range, there was absolutely no reason why you couldn't get around the world.

Spirit of Cardiff was built back to front. Most boats would start out with a hull design, and then engines and fuel tanks would be chosen to fit the space available for the required performance. But in most cases, ultra-long range wouldn't be a prime requirement. Designing a boat specifically to tackle a circumnavigation of the world required a different approach.

'Once we knew what engine was available to us, we knew the fuel consumption of the engine,' explains Alan. 'The reason we used the particular Yamaha model we did was because it was the only one that I felt was capable of doing what we wanted within our range of sponsorship. We had other offers, but none of the other engines were what I thought would be up to the job.'

'Once we knew how much fuel it would use, we then calculated the length of the longest leg of the route I'd chosen, and built fuel tanks to accommodate it. They dictated the size of the boat. That was it - simple. We built a floating fuel tank.'

Alan had known naval architect Alastair Cameron since the late 1980s, and Alastair had been instrumental in designing other boats for Alan prior to Spirit. The way the hull was constructed meant that the high cost of the boat could never be seen, because it was all hidden away. In order to fit in the required capacity fuel tanks, Alan wanted to take out some of the longitudinals - reinforcing bulkheads which run from front to back - or rather, not put them in, which Alastair was quite concerned about. He thought it would weaken the hull. So what they settled on was to apply an inch-thick layer of foam inside the hull, and then put another hull inside that to strengthen it. The fuel tanks were designed and built in such a way that they would replace the longitudinals. A boat of this size would normally have an aluminium fuel tank, but made from stainless steel, Spirit's tanks weren't just designed to carry fuel, they were intended to provide structural strength as well. To Alan's knowledge, no one had ever built a boat like that before.

'But while the tanks are substantial,' says Alan, 'and each one took two people to lift, when the hull was laid and the tanks fitted, it only came out at 1.2 tons. The fuel tanks are part of the boat. If you took them out, you'd have a weaker boat.'

Made of glass fibre by Northshore Composites, the normal hull is three eighths of an inch thick, then there's the foam filler, then the second hull inside it, also three eighths of an inch. The keel is five inches thick. In other words, it was an incredibly strong boat, built to take the punishment of going around the world in its stride.

As far as the tubes were concerned - the inflatable collar around the hull - it was a challenge for Henshaw Inflatables, the company which made them, simply because they were so big. Two feet in diameter, and made from Hypalon - a tough fabric with synthetic rubber coating - with internal baffles to make nine separate sections, the tubes would provide the boat's phenomenal extra stability and flotation. While the hull had built-in flotation provided by the foam filler, even if the hull were catastrophically holed, the tubes would still keep the boat afloat. As we told people many times, it would take a bomb to sink Spirit. She was a high-powered life raft.

'When we first showed the boat off,' says Alan, 'the know-it-all boat-builders of the world said: "Oh, that won't work. You need to do this, you're going to puncture your tubes." History, and a total mileage adding up to nearly two circumnavigations of the world, proved them wrong.'

The concept of having a cabin, unusual for this kind of boat, came through the bitter experience of Alan, Steve and Jan's three-week crossing of the Atlantic in an open RIB in 1997. Protected by Gore-Tex drysuits, Alan and his crew were at the mercy of the elements, and lashed in the face by the sea, which Alan likens to being hit around the face by a wet plastic bag.

'It hurts. You get salt sores inside the nose and in the ears, and you're constantly spitting salt out of your mouth. It's horrible, and something I vowed I wouldn't do again.'

There had to be an enclosed wheelhouse, both for keeping water out, and for providing shade from the sun. Again, that had to work backwards.

'We wanted a substantial engine box for ease of maintenance and storage, which took up the back part of the boat. We always knew we'd have to carry extra fuel in cans, so that gave us the volume of the aft deck well, and the next measurement was sleeping arrangements and the position of the driving seat. Some people might say: "Well, if the driving position was further aft, the boat would be more comfortable," but then again, that would mean you'd be sleeping further forward, and you'd be a lot more uncomfortable. The front end of the boat was never to be used for anything other than storage - it's just too uncomfortable up there in bumpy conditions.'

Spirit took 75 days to build, from the moment Northshore was given the go-ahead, to the moment she was on the water and fully fitted out. The hull with tubes was delivered around 20 days into the process.

'It was a mad panic time,' admits Alan. 'And while that was going on, we were also rebuilding the wreck of Still Never Enough (the transatlantic boat), which had been trashed in a motorway accident in France. We'd already sold that boat, so we needed to get it into a condition where we could make good the sale and use the money to help finance building the Spirit.'

Given more time and bigger budgets, the boat would have been cosmetically different in appearance, but it had to be functional as well. The cabin had a very angular appearance about it, but it was built like that to be strong. Having said that, because they weren't building something with lots of curves, making the moulds was a lot easier.

The cabin and wheelhouse, built by Alan and Steve, was another area of the boat which attracted criticism. Everybody said it wouldn't be strong enough. The damage it did sustain - two instances of broken windscreens, was in conditions that would have inflicted damage on any boat.

'Many people looked at the boat and said the windows were too big, and that we were inviting damage. We could have used toughened glass instead of auto glass, but arguably if we had, the impacts which caved in the auto glass windows would have caused more severe structural damage to the cabin,' explains Alan. 'The glass fibre would have broken, the window frames would have ripped out. As it was, the laminate stretched and absorbed some of the energy of the impact. At least by doing it the way we did, it was simply a case of running a Stanley knife around the seal, cutting out the broken window and putting in a new one. In hindsight, the windows should have been smaller, but even then I wouldn't have used toughened glass. If toughened glass goes, it just explodes - and shards of glass and an inflatable boat don't really make what you'd call an ideal combination.'

The boat was powered by a Yamaha ME420Sti turbo-charged

260hp diesel engine, a straight six-cylinder engine, basically the marine version of what you'd find in a Toyota Landcruiser. Given that the Landcruiser is one of the most widely used diesel engines in the world, we reasoned that we'd have a good chance of getting spares, wherever we might be. In the end, the engine performed faultlessly, requiring only standard servicing, and a couple of new fanbelts.

We could have had a jet drive, which Alan discounted at the time. In hindsight, a jet drive with no exposed propeller would certainly have been less vulnerable to collisions with debris, but you would sacrifice a certain amount of performance. We spent two and a half years testing the Yamaha Hydra drive with no problems whatsoever. It was a different story going around the world, however, although the conditions were far more demanding. 'It's a brilliant drive,' says Alan, 'but ultimately I think we just asked too much of it.'

Our backup against any problems with engine or drive was a small Italian-made 35hp diesel outboard wing engine. Stowed inside the engine compartment, bringing it into play involved heavy lifting by two or three crew members, and then taking it in short bursts. It had to be clamped to a plate at the back of the boat, a sturdy rope tied to it in case we dropped it overboard in the process. Then the fuel lines had to be connected up, usually taking fuel from one of the side tanks, and electrical cables attached within the engine box. It was unbelievably noisy, and at best we got five knots out of it, but it was better than nothing. In the end, we used the wing engine four times. It was definitely a good investment.

The fuel tanks were the biggest innovation. There was the main tank, midships, and closest to the engine, with 750 litres capacity. Then the forward tank was 1,000 litres. The two side tanks, which were put on for the Atlantic crossing, were 550 litres each. That gave us a total fuel capacity of 2,850 litres. For really long legs up to 1,250 nautical miles, we'd take another couple of hundred litres in plastic cans, stowed in the aft deck well.

All the fuel being pumped to the engine came from the main tank, so it would be topped up from the forward and side tanks. In the early days, they considered the possibility of pumping fuel about from one part of the boat to another to help balance it, rather in the same way that Concorde trims itself inflight. In the end, Alan opted for a rather more basic system with a series of three electric pumps which would pump either the side tanks into the main tank, or the front tank into the main.

'While we had one fuel pump problem around the British Isles,' he admits, 'we were plagued with them around the world. We were buying proper marine fuel pumps, and they just weren't lasting.'

Fuel filtering was critical. We were reliant on having clean diesel, but by the same token, we knew that there would be places where we'd be putting dirty fuel into our tanks. The Soltron additive that we used was extremely effective, neutralising impurities, and improving fuel economy. We would filter the fuel as it was pumped from either the forward or side tanks into the main tank, and again when it went into the engine, so it was well filtered, ensuring it wouldn't contaminate the pumps or burn the injectors. A lot of expense went into that, although you would never see it.

Before we crossed the Atlantic in 2001, the boat had a pair of hydraulically operated trim tabs fitted. These were designed to deflect the water as it came past the transom - the back of the boat - and lift it higher out of the water, thus setting the bow further down, improving its angle of attack. When we set off around the world, the electrical circuits controlling them went wrong, and by the time we reached Gibraltar, the trim tabs were in terminal decline. One of them was seriously damaged by the collision with the Maltese fish farm, but in essence, the loss wasn't that great. Trim tabs work well when the boat is at speed, but at slower speeds, they made no difference to the boat's handling.

The navigational equipment was the only part of the boat not fitted out by Alan and Steve. Raymarine descended on the boat with boxes of equipment, and just said to Steve 'Cut a hole here, cut a hole there.' Alan and Steve didn't have a clue what they were fitting. They simply said: 'Trust us.' The net result was a system that meant we didn't even have to drive the boat. It was so sophisticated, so well thought out, all we had to do was make sure nothing was coming in front of us. All the instruments in the boat spoke to one another through a high speed bus system, and if necessary, the boat could be operated by remote control from anywhere on board.

Once we lost the budgets to fully refit the boat, we couldn't develop all the things which would have given us a few more creature comforts. With the right money, the sleeping arrangements would certainly have been more comfortable. That's not to say we still wouldn't have got hurt, but maybe not quite so much. The original sleeping layout was with the two people off-watch sleeping across the back of the cabin, one on a bunk, one on cushions on the floor. It was OK, but it had a drawback in that anyone else would have to climb over two sleeping bodies to get to the door, and, as the tallest of the crew, I slept permanently scrunched up.

The last refit included changing the sleeping positions by running them along each side of the cabin, with feet actually inside the boxes which supported the front seats. In recognition of my height (six feet), Alan cut out the front of the seat box on the port side, so my feet would have a bit more room. It certainly gave me more room to stretch, but it was a disadvantage in heavy seas, where I might have appreciated something to brace against. And there was always the likelihood of getting my feet kicked by anyone sitting in the navigator's seat while I was trying to sleep.

There would have been more sound proofing in the engine box, and in the cabin, so the noise level would have been a lot less. In cooler conditions, with the door on, it wasn't too bad, but in hot weather the sound of the engine intruded on everything. Having said that, we simply got used to it. The last refit before we set off cost £2,000, when the original budget was £8,000. All the things that went were the creature comforts. The biggest expense in that refit was the outside shower and toilet platform at the back of the boat. It had to be right.

As for basic facilities, they were just that - basic. Alan had toyed with the idea of a small toilet, not inside the cabin where it would have taken up too much valuable storage space, but in the well in the bow. Given the seas we encountered, it may well have not been usable for much of the time. In rough conditions, we simply used a plastic bucket, stopping the boat if necessary, and in calm conditions going off the back from the small dive platform. Basic, but functional.

While normal boats might have a galley, most of the time, we simply used a camping stove. When we took the boat to America in 2001, we had the luxury of a microwave. It worked well, although there was the exciting moment when Steve managed to knock the on switch while snuggled up in his sleeping bag. It wouldn't have mattered much but for the fact that there was some paper packing inside to stop things rattling, and it caught fire. I happened to be sleeping on top of it at the time. There's nothing like a conflagration to wake you up smartly.

When it came to safety, we went strictly by the rules, and then some. The UIM's rules dictated that we had a four-man life raft, even though the boat itself was essentially a very large powered life raft. That weighed 100 kilograms. We elected to take a sea anchor after studying sea patterns in the Pacific. In really big seas, we'd deploy the sea anchor, basically a 4.5 metre diameter parachute on 300 metres of line which would keep the bow pointed into the waves. It incorporated a heavy chain to stop the line from snatching. That weighed 60 kilos, and we never used it. We felt the boat was more comfortable lying to in really big seas, just bobbing about. The life raft and sea anchor added to the fuel consumption - it was like having two extra crew members in weight. Without them, we could have made significant fuel savings, and at no real cost to safety.

In fact, it was the rules that nearly scuppered us at the beginning of 2002, when it was pointed out that we hadn't followed the UIM's rule requiring a vessel to be built to comply with a number of safety regulations pertaining to large commercial sailing and motor vessels over 24 metres in length. When the UIM had drafted their rules in 1997, they never in their wildest dreams imagined that a vessel of just 10 metres might attempt the world circumnavigation record. With the help of former RYA Powerboat Manager and record-breaking powerboat racer Peter Dredge, the UIM granted us a dispensation on the rules to enable us to go ahead.

Even if a little rough around the edges as far as creature comforts were concerned, Spirit was built to be safe and sturdy, and ready to take on the mammoth task before her. We all had 100 percent confidence in her.

20
THE EMPTY QUARTER

Good luck guys on the rest of the trip. Looks like you might need it given the waters that you now are travelling.
Website posting from Jon Jonsson.

Thursday 23rd May

It's just coming up to four in the morning. There's been light in the sky since three, but now a cherry red sun, noticeably flattened as it creeps over the horizon, is rising above the creamy smooth surface of the ocean. We're working our way along the south-eastern coast of Hokkaido, with the Kuril Islands stretching out before us all the way to the Kamchatka Peninsula.

I never really thought before how birds go to sleep on the sea, not just seabirds, which you might expect to find floating in groups on the surface, but migrating birds as well. But it's only the seabirds that try to keep up with us once they take to the air, thinking perhaps that we're a fishing boat with some easy spoils. Yesterday we spotted a Laysan albatross - its wingspan of a good six feet supporting it with barely any movement as it wheeled effortlessly over the waves.

It's cold, too. For the first time last night, my lightweight Snugpak sleeping bag - too warm to use during our spell in the tropics - is now just a little chilly, so it's time to bring out its heavyweight brother to cope with the next week or so in the North Pacific.

Breakfast this morning is a bowl of granola (the nearest thing we could get in Japan to muesli) followed by a very satisfying soft-boiled egg in toast sandwich and a steaming mug of tea. The biggest surprise of the night has been the calm state of the sea since leaving Muroran. With no wind worth speaking of, and just a slight swell, we've all managed to get some quality rest to make up for the previous night's torment, and we've also made a reasonable dent in the mileage to Petropavlovsk-Kamchatskiy. The world is definitely a much better place this morning, even if it is damned cold.

We clear the end of Hokkaido, moving on to the first of the Kuril Islands, some of which are not much more than rocks. So now we're in Russian territory, and an hour ahead of Japan. The islands, which Japan regards as its Northern Territories, were occupied by Soviet troops at the end of World War Two. Although the two countries restored diplomatic relations in 1956, they never signed a formal peace treaty because of their dispute over these islands, and much of that centres around their rich fishing grounds, and the fact that they afford a clear run out into the North Pacific from Russia's major eastern port Vladisvostok. The island chain is also one of the great volcanic hotspots of the world, generating frequent earthquakes and tsunami (tidal waves).

Alan proves the gastronomic adventurer once more, tucking in to a tin of crab. 'It's got bits of crushed shell in it,' he observes with an element of distaste, before slinging the half-eaten contents over the side.

I've been sitting in my office bunk with my lightweight sleeping bag wrapped around my legs to keep warm. We sort out which of the big Snugpak bags belongs to whom, and I swap over. The result is instantaneous. To think we'd stopped using them two or three days out of Cardiff because they were too warm. Now they're perfect. We've also made the transition to thermal underwear, fleece jackets and warm hats. I think it'll be a while before the sandals come out again.

Steve and I put our watches on one hour to be correct for the Kuril Islands, but Alan has put his on two for P-K, so he's in the right time zone for phoning. Oh well, it'll all adjust together eventually.

As the afternoon progresses, the sun disappears, and we're in thick fog, which promises to be even colder. I assume that there can't be much wind, but Alan reckons about 10 knots nonetheless. Certainly not too uncomfortable, and we're still doing around 17 knots.

Friday 24th May

From the frenetic activity of fishing boats along the Japanese coast, the passage along the Kuril Islands feels rather like venturing into the empty quarter of the Sahara Desert. We've seen absolutely nothing in the way of shipping or small boats.

During the night, we've crossed through the line of the Kuril Islands to follow their western flank in the Sea of Okhotsk. The hope here is for a little shelter from any wind coming from the north-east, and it knocks a few miles off the overall passage to Petropavlovsk-Kamchatskiy. Although the wind has picked up a little, we're still making 15 knots. With around 500 miles to go to P-K, we could arrive there by late Saturday night provided the wind gets no stronger.

As the sun rises at just after 0400 on Friday morning, the sight which greets my eyes looks more akin to South Georgia. We're just a couple of miles offshore from the island chain - rugged mountains wreathed in mist rising straight out of the sea, their dark silhouettes given shape and texture by the lines of snow which fill their numerous gullies.

Here and there the mountainsides descend to shallow saddles which sweep down to isolated beaches. The sort of place a shipwrecked mariner might head for, but not very welcoming or hospitable even so.

It's not freezing, but the temperature can't be much above. It feels colder because of the damp. There is a heater in the boat's cabin, but at these temperatures, it's pretty ineffective, and an icy draught comes through the gaps around the door at the back since we have to keep it ajar to stop the windows misting up.

Alan and Steve are asleep, and by the time they're awake, we've driven into a large bank of fog. The Kuril Islands are indeed a sight of wild and rare beauty, and one which I guess very few have the privilege of witnessing.

Breakfast is a bowl of cereal, plus a mug of tea. I follow it up later with an apple, one of the delicious enormous ones bought in Muroran. As the day wears on, the conditions get more bumpy. We're still making around 16 knots, but not very comfortably. The time in P-K is rather ahead of what I'd expected (gleaned from Alan's mini-Atlas) so now we're 12 hours ahead of BST. Which means we've had a short day today. Perhaps we'll have dinner for lunch, or maybe vice versa.

But whatever time we are now, Nadia has told us that the

immigration people in P-K don't want us turning up after 1500 Saturday, and we know we won't make it in until long after that. Whatever happens, we won't get fuel till Monday, but it would be nicer to spend Sunday on dry land instead of drifting around in uncertain conditions offshore.

Saturday 25th May

After a rough night in the Sea of Okhotsk, the water has flattened off nicely. We've passed a few more islands, and now we're coming up on the southern tip of Kamchatka, a peninsula of stunningly spectacular snow-clad volcanoes. We've even had a fair smattering of wildlife, from watching the comical efforts of puffins racing across the water like demented paddle steamers in their efforts to get airborne, close encounters with dolphins and seals, and we've seen our first couple of killer whales, their distinctive sail-like dorsal fins slicing through the water.

The Russians have now decided we're not allowed into Petropavlovsk-Kamchatskiy harbour until Monday morning, despite the fact that we could easily get there by Saturday night. The latest they could accept us Saturday is 1300, which they extended to 1500, neither of which we can make. So we're expected to anchor offshore until Monday morning.

We've accepted we can't refuel until Monday morning, but not that we can't go into a harbour and tie up. After all, Kamchatka is supposed to be very beautiful, and our hosts on the ground would be in a position to show us some of it on Sunday. But sadly that's been denied them.

We've pointed out that we're only a small craft which will be on the verge of running out of fuel, we've pointed out that the only anchor we have is a sea anchor designed to stabilise us in dangerous conditions. We've even offered to pay extra (they're charging us enough already) but none of these has persuaded them to make an exception for us.

Our options now are to make reasonable passage to Kamchatka and find a quiet bay somewhere, or to slow down. At the moment we're making just 10 knots, which will get us there on Sunday, but we have to find the happy medium fuel consumption-wise. It's possible to go too slow as well. In the meantime, we can do no more than enjoy the starkly beautiful scenery and wildlife, and we'll worry about what happens in P-K when we get there.

Of all the reasons for which we might not come home with the Cable and Wireless record, the weather is the easiest to understand and to bear. Even the unforeseen mechanical problems. But the avoidable ones, like mindless bureaucracy, sheer stupidity and laziness are the most frustrating, and here I think we're about to brush with masters of all three.

As we come to the end of the Kuril Islands chain and approach the southern end of the Kamchatka Peninsula, the sea picks up again. We skirt in close to the shore to try and gain some shelter.

'Never mind about the 12 mile limit,' says Alan. 'This is more like 1.2 miles.'

More to the point we're enjoying the sightseeing, even if we are ever so slightly on the wrong side of Russia's international limit.

Coming too close to shore almost has a price to pay. We pass into a patch of darker coloured water, and before we know it, horrible straining noises are coming from the prop. We've wandered into a vast patch of seaweed - huge tentacles of vegetation floating just below the surface. The prop is well and truly tangled, but before Alan takes to the icy waters at the back of the boat with a large knife, he tries one trick - putting the boat into reverse. It works. The prop sheds the unwanted vegetation, and we pick our way into clearer water.

But the view is fantastic - volcanoes, classic Fuji cones, and mountains, partially covered by snow, wild and desolate. The sky is blue and the sun feels intense in the crisp northern air. I brave the numbing cold to spend some time outside taking photographs as it sinks lower in the sky. It's one of the most spectacular sunsets of the whole trip. And the sky's clear, so it's certainly going to be bitterly cold tonight.

21
'THEY MIGHT SHOOT YOU'

If you get any problems with the authorities, you can always call your friendly Assembly Member and MP!
Lorraine Barrett, Assembly Member, National Assembly for Wales.

Sunday 26th May

WE ARRIVE AT the pilot station at the entrance to Avachinskaya Bay just after 0730, stop timing, and stop everything to cook up a fine breakfast of poached eggs, baked beans and Spam. I'm not feeling too well this morning. I have a headache and sore throat, so suspect I'm going down with a cold.

We drift around at the first of the designated waypoints we've been given for the approach to Petropavlovsk, beneath a cliff with a large radio installation on top. On the other side of the entrance to the bay is an early warning radar establishment with several large golf ball radomes. This of course is the closest point to the United States, and during the Cold War was a major centre of military activity. It was closed to Russians until 1989, and although opened to foreigners in 1990, has been pretty well restricted. Here in one corner of the bay is Rybachiy, Russia's largest submarine base, and home to the Pacific Fleet's ballistic missile nuclear submarines.

People try to reach us on the VHF radio, but whilst we can hear them, they can't hear us. It's a problem we've had before - we're very low in the water, so our signal doesn't carry that far. But we do manage to make telephone contact with Martha, our American contact here on the ground. We explain our problem is that we can't drop anchor outside the harbour - we don't have one. And having come over 1,000 miles from Japan, we're virtually out of fuel, so we can't drive around in circles endlessly. Even so, she advises us against just coming straight in.

'What would they do if we did?' asks Alan.

'They might shoot you,' she warns. 'They did with someone else a couple of days ago.'

So we bob around in the waters at the entrance to Avachinskaya Bay. We can make out people on the cliffs on the radio installation side. Some of them are running about, which leads us to think they've just woken up from their vodka-soaked Saturday nights to find an unauthorised vessel at the harbour entrance. Are we about to be blown out of the water? It nearly happened to the Greenpeace Rainbow Warrior a few years ago - it could very easily happen to us.

Hours pass, and nothing happens. Then we hear from Andrey, our other contact, that they've managed to get special permission from the General in charge of the area for us to proceed into the harbour and tie up, but we won't be allowed to get off the boat. But we have to wait for a pilot boat to come out, and that doesn't seem to be in much of a hurry.

Eventually it appears, and we follow him into the port. It has the usual Russian-style buildings, dilapidated and crumbling, but it looks rather more picturesque than the average Russian city, with its stunning Kamchatka backdrop of snow-cloaked mountains and volcanoes. Here we find two young women in camouflage uniform, one rather stern with typical Russian artificially coloured red hair, the other blonde, not quite so glacial. They both seem very suspicious of us. As I clamber onto the quayside and advance to shake her hand, the stern one stretches out her hand like a traffic cop. I mustn't approach any further. OK, so I've not washed for a few days, but really! Then her officer appears, who boards the boat to inspect our passports, and promptly bangs his head in the low doorway. We're off to a good start.

When Andrey, our agent, appears, he can't believe that all the standard paperwork which has been filled in for a visiting ship has actually been bent to apply to a 33ft boat. The blonde girl asks where we sleep, and I try to explain. Trying to put into simple words the concept of two seats which are really bunks with your feet inside the front seat boxes proves a bit too much for me, so I point at the cabin and say lamely: 'In there.'

After the initial formalities, we're told that because we can't be cleared by immigration until tomorrow, we have to stay with our boat, and we can't go further than a 20 metre radius on the quayside. This seems vaguely absurd, so the moment they're gone, I amuse myself by climbing a nearby crane, which provides an interesting alternative camera angle of the boat. Afterwards I trot back to have a few of Maretoshi's beers with Alan and Steve. It's quite pleasant to find ourselves with nothing to do, relaxing with a beer in hand. But ultimately, it's damned cold sitting here.

Later, Marina arrives with Irena, her friend. She's the boss of the travel company Pacific Network, and she's brought us some food. In fact, it's a whole chicken each, very nicely cooked, with some Uzbek bread and tomatoes. There are some other supplies as well, including a bottle of vodka and a bag full of books.

I end up with Michael Crichton's 'Airframe', which I start reading to myself, but then Steve wants it out loud. It's a change from his usual: 'Tell us a story, Clive.' So instead of making something up, or reading one of the travel features archived on my Psion, I have Michael Crichton to help me out. All 420 pages.

We erect a few curtains around the cabin - towels pinned up over the windows. Makes it a bit more conducive to slumber, and keeps the prying eyes at bay. We're being visited every two hours by border guards, making sure we haven't nipped off to a nearby bar. And we've noticed at least three points around the harbour where there are lookouts in towers, no doubt keeping a friendly eye on us. They needn't have worried. We're so knackered we end up turning in at around 2030.

Monday 27th May

I wake up as though from a drugged sleep. It's just before 0800, so I've slept for nearly 12 hours. I guess running a powerboat as a three-man crew does take it out of you. Surely it can't have been the three cans of beer?

Whilst there are one or two old rusting containers on the quayside suitable to nip behind for a pee, we decide they might be less than pleased if we do the same for more substantial matters. So Steve and Alan decide to have a poo on the bucket inside the cabin. This is not conducive to the best atmosphere, but it is relatively out of sight.

It's just as Alan has his trousers down that Martha arrives with three young girls in tow. Fortunately the tide is nearly out, and the boat quite a long way down from the quayside - otherwise they might have seen an unexpected side to their English visitor. The girls are exchange students, two Russian and one from Brazil. Martha's American, married to a Russian, and living 15 miles outside Petropavlovsk. They take a few photographs of us, and as we're chatting, the first in a succession of officials arrives, customs, followed by immigration and health.

Naturally I'm disappointed to have missed my opportunity with the bucket, so I ask Martha to ask one of the guards if there's a toilet I can go to. One of them takes me at an unbelievably brisk pace - even for my long legs - to some grim concrete building along the dock. Inside, it's nicely warm. Then up a flight of stairs with 1950s style wrought-iron banisters to a toilet on the first floor, a dimly lit windowless room, with a cubicle whose door doesn't quite fit the frame.

Inside, the toilet pan is set at low level into a concrete platform raised about nine inches above the floor. So it's a question of crouch rather than sit, and it appears that one or two previous users haven't been too successful with their aim. But I am surprised to find not just toilet paper, as opposed to the damp torn up strips of newspaper I tend to associate with Russian public conveniences, but soft toilet paper at that. Even so, it's not a place in which to linger, particularly as the paper mustn't be flushed down the toilet. There's a separate bin for that, which presumably means the waste plumbing isn't up to much. And this is one of the main contributors of technology to the International Space Station! I emerge to find my man has been waiting outside for me, and he escorts me diligently all the way back along the quayside to the boat.

It's chilly standing around, but at least there's a certain amount of fun to be had filling in forms. The lady from the health department is immaculately dressed in very expensive clothes. She hands me a health declaration to fill in. Have we come into contact with plague or rats? Has anyone been injured? Have any crew members died? I answer this one with: 'Not yet'. Another asks whether we're suffering from any kind of disease. 'Possibly mental' seems appropriate. They think we're crazy, anyway.

After they've gone - Martha disappears for half an hour, but in fact we don't see her again - we're back to more waiting for our immigration and port clearance papers. A young man called Yevgeny comes by and we have quite a chat. His English isn't that good, but he also has a reasonable smattering of French and German to match my less than reasonable schoolboy smattering, so we manage to communicate quite well. He tells me his grandfather was German - taken prisoner by the Russians during the war, and ended up in Russia's Far East, serving two years in a prison camp. Yevgeny hopes one day to be able to visit Dusseldorf, home of his German family some time.

'It takes time to get the visas,' he tells me. He produces a handful of coins. I think he just wants to show me, but he says I should keep one as a souvenir. I take a two rouble coin. Later he returns with a bottle of Russian beer for each of us. There's no doubting the natives are friendly, even if the military types are a little frosty.

Eventually our paperwork is sorted, and we're driven up into town for a swift sight-seeing session. We're allowed one hour before we have to be back at the boat and under way. There's not a lot to see, but we do a quick tour of a typical Russian department store, which provides a certain amount of entertainment. The concept of shop displays and window-dressing are alien here. The goods are simply piled up on shelves, and whilst there's a degree of demarcation between clothes and hardware, you still might find a toaster sitting next to a chainsaw.

Alan exchanges $25 thinking we might find something to buy, even if it's only a cup of coffee somewhere. But we're out of luck, so weighed down with several hundred roubles, we wander back to the boat. We don't have to wait too long before the final paperwork giving us clearance to leave is sorted. Strangely, the red-haired woman who was so stony-faced yesterday seems slightly more affable today, and even breaks into a smile at one point.

When we finally get away, it's very nearly 24 hours after arriving. Clearly Russia is another place where the concept of urgency and world records has yet to arrive. But as Martha explained to us: 'Doing things here is not so much about speed and efficiency, it's keeping people occupied.'

The stop has actually cost us a lot less than we anticipated, just $1,600. We untie and set off into cold Avachinskaya Bay. The boat is rather sluggish, but we're punching a tide, and we're fully laden with fuel. Still, we're excited to be on our way to Adak, 957 miles to the east in the Aleutian chain which divides the North Pacific from the Bering Sea. At least we know that there we have rather more of a welcome waiting for us. We're virtually halfway around the world, and by the time the night is out, we'll be on our way home.

22
THE GREAT AMERICAN DREAM

Whatever you do, don't ask me for any money.
Howard Stringer, Chairman of Sony Corporation North America, speaking to Alan Priddy, 4th April 2001.

That boat must be worth big bucks. What's that bumper all about?
Overheard in diner, Gloucester, Massachusetts.

IT WAS TO be our last big trip before going around the world, and originally the trip to test out the floating fuel drogue which would extend our range for the big legs across the Pacific and Atlantic. We wanted to do it by taking on Cable and Wireless Adventurer's last two port-to-port records, from New York to Horta in the Azores, and from there to Gibraltar.

There was another reason for fitting in a transatlantic crossing. While we had no hope of matching the speeds across the Atlantic from the likes of Richard Branson and the Aga Khan, we could nevertheless establish a record for the fastest crossing of the Atlantic. The reason was that the Union Internationale Motonautique (UIM) had the previous year changed the finishing post for powerboat transatlantics from Bishop's Rock in the Scillies to Lizard Point on the Cornish mainland, thus leaving it wide open for a new record, even with our dog-leg of a route via Gibraltar.

It would be my biggest ever trip on the boat, and for Alan, Steve and Jan, a revisitation. They'd crossed the Atlantic in the Spirit of Portsmouth in 1997, and this would make them the first people to cross the Atlantic twice in a RIB.

Unfortunately, we didn't get the funding we wanted to develop the fuel drogue, so Alan devised a route which would put a refuelling stop roughly halfway between New York and the Azores - St John's in Newfoundland.

It wasn't just to be a question of shipping the boat over and driving her back. Sponsorship hadn't been overly forthcoming, so we decided to embark on a promotional tour of the Eastern seaboard to see what interest we could whip up in the USA. Somehow we thought that raising money would be easier in America, where we felt they were more open to enterprise. Britain is great at basking in the reflected glory of its adventurers, but even Ellen MacArthur had been forced by the declining economic situation to go to France in search of funding.

But it wasn't all doom and gloom. With the help of Cardiff MP Alun Michael, Alan had managed to get the trip part funded by Cardiff Harbour Authority and Cardiff County Council, the deal being that we would promote Cardiff and Wales whilst out in America - particularly valid as the whole country was reeling from the terrible effects of the foot-and-mouth epidemic. Come what may, we would return to Cardiff on 2nd June to take a starring role in the official opening of the impressive Cardiff Bay Barrage.

To that end, we were helped out by our champion Alun Michael MP. He put us in touch with the Welsh Development Agency (WDA) in New York, and brought the 'old boy network' into play. Chris Jones, former chairman of Barclays Bank and leader of the Labour Party in North America, was asked to provide what assistance he could in opening doors. Alun also asked another old friend, Howard Stringer, KCMG, for a small favour. Stringer, naturalised American but a native of Cardiff, was chairman of Sony Corporation North America. He offered to throw a reception for us in the lavish Sony Club on the 35th floor of their impressive offices in Madison Avenue, Manhattan. There was even talk about inviting New York's newly-elected Senator, Hillary Rodham Clinton. If all that didn't open doors for us, nothing would.

The boat was shipped out from Southampton to Newark, New Jersey, by Peters & May and Wallenius Wilhelmsen, and on the 29th March, Alan and I flew out to New York with road crew chief Keith Walker. We arrived in Newark the next day to find Spirit on the dockside, but with the jockey wheel of her trailer retracted, so she was sitting bow down. They'd had torrential rain over the last few days, and water had run inside the cabin, saturating all the carpets.

Keith and Alan set about getting the boat lifted into the water, becoming absolutely soaked in the process, while I filmed proceedings from the comfort of a van. We then took the boat round from Newark to Chelsea Piers, on the west side of Manhattan, originally built to accommodate Titanic, and now turned over to various leisure activities after many years of decline. I shall always remember the surprise of the reception staff in the Park Avenue offices of the Welsh Development Agency when we turned up, me just moderately wet, Alan and Keith positively saturated, with water gathering in puddles around their feet.

We chatted over the form for our presentation at Sony next week, then headed back to Chelsea Piers. We still hadn't dried out properly, and we had the prospect of sleeping in a boat which was cold and wet - we couldn't afford to stay in a hotel. The only place we could find nearby that was warm and dry was a bowling alley. We spent five hours there.

When, as needs must, we decided some form of alcoholic refreshment was essential to take our minds off the misery of living like tramps for a week in the Big Apple, we were accosted by a security guard. He asked if I could prove my age. I suggested he might pay closer attention to the evidence of his own eyes - my grey hair and the lines on my face. Maybe under 21s age quickly in New York - I ended up showing him my press card, upon which he presented me with a paper wristband. I screwed it up in disgust. Alan, on the other hand, was bloody-minded from the start, refusing to co-operate at all. The poor man left us in search of less troublesome punters.

After a brief look in the micro-brewery in the golf club next to where the boat was moored, Alan asked someone if there was anywhere rather more lively in the vicinity. We were directed to the Red Rock West Saloon, as close as you can get to a bikers' bar, with loud rock music, and smutty barmaids dancing provocatively on top of the bar. Our first day in Manhattan, and we'd found our local.

Over the weekend, we checked out a fantastic place to show off Spirit. At the lower end of Manhattan, in the shadow of the Brooklyn Bridge, and with the twin towers of the World Trade Center nearby, was South Street Seaport Museum. It had a number of impressive floating exhibits, including the old 1908 Ambrose lightship, which appeared to have space next to it where we might moor up. This to us had some significance in that we would be starting the record run from the modern automated Ambrose light outside New York harbour. There was also Pier 17, a large shopping mall adjacent to the museum, which we reasoned might be good for sponsorship, and if nothing else, would mean the boat would be seen by all the shoppers going in and out of the mall.

In the evening, Alan decided it would be a good idea to ring WDA boss Chris Sheehan's home, just to check everything would be all right for our meeting with him in the morning. His wife answered the phone, in tears. Chris's father had died, and he had had to jump on a plane back to the UK. Why, we wondered, had nobody tried to get a message to us? Suddenly we were panic-stricken that everything would fall apart.

But as we found out when we went in to the WDA offices on the Monday morning, everything was in hand. Jane Lohrer, in charge of their Boston office, had flown down to take over, and we were provided with our own office and telephone line, along with any secretarial services we needed.

We had a brief meeting with Chris Jones, who gave me one or two contact details, and then we adjourned back to Chelsea Piers, where we test-fired the tracking system which would plot our position on the website as we crossed the Atlantic, updated every hour. For some reason, it placed us in Tel Aviv.

Wednesday 4th April was our big day. We dressed up in smart suits, and took our presentation equipment to the Sony Club. There was a good turnout of people from a wide variety of companies, although we suspected some had just turned up for the party rather than any real interest in us.

Then Sir Howard entered the room, making a short speech to welcome the guests. I didn't quite understand why, as someone who was a naturalised American before his knighthood was conferred on him, people were addressing him as Sir Howard, but perhaps I'd missed something. His remark to Alan at the beginning of the reception left us in no doubt of the state of play. He'd agreed to throw the party as a favour, but that was as far as it went. He'd had too many people trying to play the Cardiff card already with requests for financial support. He introduced Alan, who ran through the presentation in his usual slick style, ending up with: 'We're going around the world next year. Do you want to come with us?'

It ended up with two people signing up to support us straight away, although they had in fact previously agreed to do so. The hope was that by volunteering their support in public, they might generate a tidal wave of opening chequebooks. Sadly that didn't happen, but we amassed a good collection of business cards and contacts to follow up.

Alan, Keith and I flew back to the UK at the end of the week for Easter. We had just nine days at home before Alan and I flew out to New York again, this time with Steve, and Jan, who would be with us just for the weekend as we established the boat at its new base at South Street Seaport Museum. In that time, the weather changed from cold, wet and miserable, to warm and sunny. Before I knew it, I had a humdinger of a cold.

With our close proximity to Wall Street, we saw a lot of people from the financial district wandering out onto the pier with their packed lunches. The boat looked great, and we had banners explaining what we were doing, and we'd all pitch in handing out leaflets and entreating people to sign the ship's log for $5. We'd have a steady stream of interested people, all amazed that we could consider crossing the Atlantic in a boat so small, or indeed to go around the world. There were quite a few holidaying Brits, as well, and indeed a number from Cardiff. We even had several showing serious interest in major sponsorship.

The most exciting of those were the people from the communications company Global Crossing, who paid several visits to the boat over a number of days.

'Would you consider changing the colour of the boat and completely re-branding it?' they asked Alan. Given the lack of support from the business community in Cardiff, Alan was willing to consider anything, including changing the boat's home port and renaming it. It suddenly became even more interesting when they said: 'Would $5 million be enough?'

More visits ensued, and subsequently we followed it up back home. But it all became rather hypothetical when Global Crossing went into Chapter 11 bankruptcy in January 2002.

From New York, we set off, without Jan - he had to be back at work tending to the sick - on our promotional tour of the Eastern seaboard, starting out with Baltimore. This proved to be an interesting parallel with Cardiff. The redevelopment of Baltimore's Inner Harbor over some 25 years was taken as the model for the waterfront development of Cardiff Bay. The harbour area had been very like Cardiff's, dingy and run-down. They'd revived their waterfront, turning it into a traffic-free precinct with shops, restaurants and bars. It had an open, friendly cosmopolitan air, and its modernity was nicely set off by the historic warship USS Constellation.

Our first impression of Baltimore was of its cleanliness, vibrancy and very friendly people. So we were rather surprised to meet a local policeman who told us that Baltimore's crime rate is high, with 300 murders a year. There are definite no-go areas in the city. Our last night in Baltimore was marked with a shoot-out - with 75 shell casings found the following morning.

But the people here were incredibly welcoming. One of our neighbours in the marina was Stan 'Bob' Boardman, owner of a chain of car washes called Water Works - inspired, apparently, by the Monopoly game. He was quick to tell us the extent of his wealth - around $20 million - and that he had a collection of Rolls Royces.

We went out with Bob and his girlfriend Alicia one night, where they introduced us to an interesting drink called an Irish car bomb - a Guinness with a small glass of Baileys and Irish whisky dropped into it, and downed in one go. After three pints of the stuff, along with a lot more beer, we all felt a bit fragile the following morning, but Bob kept a lower profile than the rest of us. Even so, Bob was a lot of fun. Speaking with a typical southern drawl, his favourite exclamation was: 'Good God', pronounced 'Good Ga-a-awd' with a slow wobble of the head.

If there's one thing I wouldn't miss about Baltimore it was the atmosphere. Heavy with pollen, it was definitely hay fever city. My cold from New York went from bad to worse, leaving me coughing and spluttering all the time.

Our next port of call was Hyannis, on Cape Cod. The yacht club here is the Kennedy family's club, the members here all pretty well-heeled. Having come to somewhere smaller, where everyone was interested in boats, there was no shortage of people wanting to find out about the project, and, it must be said, to ply us with drinks.

The manager here was Dirk Isbrandtsen, and his English wife Diana was instrumental in setting up our appearances both here, and in the beautiful little town of Marblehead, where they live. Diana had the delightful tendency to refer to Alan, Steve and me as 'the boys', which did wonders for our middle-aged egos. Sadly for Diana and Dirk, they were to lose their eldest son Erik later that year. An industrial sales trader for Cantor Fitzgerald, he died in the World Trade Center on September 11th.

Boston was our next major stop, but things weren't as well set up for us. We'd had a hotel booked for us to do a presentation, but when we discovered how much it would cost, we decided to take it to Marblehead, home of the Boston Yacht Club, about 40 minutes drive away. Boston proved a short stop. After the obligatory drink in 'Cheers', the bar which inspired the long-running TV programme, and a photo session with Spirit close to 'Old Ironsides', the USS Constitution, we headed north.

We'd noticed that Gloucester, Massachusetts, home of America's fishing industry, and the place at the centre of the book and movie 'The Perfect Storm', wasn't that far up the coast. It was more a question of satisfying our own curiosity that compelled us to go.

As we pulled into Gloucester, we spotted a number of the longliners of the type seen in the movie. The names were very similar to Andrea Gail, the boat which was lost at sea and whose fate was at the centre of the book and movie. It was obviously a tradition here - Theresa Marie, Grace Marie.

The wharf featured in the movie was on the Harbor Loop, now with the Adventure, the last of the old fishing schooners moored up to it. The timber decking was covered on one side with weathered plywood which looked suspiciously as though it might once have housed the track for a camera dolly, although I was assured that it simply made the rather gappy decking somewhat safer for the tourists to walk on.

The Crow's Nest pub, seen in the movie as a rather charming shack at the end of the wharf, was pure fiction, a timber facade erected around a rather uninspiring concrete building, the plugs in the walls used to hold it all up still visible. The real Crow's Nest is just a short walk away on Main Street, and whilst undeniably it had character, it was rather more bland than its movie equivalent. Here I met one of the barmaids, intriguingly named Rufus, a lady who had worked at the Crow's Nest for twenty years, and who remembered the crew of the Andrea Gail well.

'Yes, they used to come in here a lot' she said. 'Everyone was very sad when they were lost.'

Inevitably, things have changed since the book in 1997, and the subsequent movie. Now the Crow's Nest has T-shirts and caps on sale, and the walls of the bar are plastered with photographs of the bar's staff and locals with 'Perfect Storm' stars George Clooney, Mark Wahlberg and Mary Elizabeth Mastrantonio. At the height of the film's popularity, they were selling 3,000 T-shirts a day.

But inevitably, there had been a shift in clientéle since the movie. Although many of the locals had stuck with the place (and I'm convinced I spotted the grizzled old character who muttered 'Flemish Cap, lots of weather out there'), I felt that there was a strong tourist element there now. Hiding amongst the 70s rock classics on the jukebox was the 'Perfect Storm' soundtrack.

By contrast, just across the harbour we found Pratty's, a bar as rough and ready as you can expect, and probably a more accurate representation of what the Crow's Nest used to be like, with several pool tables and dingy decor. Here I was told to wear something dark, 'so the blood doesn't show too easily.'

'I don't know how to play American pool,' admitted Steve.

'You have to hold the thin end of the stick instead of the thick end,' explained Alan.

'Why's that?'

'It hurts more if you have to use it to hit someone!'

But at least the beer was cheap, and the jukebox featured some of the best tracks from the Doors and Lynyrd Skynyrd.

My best find of all in Gloucester was a chance meeting with Gloucester's living legend, 90 year-old Captain William Shields. The last of the schooner fishing boat captains, Shields survived a capsize in a horrendous storm in 1938, and again narrowly escaped death three years later when the Japanese bombed Pearl Harbor. Jacques Cousteau was a personal friend, and Shields was involved with the Alvin, the submersible used by Robert Ballard to locate the wreck of the Titanic. Shields was accompanied by his son-in-law,

Bill Harmon, who also happened to have gone to school with Billy Tyne, captain of the ill-fated Andrea Gail.

'After what happened in 1991,' he said, 'you'd never get me out on the water.' Over a cup of coffee, I explained to them what Spirit of Cardiff was all about, and gave Bill Shields a copy of the brochure. 'You going across the ocean in that?' he exclaims. 'Take my advice. Go home by plane.' But it was a different story when he saw the boat for himself. 'OK,' he said. 'I think you might make it in that.'

Next to the main fishing harbour, and moored up alongside Cape Pond Ice (whose T-shirt was worn by Bugsy in the movie) was the Lady Grace, the fishing boat which took the part of the Andrea Gail in 'The Perfect Storm'. She was a fairly faded green, with a darker patch on the bow obscuring her alter ego, and her original name reapplied in fresh white paint. I suspected that the filmmakers, rather than having her entirely repainted, used some kind of digital wizardry to get the green paint all the same shade. The real give-away was one of the oil drums on her foredeck, bearing the letters 'AG'.

From Gloucester we made our way to Marblehead, an attractive little town steeped in history. There are many wonderful old buildings here, including the late colonial Jeremiah Lee Mansion, dating from 1768, and one of the finest examples of Georgian architecture in America, and the Lafayette House, with a chunk taken out of one ground floor corner. Legend has it that General Lafayette's carriage was too large to pass by the house when he visited Marblehead in 1824, so the corner of the house was removed. The Boston Yacht Club, founded in 1866, is one of the oldest in America, and as in Hyannis, we had genuine interest from the boating people. Here we threw our Boston reception, and did a few more interviews for newspapers and TV. We also managed to get our first night in a proper bed for about three weeks, staying with Diana.

We'd met Terry Ryan at the Sony Club do in April. There in his capacity of Director General of the Wales North America Business Council, his main claim to fame was in starting up the telecommunications company NTL, which had its UK headquarters in Cardiff. He was sufficiently taken by Spirit to want a ride in her, so we offered to give him a lift from Marblehead to New York. It was a pleasant journey back, particularly the early evening transit through the Cape Cod Canal, after which Terry snoozed for the rest of the journey. We knew he was shortly to take retirement from NTL, and Alan was hopeful that his parting shot might be to sign off a large sum of money in support of a worthy cause. Sadly, it didn't happen.

Our final five days in New York were spent preparing the boat and ourselves for the crossing. We set off in blazing sunshine on Saturday 19th May. A small crowd gathered on the pier at South Street Seaport Museum to see us off, but the only media coverage we had was from the New York Office of Britain's Press Association. The one thing we'd found was that trying to get newspapers and TV stations in New York to cover anything at a weekend was a waste of time. Their offices all ran on skeleton staffs, presumably in the mistaken belief that no news happens at weekends.

And whilst it was almost unbearably hot in New York, we knew that what we were heading into was a lot less enticing. In Alan's words: 'Bertie has given us the weather forecast from hell.' We should have had the wind behind us all the way up to Newfoundland, but it was going in the wrong direction. We would be punching head seas. Worst still, we'd heard from Keith Walker, already in St John's setting up our refuelling stop, that the temperature was below zero, and there was snow on the ground. There was a strong possibility that we'd have to contend with ice - something which Alan, Steve and Jan didn't relish. Not having been close up to it before, I was rather more excited about the prospect.

For Alan, Steve and me, it was simply a relief to put to sea and get on with the job of trying to break records. For the past month we'd run ourselves ragged doing the promotional tour. Whilst people back home thought we were enjoying an extended, very glamorous holiday, we were working hard, and living in squalor. When subsequently we reported back the most important message - that Cardiff and Wales had a huge problem regarding lack of awareness in the USA, we were ignored. Strangely, it was a different story when First Minister Rhodri Morgan discovered exactly the same thing when he visited the States six months later. Only then did people sit up and take notice.

It was the night before we arrived in St John's that was potentially the most scary. We'd had an ice warning, and by now the weather had turned to give us a big following sea. It was pitch dark, and as we surfed down huge waves, we had no way of telling whether there might be anything large and unfriendly at the bottom.

We arrived in St John's 12 hours behind schedule, relieved to be ashore after around 66 hours at sea. There to meet us was Keith Walker, along with local man Egbert Walters. Egbert, who has family connections in Wales, had discovered the visitor centre in Cardiff Bay, and promptly offered his services. As general manager of the Community Food Sharing Association in St John's, he'd taken a charity turning over 600,000 Canadian dollars a year into 12 million. In other words, Egbert was a master of the art of blagging, and he proved it by whisking us to the local Quality Hotel, where he'd arranged the free use of a room so we could have a shower.

The TV and radio people in St John's didn't quite know what to make of us. Early summer is known there as the 'silly season', when people from all over the world come to St John's to cross the Atlantic by a variety of means. Having made it into the harbour in atrocious conditions, they couldn't believe we were going to head back out into them. Some were of the opinion that what we were intending to do was nothing short of suicidal, and in fact they followed up on our progress just to be sure we were all right.

We crossed the Grand Banks in mountainous seas, but as it flattened off, so we had another setback to our dwindling hopes to take Adventurer's New York to Horta record. We were heading for our own version of 'The Perfect Storm' - two converging depressions, dead ahead of us. As the head seas became more and more uncomfortable, with waves going in one direction and the swell in the other, we slowed down progressively. Eventually we had to admit defeat, switching off for a while and drifting.

We arrived in Horta, battered, bruised and slightly damp. We'd lost the first record, so we decided to extend our stay to get everything properly sorted for the next leg, and to give ourselves some time to recover. We stayed for 26 hours.

As we came to terms with the fact that we'd been beaten by the weather in trying to break Cable and Wireless Adventurer's New York to Horta record, we were already faced with a dilemma for the next part of the trip. The chances were we could still do the Horta to

Gibraltar leg and take their last port-to-port record. The trouble was, the weather was on the turn in the eastern Atlantic. There was no guarantee that we would then have enough time to get back to Cardiff by 1600 on the 2nd June, ready to be the first boat officially to pass through Cardiff Bay Barrage.

So we set off from Horta, heading straight for Lizard Point. It was an idyllic crossing, with beautiful sunshine and calm seas. But as we closed on the Lizard, we did have a moment of concern. Having run the boat for two legs using a special fuel additive which promised an eight percent improvement on fuel economy, Alan had decided to do this leg without, to provide a means of comparison. After 1,239 miles, we were literally running on fumes, and lucky to make it in to Falmouth after registering our arrival at the Lizard over the radio with Falmouth Coastguard.

We arrived at Cardiff Bay Barrage bang on time, with a spectacularly noisy display of daylight fireworks as the inner lock gate opened and we passed into Cardiff Bay. We hadn't taken Cable and Wireless Adventurer's New York to Horta and Horta to Gibraltar records. But our six and a half day voyage to Horta still counted in the 30 to 50 feet powerboat class, and we'd crossed the Atlantic in something over 10 days, so we'd notched up yet another two world records in Spirit's growing tally.

As for the state of the project, we'd come home with a few leads to follow up, but nothing firm in the way of sponsorship from across the pond. Alan even wrote to Terry Ryan to ask him what it was that people didn't like about us. What were we doing wrong? Why weren't they interested in sponsoring us when they'd happily pour money into something else? He didn't receive a reply, and neither did he receive any cheque from the Wales North America Business Council, pledged at the Sony reception in April.

It was a less than auspicious return for other reasons. Alan was faced with mounting debts. While the Cardiff Harbour Authority money had helped, it didn't plug all the holes. The visitor centre had been substantially refurbished on borrowed money, in the mistaken belief that promises made would be kept. They weren't. On arriving back in the UK, Alan had to go to court to enter into an Individual Voluntary Arrangement (IVA) in order to phase the paying back of the project's creditors.

In any event, any hope for American financial support for the project vaporised three months later. If taking Spirit of Cardiff across to the States was any kind of dream, that dream certainly shattered on September 11th.

23
ALONG THE ALEUTIANS

Class 10 have been following your journey on the internet by using an interactive whiteboard in our computer room. All of us are able to read your reports and view your photos... shame you don't have a webcam... or do you? Good luck on the rest of your record breaking quest! We will continue to follow your journey.
PS. Thanks for making Geography a little more interesting!!!
Website posting from Class 10 Deighton Primary School, Tredegar.

Clive's reports do not describe the hardships on board or the physical condition of the crew.
Email from Spirit of Cardiff visitor centre volunteer.

Tuesday 28th May

I WAKE MOMENTARILY at around 0600, well before my second watch. Steve is in the navigator's seat trussed up in his sleeping bag, fast asleep. So who's on watch? Alan had relieved me from the first watch, so I assumed the order would be the same. I close my eyes and doze off again. By now I don't care if we are all asleep - there's nothing else out here in these wild desolate waters anyway. I'm shaken awake by Alan half an hour later. Steve is in the other bunk. Have I been imagining things? Am I going mad? Or did Steve sleep right through his and Alan's watches? There are times when sleep deprivation has you hallucinating, playing all sorts of ridiculous tricks on your mind. Maybe I dreamt it, or maybe it really happened. I'm so tired I really don't care any more.

I nip outside for a toilet moment with a plastic bag liner in the bucket. When I finish I check the wind direction and lob the bag overboard in what seems the most appropriate direction. In my haste to get back into relative warmth and dryness, I fail to tie up the top, and as I throw it, the wind catches it and forces a crash landing further back on the port tube. Worried the contents may spill out, I'm contemplating crawling back to give it a prod, when the wind catches it again. The plastic bag on the wet tube has a certain level of adhesion, but slowly it slithers like a large white slug towards the stern. It hangs on at the end for what seems like an eternity before the sea finally claims its dubious prize.

We've taken a more southerly route towards Adak in the Aleutian Islands, and our first US landfall, in order to miss the 35 knot winds which have been gathering behind us over Kamchatka. So far we've made reasonably good progress, although outside it's cold, grey and miserable. I really can't wait until we're coast-hopping down the US west coast in nice warm sunshine. We're getting a lot of cavitation as well, where the prop races as it comes out of the water when the stern is lifted up by a wave. Even so we're making reasonable speeds, averaging 15 knots, and getting up to 20 knots at times. I've read out another large chunk of 'Airframe' this morning, and I'm starting to get into it now. My audience of two certainly seems to be enjoying it.

We decide to put our watches back to Alaska time. Well really, we're putting them three hours forward. It's the date that's going back. So then I realise I shall have to do two Tuesday updates. Today's Tuesday update was a short bit about crossing the International Date Line, kinked at this latitude to accommodate the Aleutian Islands. Tomorrow's Tuesday update will have to be about something else.

Our main meal is poached egg, ham and beans, another culinary masterpiece. It goes down nicely, but oh for something with potatoes or more variety. It's strange how the time doesn't seem to be in sync with the light. It doesn't get dark till gone midnight, but then we are still 500 miles west of Adak, at the southern fringe of the Bering Sea, which at this latitude must mean a difference of an hour.

We seem to be in the middle of a large depression. The skies are heavy and dark, and according to the barometer built into my wrist watch, the pressure's down to 988 millibars. The sea is bumpy, with large following swells. Not enough to give us a good speed, though. We're down to nine or 10 clawing our way uphill, with 13 or 14 for the occasional bits of surfing.

'I'm a bit worried about the weather!'

If it had been any of the three of us on board Spirit of Cardiff, you might perhaps understand. But this is Bertie, on the phone to Alan during his daily weather briefing. Normally Bertie talks in purely technical terms, relaying the information he's amassed, and his forecast as to what the weather's going to do. But when Bertie ventures into more emotional language, we're worried that he's worried.

We're in the middle of one depression, and there's another following hard on its heels at 20 knots. The dilemma now is when we get to Adak, do we try and outrun it, or sit tight? Apparently it's clear behind the depression, and the passing low would turn the northerlies we need to get from Kodiak, our next stop after Adak, south-east to Telegraph Cove in British Columbia and onwards.

By late afternoon, the sun has come out. It's quite strong, and for the first time in a week the cabin feels warm. It's just nicer having sunshine anyway. It's no less bumpy, but it feels more hopeful. We're now around 350 miles from Adak - I wonder what time it'll get dark tonight.

More than anything I'm hoping I can get into a shower and wash my clothes. Neither the clothes nor I have washed for an entire week. At least in warmer conditions we can take a shower at the back of the boat. My trousers look positively disgusting. There are various unmentionable stains down the fronts of the legs (I never was very good at judging wind direction), then there's the spilt soup, bits of chicken and tomato from our picnic in P-K, along with the black oil stains probably picked up from climbing the crane. Steve and Alan are in a similar state, and I get the overwhelming sense that people in Adak will get an overwhelming sense of us.

As the evening wears on, the sun disappears. Menacing dark clouds gather overhead. The waves are turning into monsters, coming at us from behind and to the starboard beam. I hate beam seas because I don't feel comfortable with the rolling motion. It seems as though we have the runaway train effect of a big following sea along with the roll of a beam sea. It feels completely out of control to me, and I'm not looking forward to doing watches tonight, particularly if it gets so dark I can't see the horizon. Give me a slow and painful head sea any day. Alan rather confirms my fears when he says 'Well, this is going to be interesting in the dark.'

Wednesday 29th May

It's the fact that it doesn't get dark until around 0100 that throws the watches into disarray. We stop and have a brew up at midnight. I opt for a hot chocolate, hoping it might help me get a couple of hours sleep, while the others go for coffee. My first two hour shift starts at 0300, by which time it's pitch black.

Alan hands me my water bottle after I attempt to find it. It's almost empty, but more to the point, one side is curved in rather than out. That can only mean one thing - the air pressure has increased since I last had a drink. I check it on my barometer. Yup, the air pressure's risen from 987 millibars to 995. That has to be a good sign.

We pass Gareloi Island in the early afternoon. It's quite small, about five miles across, and it looks rather Scottish, with green lower slopes, upper slopes still with some snow, and bare patches of dark brown where the grass has been covered for the winter. Then two more Aleutian Islands, Tanaga and Kanaga, also with snow on the upper slopes, tops of mountains disappearing into the clouds. Eventually, after a bumpy and exhausting ride, we arrive at the next one along - Adak, skirting its northern shore to make the harbour on the eastern end of the island. We're met outside the harbour by a small boat, and we zip along straight to the fuelling berth. The pier is a long way up, and the ladder is far enough away that we can't actually climb up onto dry land. So we have to stay on the boat whilst we're refuelling, which is probably just as well. The guy refuelling us tells us he often has to wear a harness to prevent him being blown off the dock.

I'm up in the bow, talking to Joe Galaktionoff and Jay Stewart in the boat which came to meet us. I tell them about some of the places we've visited where the average temperature is 70º F, when Joe says: 'The only 70 we get here is miles an hour - the wind.' Adak has the dubious title 'Birthplace of the winds', and bad weather here is the norm. It's definitely not the place to come to if you're a fan of sunshine.

The island is virtually treeless, with just short tundra vegetation grazed by roaming caribou, and I'm told our view of snow-spattered hills disappearing into the clouds is very much the typical one. The buildings are functional, as one might expect for a former US military base, but they do get a few cruise ships stopping off here each year, including the mega-ships of Carnival Cruise Line.

'That's always a bonanza time for the shop and restaurant,' says Jay, 'and lots of people do wildlife tours.'

Once we're fuelled up, we take the boat round to the small boat harbour, after which we're whisked off to our accommodation in Adak. We're staying the night here to recover from the hammering we've taken over the last three days, because there just comes a point when you can't push yourself further. We're in the Sandy Cove Hotel, but this is no conventional hotel. It's basically self-catering, but serviced in one of a streetful of houses built from kits, former married quarters for the base. The house has only two bedrooms, so Alan nobly opts for the couch in the lounge, although we suspect the proximity of a huge back projection TV might have had some influence.

Then it's time to rip off our stinking clothes and bung them in the washing machine, then take a shower. It's fantastic to have a wash and clean up after a week.

We're picked up by Bill 'Shipmate' Wooten early evening, and we head over to the Bake and Tackle restaurant, a former McDonald's. Here we have one or two beers and chat to a few people. I end up talking to Kjetil Solberg, the Norwegian President of Adak Fisheries. After I tell him all about the boat, and the trip, he says he'll buy us the fuel for the next leg. When I tell him we've already got it and paid by credit card, he says he'll make sure the slip isn't processed, and he'll have the transaction put through his company. As if that wasn't enough, he reckons his business rivals in Kodiak can probably be persuaded to foot the bill for the fuel Kodiak to Telegraph Cove. Given that we still don't have sufficient funds to get home, this comes as a very welcome surprise. So he gives us his business card with a message scribbled to them, and an Adak Fisheries baseball cap just to hammer home the point. Sadly it doesn't work, but it feels good at the time.

I wonder why it is that people want to live here - it doesn't seem to have much going for it. The weather's bad, Anchorage is a five hour flight away, there are only 100 people here, which of course has its plus side from the point of community, but minus inasmuch as everybody knows what everyone else is up to. The answer of course is that while it's not everybody's cup of tea, some people like to be out of the rat race and away from normal town or city life.

We have our meal - a salad, with steak and lobster, and mashed potato and corn on the cob with a cup of melted butter. It's absolutely fantastic. After that, we go for a little tour of the island with Shipmate, a Colonel Sanders look-alike with a splendid turn of phrase (no sheeyut!), and Rex and Violet, who run the Bake and Tackle.

Adak was once a huge military base. The airfield has two runways big enough to land 747s (although not quite long enough to take off fully laden). There are lines and lines of accommodation blocks, including one that was still under construction when the base was being closed. The moment it was finished it was boarded up along with the other blocks, and so was never occupied. At the time the base closed in the 1990s there were 6,000 personnel here, but in its real heyday there were as many as 90,000. It started up in World War Two with the army and air force - then it was taken over by the US Navy. Now the population is around 100, mainly people involved with fishing, with 25 of school age. The school here caters for all grades. In general, while there are people and vehicles to be seen, the place has a slightly eerie ghost town feel to it.

Both Rex and Shipmate had done military service on Adak, and liked it so much they came back to live here. Rex was a military policeman, whilst Shipmate worked with the nuclear (sorry, noocular) weapons - bombs and torpedoes - which were housed here. There was also a massive amount of conventional ordnance stored here in magazines dotted all over the hillsides.

We take a look in the club which opens Thursday, Friday and Saturday, also run by Rex and Violet. Here on the walls are lots of photographs of Adak from the war years and afterwards. Obviously the Cold War era was important here, as Adak was a front line base. Not only did they have a nuclear arsenal, there was also a sophisticated communications base which could signal American submarines anywhere in the world.

Then we head off out into the wilds. Further away from the built-up part of Adak, we can see numerous places in the hillsides cut away where once Nissen huts stood. There were hundreds. We also pass Adak's forest, a tiny clump of conifers. But it's near here that we're up on a hill, and across the valley we see three caribou. Shipmate does a fair bit of hunting, and is regretting the fact that he doesn't have a rifle with him. He's already bagged eight caribou this year, and he does a lot of fishing as well. Amazingly, while the cod are big, the halibut is the most prized catch, and it seems they virtually throw themselves onto your fishing hooks.

We stop by at an inlet where the tide is coming in with ferocious speed. This is a prime spot to see seals, and we're not disappointed. Rex explains that the longer we stay here, the more inquisitive they become. We stop on a small single-track bridge, and as we're talking the heads popping up get closer and closer.

As we're about to drive off, we notice we have a flat tyre. We could drive back into town on it, but it would trash the tyre entirely. So we radio for help. It's not long before someone comes out, picks up Shipmate and takes him back to collect another truck, and we all get back OK. A great illustration of community spirit. But amazingly, the van is left blocking the bridge.

'It'll be OK there till the morning,' says Rex. Clearly no great danger of huge tailbacks of traffic here.

Back at the house/hotel, Alan conducts a telephone interview with a reporter from the Welsh Mirror. It doesn't go well. The reporter clearly thinks we've already failed. I listen to Alan doing his best to keep his cool. We said we'd circumnavigate the world in sixty days. We've just passed the halfway point, and we've taken just under two months to get here. All the questions are loaded. We're not going to break the Cable and Wireless record, so we're failures.

Trying to circumnavigate the world via a route which has never been done before isn't enough for some people! Never mind the fact that we've taken a 33ft powerboat through some of the most inhospitable conditions anywhere on the planet, and that provided we get back to Gibraltar, we'll still get the under 50ft record. We're proud of our achievement, given that there were many who thought we wouldn't even get this far. But clearly, to some, we've failed.

Thursday 30th May

After breakfast, we go to shop for our provisions before heading off to sea again. The store is in the old base community centre, and as you might expect, it has virtually everything you might want under one roof - food and drinks to clothing, footwear, magazines and electrical goods. Of course the prices are quite high, but then again the goods do have to be shipped a long way. Alan buys himself a smart pair of shoes, soft and warm.

'It's amazing,' he says. 'I've had a headache for days, and the moment I put these on, it's gone!'

While Alan and Steve go with Rex to take the supplies to the boat, I trot back to the house to connect up to my email. I manage to drop Psion number two on the concrete floor of the conservatory - thankfully the screen is still intact. It's very difficult getting a solid connection, though, but I do manage to download the important emails.

One of them is from the visitor centre. It's critical of my updates, saying I'm not conveying enough of the pain and misery, and that travelogues don't sell newspapers. Having established that the main thrust of my updates was for the website rather than the Echo, and that I have actually described the hardships when they've happened, I don't think it's a fair comment, and I'm quite upset by it. Were I not feeling so fragile from the effects of the voyage, I wouldn't have given it a second thought. Anyone who finds fault in anything I write would clearly have to be regarded as insane.

It seems incredible that people can feel able to criticise what I'm doing, when they wouldn't dream of saying anything negative about Alan or Steve's functions on the expedition. Neither would I say they're in a position to be literary critics. The fact is that people would tire quickly of it if I portrayed blood and guts every day, and from the website forum, the bits where I describe the natural beauty excites far more comment than anything else. That surely is the reason why visitors like Class 10 at Deighton Primary School in Tredegar return to follow our progress day after day.

Alan and Steve return from loading up the boat, and we go back to the Bake and Tackle for a bite of lunch - I have a cheeseburger and fries. By now Steve is thoroughly envious of Alan's new shoes, and wants a pair himself. So we drop by at the store once more on the way back to the boat. Unfortunately he's out of luck. Alan had the last pair. But he's hopeful he might get some in Kodiak.

And then it's time to go again. I wish we could stay longer. We're amazed at the kindness and generosity of everyone, and humbled to think our short visit has brought a little colour to people's lives here.

As we negotiate the notorious Atka Pass from the Bering Sea back into the North Pacific, the sea is unbelievable. We've been warned that numerous boats have come croppers here, and it's not hard to see why. It's positively boiling - it's shallower because of the ridge upon which the Aleutian chain lies, and it's made worse by the wind going against the current. Alan has taken manual control of the boat, but even with the throttle off we're doing five knots, although he has to give it a certain amount to maintain steerage. It's more like white water rafting, shooting the rapids, than out at sea. Fortunately it doesn't last too long, and we return to more regular rough conditions.

24
PERCEPTIONS

You couldn't make this stuff up - if it was fiction they would never swallow it!
Website posting from Paul Saye.

WE DID INCREDIBLY well at getting media coverage from TV, radio and newspapers in Wales. We did very well in getting coverage in the boating press, where we probably achieved Alan's goal of being the most photographed powerboat crew in the country. We were headline and front page national news virtually everywhere we went around the world. So why did the British media never really latch on to us?

When we set off, things definitely weren't in our favour. The Queen Mother had died, though why that should warrant nearly two weeks of media hysteria to the exclusion of more exciting things being done by the living was a question which bugged us as only it could for anyone not actually back at home and immersed in the nation's grief. And then the World Cup in Japan and Korea took over. We just didn't get a look in.

But even before we set off, we could never get national newspapers interested in following us. We'd had plenty of coverage on Sky News and ITN, even of events that I didn't consider particularly newsworthy, but apart from the few features I managed to sell myself, the newspapers would simply go as far as regurgitating short paragraphs about us put out on the wires by the Press Association. I can only assume that they didn't think it was sexy enough as a story.

The common misconception was: 'Well, it's a powerboat. What's so difficult about going around the world in a powerboat? Surely sailing is far more difficult.'

The truth is that the exact opposite is the case. Like round the world sailors, we had sleep deprivation to contend with; like round the world sailors, we ran the risks of hitting debris in the water - even more so since we were not so far offshore, and potentially it would do far more damage; like round the world sailors, we had to make the best of the weather. Unlike round the world sailors, we also had to refuel in places where people were anything from dilatory to openly hostile to us. We suffered injuries, illness and extreme fatigue; we had guns pointed at us and were intimidated into handing over money in order to gain permission to leave port - all in order to challenge a world record which had been set in 1998 and never previously seriously challenged. And yet the British media weren't interested. Why is that? What was it about our story that failed to capture their imagination?

'I suppose it has to be an ignorance of learning or understanding,' muses Alan, 'and by that, I don't mean the reporters are stupid. It's just the fact that they don't know. They're not aware of the complexity and the risks of taking such a small boat around the world.'

I always found it somewhat amazing that the media could pay a huge amount of attention to events like the Paris-Dakar rally, or the Camel Trophy (which I myself have covered), and not to get excited about something which, if successful, would rightfully add up to a large slab of national 'feelgood factor'.

Had we achieved the original budget we wanted, we may well have made more of an impact. We would have had a budget to hire a public relations company to increase our media profile. And with a large title sponsor, we would undoubtedly have been able to ride on the back of their own PR machine. As it was, whatever coverage we could get was down to the sterling efforts of our volunteers. Whilst I was capable of turning out press releases, getting them in front of the right people and acted upon was another matter. That's where a PR company would have been able to help. But PR companies cost money. In a sense, it doesn't matter whether you have a good story or not if you have good PR, because you'll get the coverage. But it's sad to say that a good story without PR guarantees nothing.

Interestingly, we were able to draw a direct comparison with another British maritime record attempt taking place at the same time. The Skandia Ocean Row team were attempting to break the record for rowing across the Atlantic, also becoming the first to make a landfall on the British mainland. They were doing it in an advanced carbon fibre boat originally built by Pete Goss (winner of the Yachtsman of the Year award the year Alan and crew came runners-up), and sold off when he went bankrupt after the loss of his boat Team Philips. There's no doubt that we were envious of the fact that Mark Stubbs and his team had managed to get support from Skandia, and that they seemed to be doing so much better than we were on the media front. Maybe because the media thought that human endeavour was only valid for human-powered vessels. Being beaten black and blue in a powerboat didn't count. But Skandia clearly felt they couldn't back a project without putting their own PR effort into it. Had Cardiff Marketing been as supportive as they claimed at the time, they could very easily have helped.

We also couldn't get our heads around what we'd heard that BBC Wales were making a documentary about the Ocean Row, when their project wasn't even based in Wales. They'd even had a camera crew with them in St John's while they were waiting to get their weather window to depart. Not that I'd expect BBC Wales to have any kind of regional loyalty when it came to programme-making, but why would they think rowing across the Atlantic would be any more interesting or visually exciting than what we were doing? The Ocean Row website journals referred to big waves, but the fact is that the weather conditions they experienced were nothing to what we'd had in the north Pacific, and their story would be very much a two-dimensional one compared with ours. After all, we'd had some incredible refuelling stops, we'd passed stunning scenery, as well as recording all the little moments and dramas that make up life on board.

It's easy to sound bitter when you see others apparently doing better, and that wasn't the case at all. We know that they would have had the same agony in raising sponsorship, and awareness about their trip. They got lucky and we didn't. We were sorry to hear that the Ocean Row team had to abandon their attempt when the boat's rudder broke. And yet they still managed to get the media coverage. It was, and shall remain, a mystery to us.

Where we did receive coverage, not all of it was that fair to us.

When we passed the 60 days mark, some stories had us written off as failures, without taking up on our positive outlook, which was that we were battling on regardless, and that provided we made it home, we would still claim a legitimate world record. It's easy to come up with the 'Hopes dashed' kind of headline, but we always thought the British public appreciated anyone who plugged away against the odds. Not this time, it would seem.

Whilst our own website was full of postings from people anxious for our well-being, willing us on, doing their best to raise a few extra pounds to help get us home, other website forums were less sympathetic. Motor Boat and Yachting's forum was full of messages from people who didn't understand what we were doing, who thought we hadn't planned the expedition properly, and who thought we had a cheek asking people to cough up money to help us after setting off underfunded and then getting into difficulties.

We were also criticised for taking overnight stops here and there. Sometimes it was because we arrived in the evening in places where fuel wouldn't be available until the morning, but by the time we were going round the top of the Pacific, it was because we were at the end of our tether.

The people who accused us of turning the trip into a holiday when we had overnight stops here and there were ignorant. They had no idea of the injuries we were sustaining, and the general debilitating effect of being battered day after day. Only anyone who has done more than 50 miles in a powerboat would have any real idea of what we were going through. We were suffering, pushing ourselves beyond the limit, day in, day out. When we got to Alaska, we were all physically and mentally shattered.

25
A LONG WAY TO GO FOR A BARBECUE

It is really amazing on the part of the crew of the Spirit of Cardiff. It requires a great amount of courage, character and conviction to undertake a journey like this. I am greatly impressed and pray for their successful completion of the grand, and risky journey that they have undertaken.
Website posting from Mohammed Jameel.

Friday 31st May

THIS MORNING WE pass the Islands of Four Mountains. Not that I see four, but I can make out two magnificent cone volcanoes, their upper slopes covered in snow. Annoyingly, the only sunshine we can see is hitting these mountains. Where we are is overcast with heavy grey clouds. We're in big following seas, with the boat fairly well throttled back, so we're doing between eight and 16 knots.

We've made good progress considering the conditions - 250 miles in 24 hours. But we have burnt a lot of fuel. Still, if we need to, we can always call in to Dutch Harbor - the main settlement in the Aleutian Islands - for a top up. There was a point during the night when Alan said the boat was literally turned around 180º by the heavy seas, another when we surfed down a wave at 26 knots. That's scary! Sometimes in bad conditions we'll go slightly off course in order to get an easier ride, but in this case it wouldn't have been possible. We'd end up where we started.

It's been a bit of a lazy day for me. In honour of the Queen's Jubilee, Alan relieves me of doing the Spirit of Cardiff website journal today with his own nicely timed rant at Cardiff, pointing out that although some have rallied around and replaced the Carter money, we're still short. The problem is that all the extra expenses involved with unexpected stops, and shipping mechanical parts, have increased the financial drain. Fort Lauderdale will be the end unless we get another $10,000.

I read out another chunk of 'Airframe' until my eyes get tired, then snooze for an hour and a half. The air pressure has risen, which is good. The evening is beautiful, and the sea has flattened off considerably. It looks as though we could get in to Kodiak by Sunday evening. Alan's plan is to overnight in Kodiak if that's the case. A most welcome idea, even if it does eat into the time. While Adak was equally welcome, there's a cumulative effect which even one night ashore won't cure. The North Pacific has certainly been the most taxing part of the trip, physically and mentally.

Tea tonight is a surprise dish - baked beans, Spam and poached eggs. It goes down well, as does the little tub of dessert which follows. But I still yearn for proper food with vegetables.

It transpires that we shouldn't have stayed in Adak because we didn't clear US immigration. Customs have been a bit more lax about the whole matter. Naturally, our view is that they should go and talk about it to someone who gives a toss. Clearly the people who so generously hosted us in Adak didn't.

Saturday 1st June

Apparently the weather forecast for the next few days is good. It bears out the evidence from my little watch, which shows the air pressure rising. Indeed, according to Bertie, it looks as though we could be OK all the way down to Panama. But there may be a few blips until we get to British Columbia and pick up the northerly trade winds.

The only thing now is whether we'll get as far as Panama. Alan does an interview for HTV Wales, and while he points out that technically we have enough money to get the boat to Fort Lauderdale, he may still be forced to call off the attempt in San Diego. He wants to be left with enough funds to get the crew home if it comes to it, and presumably to berth the boat somewhere suitable until it's sold.

I receive an email from Nadia saying 'Nice journal page today - you are getting the hang of what needs to be said.' I think it's a bit patronising, and of course she's referring to Alan's rant, which while well-timed and needed to be said, would become a distinct turnoff if the journal maintained the same tone every day. I shall carry on doing it my way.

As the day wears on, the sea becomes more and more glassy. We haven't seen it like this since the Philippines. At one point we think we're coming close to a log floating in the water. Then it moves. It turns out to be a couple of seals, or maybe sea lions. One of them is huge - it might perhaps be a walrus. They told us in Adak that walruses sometimes climb onto the aft decks of fishing boats to enjoy a quick snack. Let's hope no walrus thinks we're a fishing boat.

The pressure is still rising, now up to 1003 millibars. But later on, early evening, and a slight wind springs up, enough to make it uncomfortably bumpy.

Just before eight, we see a thin line streak across the surface of the water, passing around us in a wide arc. We've seen the spouts of a fair few whales over the past few days, but this is no whale. The line has a regularity about it, and the coloration very similar to the line of exhaust in Spirit of Cardiff's wash. The front edge of it is travelling at speed - over 20 knots. It can be only one thing - exhaust gases venting from a passing submarine. But whose is it - American or Russian?

It gets rougher as the night wears on. We start the watches at 2200, and I get the first four hours in bed. Except it's utterly impossible to sleep. We're being thrown about mercilessly.

Sunday 2nd June

After my first watch from 0200 till 0400, I go back to bed, but to no real sleep, although I guess I drift off at some stage. I wake up at about 0600 to hear Alan and Steve having harsh words. Steve has had enough of the whole thing, and is ready to throw himself over the side. He's not joking.

'I'm not responsible for the weather,' says Alan. 'It's not just you that's hurting. We all are.'

'F*** it, I've had enough,' snaps Steve.

'OK then,' says Alan tersely, 'I'll shut the boat down. Get some sleep.' There are times when arguing would be pointless and counter-productive, and this is one of them. But then Steve realises he may have gone too far.

'Well all right, but just for a couple of hours.'

That, for anyone looking for evidence of conflict among the crew, is the nearest we get to a row in the whole trip. Apart from the odd few snapped words and moody moments, that's it - a testament, no doubt, to all our characters.

We take the northerly route to Kodiak, hopeful that we may gain some shelter in the channel between mainland Alaska and Kodiak. It's a gamble that doesn't pay off. As it is, today is easily the most uncomfortable day so far. We may have seen bigger, more dangerous seas off Japan, but these ones take the biscuit for sheer pain.

The motion goes in several planes, the bow pitching up and down, but with rolling from side to side as well. So as we forge ahead, the bow pitches upward. Everybody leaves their seat or bunk. The bow pitches downward, leaving us weightless for half a second before we fall back down. By then the boat has pancaked into the sea with a sickening crunch, and we crash land back into our respective seats and bunks, our spines compressed that bit more. But there's a rolling motion, so the whole catalogue of movements goes something like: Up, weightless, down, ouch; roll left, ricochet off a wave, ouch; roll right, ricochet off another wave, ouch; up, down, ouch. It goes on, and on.

Midday, and Nadia is on the phone.

'I'm going to overnight in Kodiak,' Alan tells her. 'We've all taken a lot of punishment.' We're exhausted and hurting after our battering, and Alan believes it would compromise safety for us to carry on without proper rest first. But Nadia clearly disagrees.

'I'm working here 24 hours a day,' she replies. 'The least you can do is keep going.'

'Nadia, you don't understand what it's like out here,' says Alan. Which is fair comment. I think it's pretty hard for anyone to understand the torture we're going through.

We round the northern end of Kodiak. It's beautiful, the mountains, some snow-clad, others green and tree-covered, glow in the late afternoon sun. The fact that it's the first time we've seen substantial numbers of trees since Japan has cheered me up enormously. We turn into Kupreanof Strait, with Raspberry Island to our left, heading for Whale Passage. We've reached the most northerly point in the North

Pacific, and now we're heading south-east. More to the point, finally we're gaining some shelter.

We keep our eyes skinned for bears, but there's not a single one to be seen roaming the hills, which are incredibly green. No wonder they call Kodiak the Emerald Isle of Alaska. We do see lots of seals, lying back in the water with their flippers folded in front. Then as we get closer they dive under the water. We spot one or two eagles, too, and as we cross one inlet, a couple of humpback whales.

The final approach into Kodiak is through fog, so it's all three of us up front, Steve at the helm, Alan at the radar and chart plotter, taking us from one buoy to the next, with me as a third pair of eyes, trying to spot the navigation points and other possible obstructions.

Some excellent spadework by Nadia ensured we'd already made the front page of the local newspaper, who nicknamed us the 'snazzy English banana boat'. They were expecting us on Monday, so apart from the harbour officer and fuel man, we're slightly short of a welcoming committee. We are in reality a good three weeks late rather than a day early. Someone introduces himself as Kyle Crow, and asks whether we'd like to take a traditional banya, what they call a sauna in these parts. We agree, and jump into the back of his pickup truck.

Before we know it, we're sitting naked inside a small wooden shed, sweating away. It certainly helps to soothe away the aches and pains, but I'm having a bit of trouble with the way the ground is moving about.

The changing room is a mite small, so I end up getting dressed outside, steam rising from my glowing skin in the chilly late afternoon air. Kyle drives us up to our hotel, where we discover that there is actually a time difference between here and Adak after all. It's an hour ahead, so we've lost an hour. The hotel is a Best Western, and there are two rooms, one with two double beds, and one with one. Alan and Steve share, so I get the one to myself. I have a quick shave before meeting the others in the bar. Two pints of winter stout, or some such, and I'm feeling tired. Then we walk up to Kyle's house, a pretty white weather-boarded building with a red roof on the edge of town. It dates from the 1930s, and is one of the few older houses that survived the 1964 earthquake.

Kyle is a former marine, now working for the coastguard.

Amazingly, he too was born in 1953. It's becoming spookier the more often it happens. Everyone we meet who shows us exceptional kindness, all from the same year.

His wife Leona is an Aleut, a natural blonde which is extremely unusual, and very beautiful with it. She makes exquisite jewellery using tiny beads in intricate designs. She gives us each a traditional Alutiiq spirit pouch 'for our wives', although I've already decided my daughter Aislinn will have mine. Kyle and Leona invite us to dine on what they call leftovers, but if these are scraps, they certainly make a fine meal - lamb, sausage and salad, with ice cream afterwards.

Monday 3rd June

It's overcast and spitting with rain this morning. Down by the harbour is an interesting building. It's actually a ship - the Star of Kodiak. During the 1964 earthquake, the massive contortions lifted her up onto the quayside. So rather than trying to refloat her, she was turned into a canning plant. Whilst at the boat, the local newspaper sends a girl down to interview us. She's using a Nikon Coolpix 5000 to photograph us. Snap! Same as mine.

We have to complete immigration and customs, and here is as good a place as any. But it transpires we'll have to pay $195 each for a 30 day visa. Tim Brady, the officer, says that before September 11th, if he saw a deserving case, he could make his own decision on whether to waive the charge. Now he has to phone a superior in Anchorage. He does that, but unfortunately it's bad news. We have to pay. Worse still, he can't accept credit cards or cash, so we have to go to a nearby bank, and purchase three money orders. So far, the Philippines has been the most expensive officially, but now the US has leapt into the lead. It's not even as if it's a 10 year visa or anything. This one's valid just 30 days. Given that British citizens can enter the US under the visa waiver scheme for free if they happen to arrive at a 'gateway' entry point such as an international airport, we feel as though we've been mugged.

We wander back to the boat, spending more time talking to people before finally setting off at 1600. It's strange - I'd felt really weird and spaced out all during the day as we walked around Kodiak. Then when we set off I'm OK. The horrifying reality is that I've become used to being at sea, used to unnaturally violent motion. The movement is now what my body regards as normal. Walking in straight lines down paved roads is abnormal.

I get my daily journal out of the way, then finish off 'Airframe'. A good ending. Now we have another Michael Crichton - 'Sphere'. This one's a real gripper from the start.

Alan has a headache, so doesn't eat. Steve and I sample a couple of the US Army ratpacks donated in Adak by Shipmate. They're 12 years old, but just like tinned food, there's no reason why they shouldn't still be edible provided the packaging is intact. Steve has a ham omelette which looks rather like a slab of rubber, while my chicken stew seems to be the better choice. I also have a nice sachet of diced peaches in syrup afterwards, plus a solid chocolate bar. Splendid!

Tuesday 4th June

Things are definitely happening with the weather. The air pressure is rising once more. As the sun rises - yes the sun actually rises - into a sky of broken clouds, there's a feeling of cheer and optimism on board. Alan and Steve sleep well, but despite the newly extra padded bunks (we've put the Thermarest sleeping mats under the seat cushions) I don't sleep that well.

'You must have slept,' Alan tells me. 'I heard you snoring.'

We have a new music centre, kindly donated and shipped all the way to Kodiak by Dom Palmeri, so we road test it with a tape of Wings' greatest hits, followed by David Gray. During that whole time, I'm trying to email today's update and photograph - of Steve with our new music centre - carefully posed on the Yamaha box. The usual score is that about one in 10 attempts to connect is successful, but it then gets as far as part sending the email and photograph before it disconnects.

After two hours of frustration, I have to abandon the attempt because the continual use has thrashed the phone's battery. I put it on charge, and let Alan have the Psion so he can compose an email.

After those emails are done, I connect up again, and eventually everything goes, over two and a half hours after the first attempt. Great work, Iridium! There's an amusing email in from Alun Michael. Having been following the debacle surrounding Transport

Secretary Stephen Byers, and his eventual resignation, I'd written wondering whether Alun might put himself up for the job, and then designate Spirit of Cardiff an essential form of public transport to secure Government funding. He replies:

'As a local MP I'm with you, but my current Ministerial responsibilities [at the Department for Environment Food and Rural Affairs] give me greater affinity with promoting the return of the Horse and Cart than with promoting your present mode of travel, I fear!'

Just before six, the prop starts to race. Alan quickly leaps over to kill the throttle. Then when he tries to bring it back up again, it races. He puts it astern and that cures it - probably a piece of weed around the prop. It's just as well. Having to swap over to the wing engine several hundred miles from land in the middle of the Gulf of Alaska doesn't bear thinking about.

Wednesday 5th June

It's some time just after midnight Wednesday that I spot a contact on the radar, almost directly ahead, just under four miles. It's definitely a solid contact, not the scatter you can get when the radar bounces off waves. I even adjust the scale on the radar screen from 12 to six miles to double-check his distance from us. Yes, it's still there. Over the next 10 minutes it moves away from a collision course. Then suddenly, nothing. It vanishes from the screen.

Did I just watch a ship sink? Alien spacecraft? Having seen evidence of a submarine a day or so ago, I'm more tempted to think it's that, a submarine on the surface, then diving.

During my second watch, I pick up an email from Telegraph Cove saying we have to go to Prince Rupert, some 100 miles out of our way, to clear Canadian Customs. We're given a choice of three docks we can go to, and then we have to ring the telephone number we're given. Provided everything is OK, we can complete the formalities without them visiting the boat. So why go miles out of our way to make a phone call? Why not phone from Telegraph Cove?

We decide not to go. Firstly, we don't have detailed charts for Prince Rupert, so it would be a dangerous passage. Second, it might run us out of fuel. We decide the best thing will be just to turn up at Telegraph Cove and say nothing.

When I have a pee in the early evening, I'm disturbed to see several small dark lumps swimming around in the bucket. I tell Alan about it, and he says to keep an eye on it. The likelihood is that I bruised my kidneys when we took the last beating, and I'm now passing bits of blood clot.

Thursday 6th June

Today's the 58th anniversary of D-Day. And here we are, looking at the possibility of a war - maybe even nuclear - between the Indians and Pakistanis over disputed territory in the Himalayas.

My first pee in daylight seems to be clearer. I'll see how it goes between now and Telegraph Cove. I can feel a dull ache in my lower back and tummy, so I guess the chances are I did myself some internal damage which is working its way through.

I pick up an email from TV producer Tim Exton. He can't come with us from Telegraph Cove to Eureka after all. A shame, as we were looking forward to having a guest for a few days. As we come into the sound which demarcates Vancouver Island from the mainland, we stop to clean the windscreens and for a quick comfort stop.

'How about you, Clive?' asks Steve. 'Are you still pissing lumps?'

I reply that the frequency seems to have reduced, but that I'm experiencing a few dull aches in my lower back and tummy. RIBbing is definitely not good for your health!

It's wonderful to be back within the sight of land, especially the beautiful tree-clad islands on either side of Queen Charlotte Strait, but as we pass into Goletas Channel, the early clear skies and sunshine give way to clouds.

Approaching Telegraph Cove, there's a moment when we think we might have some rather military boat pursuing us. It's a large grey fast boat, definitely hot on our heels, albeit a mile or so back. We discover later it's one of the local whale watching boats.

As we arrive at the designated waypoint, we head further into a bay. But all we can see are sheds and a logging camp. The bottom end of the bay is boomed off, with thousands of logs floating there.

Eventually we find Telegraph Cove - a tiny inlet near the opening of the bay, so small we'd gone past it. We approach a pontoon, and as I step onto it, I skid over. It's leaning over, and very slippery. I gash my thumb on a nail. It's a bit of a mess.

Here to greet us is Gordie Graham, the owner of Telegraph Cove. He brings us a pitcher of beer, and as we're getting ourselves together, Ray Jones, an expat Welshman appears with his friend Bob, also from Wales, along with their respective wives. They're all wearing Cardiff Arms Park T-shirts.

Telegraph Cove dates back to 1912, when it was the place where telegraph lines for North Vancouver Island came ashore. It was an important point of contact during the influenza pandemic of 1918-19, and it later saw life as a fish saltery and a sawmill. The houses - beautiful timber buildings joined by a raised wooden walkway - have been restored, and each has a little explanatory panel detailing the history. Many of them have bird feeders hanging outside, and hummingbirds buzzing around them. These days, Telegraph Cove is the main killer whale watching centre in British Columbia.

A chap from the local newspaper appears, and spends quite a bit of time interviewing me. Eventually I get to wander up to our little cabin and have a shower. Long before we'd set off around the world, we knew we'd be treated to barbecued salmon here. Up at the Saltery pub, the salmon is sizzling and the beer is flowing. The salmon is positively delicious, a huge chunk, as well. Afterwards, I have some kind of death by chocolate and caramel cake. Yum.

After a pleasant evening in the pub, we retire to our little cabin, the Graham House, built around 1942. Alan and Steve each have a room and a double bed. I get a single bed on the landing. They turn in at 2230, while I sit up and write an update. Then I try to transmit it from the boat. It takes several goes. When I get back, I spend time going through the BBC Wales video tape, so it's ready to be sent off tomorrow.

Friday 7th June

We set off at 0900, heading south along the Inside Passage between Vancouver Island and the mainland. It's calm water compared to the open sea, but we do need to be careful to watch out for logs. There's one moment when we nearly run into a veritable floating forest. Alan shouts at Steve to throttle back just in time. The logs and smaller debris are fairly densely packed, and we nose our way through gingerly, rather like an icebreaker.

Further down, the Inside Passage opens out more, and we encounter strong currents, even whirlpools. Even so, it's still better than the open sea. We're sheltered, making nearly 20 knots, and we've got some spectacular scenery, to boot.

During the afternoon, I pick up an email from Jim Leishman. Nordhavn left Acapulco today, and is on the last leg of its circumnavigation. They expect to be back at Dana Point in California around the 20th June - when we ought to be back in Gibraltar if we were going to break the Cable and Wireless record. So we reckon that somewhere along the Baja coast will be the point where our paths will cross. It's going to be an interesting meeting.

'There's one thing against us when it starts to get warm again,' announces Alan. I look at him inquiringly.

'This cabin's starting to smell like a tart's arse!'

I'm unfamiliar with the comparison, but I take his point. We could certainly do with a vacuum cleaner for the carpet, and it and the upholstery would benefit from a shampoo.

By early evening we can see the tall buildings of Vancouver in the distance. The wind seems to have turned round, and we're bouncing about a bit more, bucketfuls of sea cascading over the windscreen.

'Could be tide, as well,' says Alan.

We're going to have to make an unscheduled fuel stop tomorrow morning. I guess we didn't take on as much fuel as we should have in Telegraph Cove. As we stop for a cup of tea, a lovely cruise ship passes us by. It's the Radiance of the Seas, which I learn later is Royal Caribbean's new ship. Based in Vancouver for the summer, she's doing cruises up to Alaska.

Coming through the southern end of the Inside Passage is not one of my better moments. It's extremely bumpy, and my insides go from just a dull ache to very painful.

Saturday 8th June

It's about one o'clock in the morning. We've been through some painfully bumpy conditions at the southern end of the Inside Passage. On our right is Victoria, in Canada, to our left the San Juan Islands, belonging to the USA. Steve is on watch and shakes Alan awake urgently.

'I don't know what this boat is up to,' he says. 'Every time I get out of his way he comes round again. He won't get out of my way.' The mystery is quickly solved as two blue flashing lights come on, and we're illuminated by a powerful searchlight. But we're not sure which side of the border we're on. It turns out to be a big 18 metre catamaran called 'Nadon', a Royal Canadian Mounted Police / Gendarmerie Royale du Canada West Coast Marine Detachment patrol vessel.

We pull alongside him and tie up. The mounties on board are somewhat bemused to find three Englishmen on a round the world expedition. They'd actually pulled us up because our mast light wasn't working. 'Sorry officer, we'll get it fixed...'

As we explain more of our story, we come clean on the fact that we should have gone to Prince Rupert to clear customs but didn't, though they don't seem overly bothered about that. Rather than being boarded, we board them. Alan hops aboard first of all to chat, then we all do, ending up on the bridge. The boat is very sophisticated, and did the North-West Passage a couple of years back, in 169 days.

The master, Jim Vardy, tells us how their job normally entails looking for drug runners. Now they're on the lookout for loony protesters trying to get to the forthcoming G8 summit in Kananaskis, Alberta. Canada's land borders are so well sealed they're trying to get in illegally by sea.

Jim tells us there's a westerly gale coming, with 30 to 35 knot winds. Would we like to head into Victoria? They'd be delighted to clear us through, they said, adding there are a lot of English-style bars there. We decline the offer, and having failed to find out where they stable their horses, we clamber back aboard the Spirit to head into the darkness. Their patrols last for seven days, and stopping us has been tonight's highlight.

The rest of the night is a nightmare for me. I don't do a watch because there's lots of navigating, so I'm lying in the back being pounded by every hard landing. My insides, which yesterday had just been a dull ache, are now screaming. At one point I'm in tears. I feel really down. If there was a way to wave a magic wand and end all this, I'd do it. I've had enough and I want to go home.

Later we pull into Westport, near Aberdeen in Washington State. This is our unscheduled refuelling stop. We also need to buy a new fuel pump, as the one which transfers fuel from the front tank to the main packed up this morning with an acrid smell of burning.

Once we sort the fuel, we tie up in the marina and seek out the chandlery. Then we head to a nearby restaurant for a burger. Whilst the Spirit of Cardiff crew can hardly be held up as examples of normal human beings, the diners here all seem a little odd. Two positively huge people sit there munching away, not saying a word to each other. Weirdest of all is the toilet. I'm used to seeing graffiti in such places, and even carved with a knife as this is, but not saying: 'May the Lord bring you safely home.'

The new pump is fitted. It's unbelievably noisy compared to the old one. Then I pick up an email from Nadia saying someone in Eureka wants to pick us up in a limo and take us to his restaurant for a meal. She'd put out the news that we were on our way to the local newspaper, and someone has come up with this nice gesture. Naturally we want to take him up on his offer.

Back offshore again, the waves are big, but there's no wind. There's not much in the way of hard landings, which is what I'd really hated. We're circled for a while by a US Coastguard helicopter. I nip outside to video him, at which point he calls us up on the radio. Alan convinces them we're not baddies, and the helicopter heads off back to shore - apparently they'd received a mayday from out here and thought it might have been us.

Sunday 9th June

Last night's sleep turned out to be rather better than the previous. I was given shorter watches on each occasion, though I'm not sure if this was to fit in with Alan's phone calls, or whether he was letting me off some. Either way, I'm grateful. There are big, big following seas out here. Every so often we stuff into a big wave, and we virtually come to a standstill. One time I'm thrown forward with quite a degree of force.

The plans keep changing. First we hear that the weather is going to be consistently bad for the next few days, so we might as well soldier on from Eureka. But by early afternoon we hear that they're recording 35 knots of wind in Eureka harbour. There's a real possibility that the US Coastguard won't let us leave once we've come in, so it looks like we'll be staying the night after all.

By some strange quirk of fate, just as we decide this, we whack into a wave and the starboard windscreen smashes. There's a split second of déjà vu, but at least this time it's in sunshine. The glass seems to hold up better this time - not so frosted.

Now we're going to optimise the time spent in Eureka, since we're going to be weathered in, and we also have a windscreen to replace. So we're moving the service stop from San Diego to here. Hopefully by the time the boat is fixed, the weather will have improved.

Our entrance into Eureka harbour is spectacular. Huge waves are rolling over a sand bar across the entrance. We learn later that it's notorious, the second most difficult harbour in the whole of the USA, and people come croppers on it every year. The first call we get on the radio is from Humboldt County Coastguard, who've watched our arrival.

'We'd just like to congratulate you on an expert piece of seamanship, coming in in such conditions.'

'Thanks very much,' replies Alan.

'But if anything had gone wrong, we wouldn't have been able to come to your aid. It's just too bad out there.'

Once we're at the marina, there are plenty of people there to greet us, including Fred Deo, who'd read about us in the local newspaper, and decided to treat us to some hospitality by whisking us off in a limousine to his restaurant for a meal. Fred is certainly one to stand out in a crowd. He's wearing a Stetson, a shirt which is stars and stripes with cowboy silhouettes around the top, and snakeskin boots in a matching red. His driver, Dave, also looks the part with a leather waistcoat.

As we've decided we have to stay at least one night, he's booked us in to a nearby Best Western hotel. He's having eye surgery in the morning (cataract removal), otherwise he would have had us stay at his house.

So we get our bags together and put them in the back of the white stretch Lincoln. We get about half an hour to clean up and change, and then we hit the road, heading out of Eureka. On the way, he cracks open a bottle of champagne, so we're really living the high life - drinking champers, sitting in the sumptuous leather upholstery of a chauffeur-driven stretch limousine.

Before going to the restaurant, we're taken into the Victorian town of Ferndale. It looks like something out of a Wild West movie, with its flat-fronted timber buildings. Here we go into a bar for a drink - the decorations on the walls are lots of old guns and revolvers, including the famous Colt Peacemaker. As I ask the barmaid about them, she lifts up my spectacles and says: 'Hey, I love your green eyes!' Most pubs I go into, the barmaids only ask for your glasses...

From Ferndale we go to Fernbridge, and Fred's restaurant, the Angelina Inn. The food is good - we have massive steaks - along with an endless supply of beer. The live music consists of a chap on an accordion, also using keyboard and rhythm box to supplement the sound. He does lots of Country and Western, but some very passable blues as well. But things liven up when everybody starts dancing, and to our astonishment, Alan gets on stage with the musician to sing a Willie Nelson number. I never knew he had it in him. Neither, apparently, did Alan.

Monday 10th June

After breakfast, Dave picks us up to take us back to the boat. There's definitely no way we're staying at the motel another night - not at $250 a room! We have a broken windscreen to replace, and one or two other things which need fixing, including the radio antenna. So while Alan and Steve get to work on all the repairs and servicing, I start writing, but there are quite a few people passing by, so it takes a while. Everyone's fascinated, and wants to talk to us. There's a photographer from the local paper who's here for ages.

I have a quick cup of coffee with a guy who bought a rather decrepit run-down sailing trimaran for $1,000. It's a bit of a wreck, and the main cabin is rather dominated by his sound system, two huge loudspeaker bins which he uses for DJ work.

Fred and Dave turn up mid-afternoon, and we head off on a little sight-seeing tour. We take the Avenue of the Giants, about 50 miles south of Eureka. This is where the giant Californian redwoods grow, including the Humboldt Redwoods State Park, the largest stand of virgin redwood in the world.

We go to look at the Founders Tree, a magnificent specimen, the lines in the bark doing a graceful twist up the trunk. The whole tree isn't much shorter than the spire of Norwich Cathedral. It's here we find out that some species of animals spend their entire lives in the canopy, never coming down to the forest floor.

Then we go to the Shrine Tree, famous as a huge hollow redwood with an opening through the trunk large enough to drive a car through. So we challenge Dave to drive the limo through - all 32 feet of it. The only slight moment of concern is where he grounds it on a hump in the road leading up to it. But Dave does it, just. So we could have set a new record for the biggest car ever to go through.

We also stop off in Scotia, one of the last company towns in the US, home of the Pacific Lumber Company. There's some interesting ancient machinery outside the sawmill museum, including a steam locomotive, donkey engine and other heavy logging equipment. When we stop off afterwards at a nearby bar, Fred buys everyone in the bar a drink. Back at the Angelina Inn, dinner is halibut. But sadly the restaurant is empty tonight, so there's not quite the atmosphere of last night.

We're driven to his house, nay mansion, in Loleta. It's big and brash, a bit like South Fork. Fred has an incredible collection of Stetsons - one for every occasion, and we've noticed that he has matching snakeskin boots for every shirt he wears. He also has numerous cars, admits to once driving a Lamborghini, and has several racehorses. In other words, he's not short of a few bob. It's not just the restaurant - he owns a bowling alley, antique shops, and buys and sells property. We each get a room for the night. Mine is vast, with ensuite bathroom with whirlpool.

Tuesday 11th June

We're up at 0700, then into Fred's truck (a huge Ford Tonka toy) into town for breakfast at a diner. Then to the marina, where it's time to say goodbye.

We set off towards the harbour entrance - scores of pelicans are heading out in formation, swooping low over the water ahead of us. A good sign, probably.

The seas are fairly heavy, but not quite as scary as Sunday. Even so, it's unusual for me to be able to see the horizon looking forwards through the windscreen from the back seat. Then a mist comes down, and it gets quite chilly. The radar starts giving odd readings until we realise that it's the fog doing it.

'Rain does it,' says Alan, 'so maybe you can get the same effect with fog.'

For a while we're running parallel to a shipping lane, and we spot one or two large container ships. Fortunately they're about two miles east of us. By late afternoon, the sea has calmed down considerably.

Wednesday 12th June

It's just after midnight, and I'm on my first watch. We're heading south-east, and about 25 miles offshore from San Francisco. Once again I'm marvelling at the phosphorescent plankton glowing in our wake, but now I'm seeing something different. Normally it's only where the water is stirred up that you see the glow, but in the dark water beyond the wake, there must be large clumps of the stuff. Every few seconds I see what looks like the mysterious lights of an underwater landing strip. Shades of 'Thunderball'. Or, since we're working our way towards the denouement of Michael Crichton's 'Sphere', perhaps what I'm looking at is something more sinister.

My second watch starts off in a memorable fashion. Steve's words 'Clive, it's time' are delivered with the solemnity of the padre arriving at my cell door to escort me to the hangman.

By midday, we've seen a major transformation. The sea is smooth, and while the air is still cool, the sun is out. The door is off for the first time in around a month, and we're barefoot. Shorts out tomorrow - yippee!

Alan has set about lots of little jobs - tidying up, fixing things. Either he's bored, or the improvement in the weather has inspired him. Then he decides we can go faster, so now we're whistling along at up to 24 knots.

We're off Santa Barbara when we see a pod of humpback whales. The boat stops, and I get some great video shots, including of their tail flukes as they come out of the water and then slip beneath the surface again. And despite the sound of the engine ticking over in the foreground, we even hear them squealing.

Later on, we have a school of bottle-nosed dolphins come right up to the boat. We throttle back so we can all stand in the bow and lean over the tube to watch them skimming along just beneath us. It's fantastic - they're close enough to touch. But then as we try to bring the revs up again, disaster.

The drive makes that familiar slipping clutch noise. The gearbox has blown, and once again we have virtually no power to the prop. Our reaction is part disbelief, part resignation. At least this time we have a replacement drive with us, and all we need do now is find somewhere to take the boat where she can be lifted out of the water. It seems Santa Barbara, 55 miles away, is our best bet. We put the wing engine on once more - now the fourth time it's come out to save our skins. Bizarrely, as we're doing this in the still ocean and beautiful late afternoon sun, we can hear the powerful puffing of humpback whales around three or four hundred yards away.

How can a moment of such euphoric pleasure be soured so quickly? We crack open a beer each, unusual for us, as we'd normally never contemplate drinking alcohol while under way. Alan decides that Ventura, although an extra 20 miles, will serve us better. We'll arrive not so early in the morning, and there's more chance of a lift-out.

So now I send an email to Yamaha asking for more help. The one thing we have learned through this is just how far we can push a single drive unit. And whilst it's fortunate we just happen to have a spare boxed up in the front cabin, it won't do the distance to get us home, that's for sure. So if we don't get another, it's all over.

26
NIGHT OF THE FLYING SQUID

We on board Nordhavn thought we were roughing it a bit on our circumnavigation until we met you and Spirit of Cardiff. You are three tenacious guys and our hat is off to you. Be careful out there. We are rooting for you.
Joe Meglen, Skipper, Nordhavn.

Thursday 13th June
DURING THE NIGHT, we hear a US Coastguard pan-pan, the international urgency call, asking boats to keep their eyes peeled after a red flare was seen being set off nearby. Several times we've pondered on the good fortune of rescuing someone. Good for them, of course, and good publicity for us. Despite having made national TV news in most of the countries we've visited, dear old cynical Britain still can't be bothered, whatever the human cost. It needs a drama of major proportions to get them even vaguely interested.

When we limp into Ventura at the Anchors Weigh Marina at 0530, it's too early for anyone to deal with us. I'm feeling tired, spaced out and most definitely not myself. Alan and Steve go off in search of breakfast, while I sloth around at the boat.

They return later, and mid-morning the boat is lifted out. Alan and Steve change drives quickly (they've had plenty of practice), and Steve glues the rubber bumper back to the front tube. The boat's showing a few signs of wear and tear, as indeed are we. Then we're off again. The sea's flat, and we're making around 20 knots. It's nice and sunny, but at the moment, the air is still quite cool. I suppose we'll get to some real heat sooner or later.

So far, I've had no email reply from Yamaha regarding another replacement drive unit, which from our point of view doesn't bode too well. The reality is that our sense of urgency is always going to be rather more heightened. But Alan has another plan. The drive we wrecked on the Maltese fish farm suffered peripheral damage only - the gearbox itself was fine. So if necessary we could get that shipped to Wilmington, North Carolina, which we hope to reach in around two weeks. The drive has only done 2,000 or so miles from Cardiff to Malta, and we'll be in cooler waters with good quality fuel, so it should still have enough life in it to get us home.

There's also the intriguing possibility that Cardiff Marketing may - finally - come up with some money, although the deal is that they would match whatever funds we can raise ourselves. But the catch is the money won't be made available until after we've passed Fort Lauderdale. It's good news, but for Cardiff Marketing to have gone on record as saying they've always supported Spirit of Cardiff rings a little hollow. This is their first piece of tangible support, and it seems unfair to make it come with strings attached.

As we approach San Diego in beautiful late afternoon sunshine, we run into a huge carpet of kelp, so thick it tangles around the prop. We end up dragging around 25 to 30 feet of the stuff behind us, and the boat virtually shudders to a halt. Alan puts the drive into reverse to spin the stuff off. It works, but then it jams up again. So again we spin it off. Eventually, after we've motored gingerly to the edge of it, the last remnants are cut away.

We enter San Diego harbour with a US Navy warship on our starboard beam. Amazingly, all the crewmen standing up on her bow are looking away from us, and towards the naval base on the other side. It's not just ships there, either, but an airbase with helicopters and F14 Tomcats.

First port of call is the fuel berth. By the time we finish and find our way across the harbour to Shelter Island Boatyard, it's gone 1900, and nearly dark. Our local contacts Dennis and Wendy Cullum aren't answering their phone, so presumably are on their way. We wait at the boatyard entrance, but they don't come. Alan and Steve wander round to Shelter Island Marina to see if they might have gone there by mistake, but all they do is return with the news that there's a splendid party with live music going on.

After debating whether to just go and find something to eat - we're starving by now - we eventually get through on the phone after talking to Nadia, and Dennis and Wendy arrive at around 2200. They'd come by earlier but hadn't seen us. Dennis Cullum was an electronics engineer, part of the 1950s brain drain to the US. His wife Wendy played lacrosse for Wales. We unload their car of all our goodies, put them into a trolley and wheel them down to the boat.

We drive off to a nearby Denny's, a fast food restaurant. I have a ham and cheese omelette, but it's not very good. On the way to their home, we pass a bizarre looking church, built recently by the Mormons. It looks like something straight out of Disney World. Eventually we get to their house after 2300. One beer and that's my lot. I take a shower, have a shave, check emails and hit the sheets at around 0100.

Friday 14th June

Despite our going to bed late, we have to be up early. Dennis has built a light aircraft, and is getting it certified by the Federal Aviation Authority today. After breakfast, we drive back into San Diego, stopping along the way to do some shopping at a supermarket. He drops us off at the boat.

Alan and Steve do the rest of the engine service, and while I'm in the office, along comes Elizabeth Fitzsimons, staff writer from the San Diego Union-Tribune. She spends quite a while asking about life on board, and hearing about our brushes with appalling weather and pirates, and of course some very friendly and helpful people.

Later Kristen Greenaway arrives. It's amazing, she doesn't look any different from Nepal six years ago, when she was one of my trekkers on a fascinating hike through the Himalayas to the holy lake Dudh Kund, south-west of Everest. On the other hand, I'm certain I do - and it's probably all stress-induced over the last two and a half months. She'd set up the interview with Liz for us, and has nothing but praise for her. Kristen is in the process of setting up a hiking trail, and when Liz did a story about it, it generated huge interest. Hopefully her story about us will do the same.

Alan decides to present the Cardiff plaque and letter to Liz for her newspaper. After she and her photographer depart, we go to a nearby restaurant with Kristen for a cup of tea and bite to eat. She's shocked at our sorry tale of woe, about the way we've been treated by our 'sponsors', and how Alan Carter left us in the lurch. She suggests we take a paying passenger through the Panama, and promptly gets on to her partner to email Liz and suggest she adds an extra line to her story about it. It'd be great if it came off. It's sad when it's time to go, but go we must. We depart at 1130, and head out to sea once more. Before too long, we're back in big following seas. When are these smooth waters going to return?

My journal update today mentions the fact that we're resigned to not breaking the Cable and Wireless record. I thought it was time I actually said something about it. The statistics which I quote at the end of each leg rather bear it out - and you don't have to be Einstein to figure out that a boat capable of averaging 20 knots can't cover over 8,000 miles in a week.

But that spawns a tiny flurry of emails designed to keep us going. Perhaps it's interpreted by our regular followers as some kind of depression, when really it's just intended as a statement of fact. The Cable and Wireless record is gone, and that's it. We've been living with the truth for a lot longer than we've let on. All we have now is the grim desire to get back. But while we've already had enquiries about what kind of reception we would like when we arrive back in Cardiff, at the moment I'm not interested in staged returns or anything like that. I just want to get home. Steve is of the same mind. He's already long overdue on the time he took off his job, and he's not even sure if he'll have a job to go back to.

We start a new novel this evening. By Robin Cook (the New Hampshire surgeon rather than British politician), it's called 'Brain'. I have a vague feeling I've seen the movie of this one.

Saturday 15th June

During the night, the following sea becomes less stop-go, and the sea flattens off somewhat, so we can maintain more of an even speed without having to worry about the throttle too much. In a following sea, there's always the possibility of ploughing into a wave in front, or of the prop cavitating, where it rides out of the water and races.

It's fairly dull and chilly to start with, but the cloud burns off to reveal warm sunshine. Even so, the air is still cool, and in the back of the cabin, in the shade, and with the draught which our flat back sucks in, it's definitely not shorts and T-shirt conditions. Alan starts out in his underpants, and even he resorts to pulling on his trousers later. After suffering severe stomach cramps yesterday, he says he feels better today.

As for me, I don't sleep that well during my four-hour session. It's become something of a standard onboard joke because I always complain that I don't sleep well. Clearly I do nod off from time to time, but it's not what I regard as quality sleep. I don't wake up refreshed and recharged - more like barely topped up with enough energy for the next few hours. And with the current pattern of watches, my sleep periods are more fragmented than the others - they get two periods of four hours, whereas I'm getting three - two, four, then two hours. The timing really all falls around Alan's need to ring Bertie at 1000 GMT every day, which of course at the moment is within the night watch period. But while Alan and Steve also tend to take naps during the day, I'm rather more restricted with the 'tippy-tappy' workload, which can only be attacked during daylight hours.

A puzzle book has appeared, presumably something from the stuff delivered to San Diego. So I take a break with a word search followed by a crossword. I don't quite finish the crossword though. There's also a pile of copies of stuff from the South Wales Echo where they've quoted from my daily journals. Despite sending them out each day with my name plastered all over them, it's generally misspelt, and there are no credits for the pictures they've used. I feel quite aggrieved that having supplied them with so much free material, they can't even be bothered to ensure I'm given proper credit where it's due. In the normal run of things, I'd phone them up and give them a bollocking, but I'm mindful that whatever their shortcomings, they're still helping to publicise our voyage, and for that, I suppose I should be grateful.

We stop at about 1800 for tea, and I get the latest position update for the Nordhavn. Alan reckons we're virtually on top of them. We try a few times on the radio, then as we set off again, we pick up a blip on the radar around 11 miles off. It could be them. There's a moment of elation as a similarly shaped boat appears out of the mist on our starboard beam. Steve is first to spot it, and we peel off to get closer. It's not the Nordhavn, and as we make an impressive close circuit around her, we don't even see anyone on the bridge.

The next contact is more hopeful. Steve sees a blip on the radar, about a mile and a half ahead.

'It must be them,' he says. 'There isn't anyone else out here.'

We get a visual on them, and this time it's definitely Nordhavn, with its distinctive 'sit up and beg' trawler profile. But as we approach, they just continue across our bow. They haven't seen us either. Alan brings us round close alongside, and suddenly there's a wave from the bridge, and then someone appears out on the aft deck.

Of course, the fact that we executed such a precise rendezvous is down to Alan getting the sums right from their last reported position at midday, and making for where they ought to be given their approximate speed and heading. But even so, it's amazing to think that we should get to find each other at all on a misty evening in the Pacific Ocean, 50 miles offshore, both of us going around the world in opposite directions.

Once we've clambered aboard, we let Spirit out on a long line so Nordhavn tows her, her engine still ticking over. Nordhavn is only seven feet longer than Spirit, but she's everything we're not. Comfortable, with cabins, toilet, shower, kitchen.

There are just three on board, skipper Joe Meglen, Dennis Lawrence and Gary Armellino. They've been on the boat from Acapulco, taking her on the final leg of her circumnavigation back to Dana Point in California. Unlike us, they've been changing crews every so often.

They rustle up some beers for us, although they're rather concerned that it isn't chilled enough. Apart from their conventional fridge in the kitchen area, they've bolted a large chest freezer to the floor of the lounge.

They heat up some hot dogs as well, frankfurter sausages in a slice of bread with mustard. Lovely. Joe tells us that all of Nordhavn's trip has seen unusual weather, so it's not just us.

The whole of the boat is really well appointed, over-engineered, to use their phrase. Alan reckons a bit under-powered, but then again, who wants to go fast when you have this level of comfort? She even has stabilisers. As I've told myself many times over the years, and particularly over the last two and a half months, comfort and discomfort are both relative concepts. The Nordhavn crew thought they were roughing it until they saw us. Our boat with its tiny cabin, two tiny bunks, no toilet, no hot water, no cold food storage, makes theirs look like a veritable floating palace. And our almost daily injury toll probably looks pretty grim to them as well.

Eventually it's time for the 'three crazy Brits' to take their reluctant leave of Joe, Dennis and Gary. By now it's dark, and we haul in Spirit, her engine still idling and running lights shining brightly, and clamber aboard. Then we cast off and wave farewell to the Nordhavn and her crew. We'd been looking forward to this meeting for weeks, first thinking we might be able to have it at a refuelling stop to maximise press coverage, then as a dramatic rendezvous out at sea as we realised our paths would cross offshore. But now, after all the anticipation, it's over. They're nearly home, while we have another 8,000 miles or so back to Gibraltar, and another 1,200 to Cardiff. I can't help feeling a little pang of jealousy, but mostly it's elation. What a great meeting, and one for the history books.

Sunday 16th June

My first watch from 2300 till 0100 sees a phenomenon rarely experienced before. I'm sitting in the navigator's seat when I see the speed counting down - 28, 27, 26 knots. Have we just hit 30 without my realising? It's still a hell of a spurt. We hit 25 on the next downhill run, and then that's it. I ask Alan, and after checking he later confirms that the instruments all went a little haywire then, including compass, so maybe it was a glitch. Or another submarine or alien spacecraft...

We arrive in the Mexican holiday resort of Cabo san Lucas on the southern tip of the Baja Peninsula at around midday, passing some dramatic rock formations just before arriving at the harbour. We refuel, then head over to another pontoon to tie up while we grab some food and go shopping. As it's Sunday, we can't complete immigration procedures, so we're granted just two hours in port.

'Steve, can you shut up the boat and put the alarm on?'

Alan calls out loud from the quayside, for the benefit of the T-shirt sellers nearby. We might as well let people think the boat is secure, even though it's easy for any would-be intruder to get in.

We find a small place that serves salads and baguettes, and eat the most healthy meal I've had for a long while. Turkey with Gouda and avocado, and the salad is nice, too. Then we find a supermarket, laying in stocks of longlife milk. Back at the boat, and we're off, exactly two hours after our arrival. It's good to be in and out so quickly, but we have of course missed out on all the paperwork.

Later in the afternoon, the sun's hot, and although we're bouncing about a bit, I strip off and have a shower, then wash my underwear, shave, and brush my teeth. It's absolutely great, and I even fit in a short nap after some intensive writing.

Nobody seems to like Robin Cook's 'Brain', so we ditch that in favour of our new acquisition from our friends on Nordhavn, Michael Crichton's 'Timeline'. I read that until the light goes - then for a short period with the cabin light on before we start the watches. It's stiflingly hot now, and I don't sleep.

Monday 17th June

We're making good progress today, 19 to 20 knots. While I spend most of the day office working, Alan and Steve try to track down the source of an annoying leak in the forward cabin. They find a crack, where it joins to the floor.

'Is it anything to worry about?' I ask Steve.

'It may be,' he replies. 'Or it may not.'

'But are you worried about it?' He shakes his head. No reason for me to concern myself, then. He reckons it may have happened back in India, when the boat was dropped into the water. The boat hasn't been made that doesn't take on a certain amount of water, and providing it stays in the bilges and the pumps can cope, it's not a problem. Once outside those parameters, it becomes a problem, and ultimately, a disaster.

The temperature is rising as we head further south. By the afternoon, we've rigged up a curtain to act as a sunshade. I even take two showers. It's really hot. Nobody else wants an evening meal, so I have an American ratpack - ham omelette (a little weird) with potato au gratin (nice).

Having said that, Alan has been suffering from upset insides for the last day or so, although he ascribes that to drinking dodgy water. By the evening, I rattle through a bit more of 'Timeline', then we start the watches. Now the sleeping bags have been stowed away, and we're just lying on top of our towels.

Tuesday 18th June

I get a slight lie in at the end of my four hour sleep, to find that

Quetzal marina, Guatemala.

Spirit moored up at the Flamenco Yacht Club. The skyscrapers of Panama City can be seen in the background.

Guided tour of the boat. L-R: HM Ambassador Jim Malcolm, Ambassador Flavio Mendez from Panama's Ministry of Foreign Affairs, Alan Priddy, Mort Deas.

Not quite what we were expecting to find next to the marina. A graveyard of double-decker buses.

Approaching the Bridge of the Americas. The first set of locks, the Miraflores Locks, is beyond here.

It's necessary to tie up while in the locks. Fortunately for us, we were able to make fast to the Falkor, a larger vessel, so our two hired line handlers had a relatively easy day.

The first chamber at Miraflores locks. The webcam is on top of the tower in the distance.

These locomotives are used to tow large ships through the lock chambers. They each cost $2.3 million.

The last set of locks we pass through is Gatun Locks, where we descend to Port Cristobal, gateway to the Caribbean.

With Spirit and her crew safely in Port Antonio after a nightmare crossing of the Caribbean from Panama, everything inside the boat is stripped out to dry off.

Port Antonio is the cradle of tourism in the Caribbean, with Trident Villas and Hotel one of the most famous places to stay in Jamaica.

Beautifully kept lawns, an ancient cannon, swaying palms and blue skies. No wonder the celebrities love to come here.

Who's pinched our skipper? Alan hops aboard another RIB for a quick chat as we make our way into Fort Lauderdale.

Getting into the harbour at Wilmington proved a tricky job at night.

Yet another TV interview. Alan poses in the bow, wired for sound, as WWAY Channel 3's Gavin Williams interviews him for the early evening news.

Halifax is beautifully sunny. I rush off into town to get my back treated, while Alan sets about getting our radar working again. It's all rounded off with a pleasant lunch in the Royal Nova Scotia Yacht Squadron.

Spirit of Cardiff arrives in St John's Newfoundland for her last but one refuelling stop before Gibraltar. Photograph: Egbert Walters

Early morning in St John's. The sun's up, and it's a beautiful day. Spirit is fuelled up and ready to set off on the long transatlantic leg to Horta in the Azores.

Spirit of Cardiff sets off from St John's on July 15th. Gibraltar, and the end of the circumnavigation, is just 2,300 miles and five days away.
Photograph: Egbert Walters

Disaster. Steve Lloyd suffers a massive heart attack.

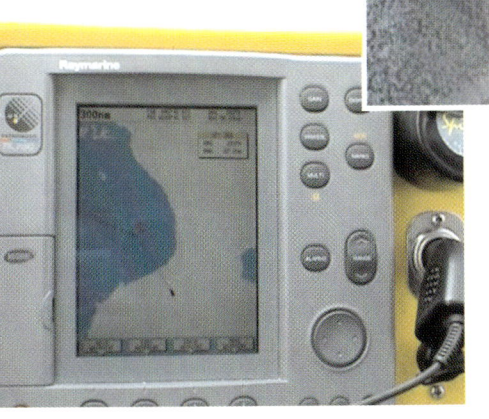

When we realise the gravity of the situation, Spirit of Cardiff is too far offshore to be rescued by helicopter. We have to turn back towards St John's and make up around 100 miles. It takes over eight hours.

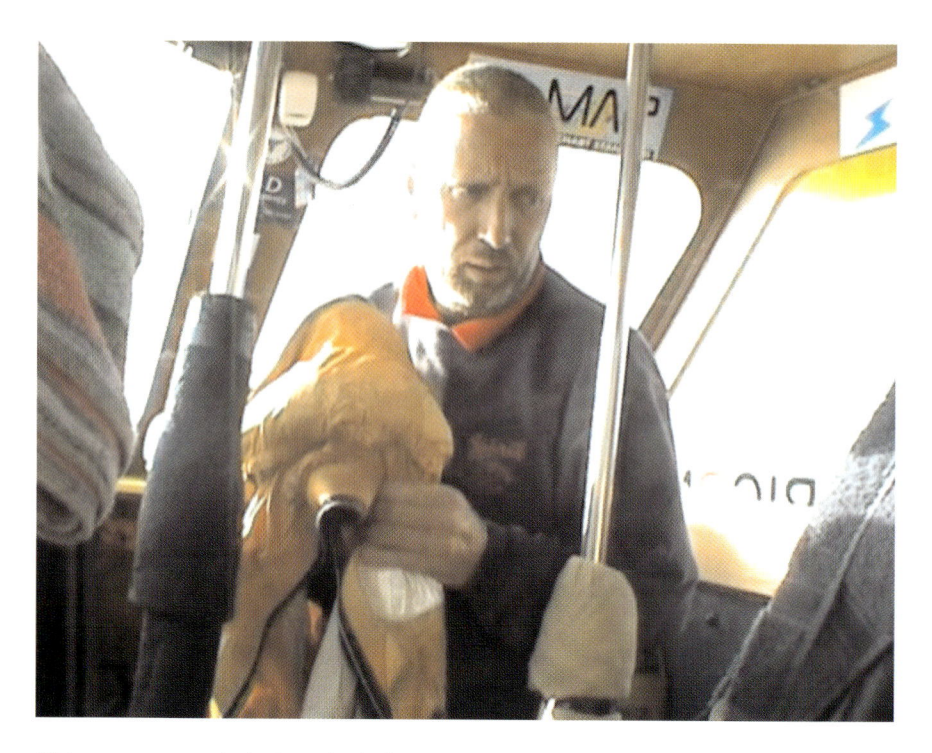

Things to get ready before the helicopter arrives. Alan gets Steve's Gore-Tex survival suit ready, then sets about removing obstructions such as flag pole and aerials.

CH113 Labrador helicopter approaches us from astern, the rotors' downdraught flattening the sea behind us. Then the first man comes down on a line.

Then the paramedic comes down with a large pack of equipment. Before we know it, Steve is being whisked up into the helicopter, and is on his way to hospital in St John's.

St John's, Newfoundland, a colourful and lively city with a huge amount of history. But whilst they pride themselves on the cleanliness and beauty of the city, the same can't be said of the harbour, where they discharge raw sewage into the water. It is this effluent which proves Spirit's final downfall.

The final ignominy. Spirit takes on water while moored in St John's harbour. We have to pay a waste disposal company to come and pump out the diesel which would have taken us all the way to the Azores.

Leaving St John's on her way back to the Royal Newfoundland Yacht Club, where Spirit is lifted out of the water and put into winter storage. The ship in the background is Carnival Cruise Lines' new ship, Carnival Legend.

we're virtually in Acapulco. It's a lot hotter and more humid here. We find the yacht club and fuel berth, but of course we're too early, so we have to wait.

We wander off to find somewhere to get breakfast. Whilst Acapulco has its reputation for glamour and glitz, we're in the less salubrious end of town, the bit that doesn't appear in the tourist brochures. The taxis here are VW Beetles, all metallic blue wings and white bodies, festooned with lights and aerials. A small two-door car with limited luggage storage seems a most unlikely contender for use as a taxi, but there are hundreds of them zipping about, and they all seem to have passengers.

The buses are weird as well. They sport all sorts of artistic spray paint jobs, some with patterns, others with airbrushed pictures with a high gloss lacquer on top to add to the sparkle. The most hilarious is one with a cartoon mouse on one side of the bonnet, and Jesus Christ on the other. They all come with loud pounding music as well, a far cry from the conservative demeanour of Eastern Counties buses.

Back at the boat, it's just down to waiting. Eventually the agent turns up and we each fill in a form. But the chances of anything happening quickly seem remote. This is the place where the concept of mañana was conceived, and they probably left it until tomorrow to do it. Having been spoiled with the wonderful welcomes at each of our arranged stops in the US and Canada, it's rather a contrast not just to be fending for ourselves, but to be regarded with complete indifference.

So we sit around in the sun, drink a few beers, and eventually wander off for lunch. As we arrive at the beach, we're accosted by various restaurants touting for our business. We have chicken with 10 chips and a sliver of salad. I've learned they sometimes serve iguana in Mexico, but this - forgettable as it is - looks pretty chicken-like to me.

Back at the marina, I jump into the pool for a quick swim, which apart from being refreshing in itself, also serves as a convenient way of washing my underwear. After more waiting, we eventually get away, late afternoon. It's cost us $350 just to get the passports stamped and port clearance signed, and we've had to wait all day for the privilege. It really is taking the mickey, particularly since they've stung us for the fuel as well. To round it all off, I have a splitting headache, the result, no doubt, of sitting around too long in the sun. Mexico? You can keep it.

Wednesday 19th June

I do two four-hour sleeps this time, and it works fantastically well. I feel really rested. I do a fair bit of keyboarding during the second watch - it is actually possible to sit in either of the front seats, do a spot of 'tippy-tappy' and occasionally glance up to check on what's about. We're crossing the Gulf of Tehuantepec at the southern end of Mexico. It's notorious for its violent winds, called, appropriately enough, Tehuantepecs. At about 0800, the first tropical storm comes through. We go from following to head sea in minutes, and suddenly it's really bumpy. Alan jumps up and knocks the throttle back, then crashes back to sleep.

The first passes us on the port beam, black and angry, with lots of rain. Once it's gone, the sea calms for about half an hour. Then comes the next one. The sea whips up, and the rain pounds down, flattening the tops of the waves. But whilst the rain is fairly short-lived, the nasty head sea isn't.

It carries on all day. When we stop for tea, we're amused to see a gull walking across the water. Or at least it looks like it as it cavorts about with a flap and a hop. Steve throws it a few bits of biscuit, and it scrabbles across the waves to get to them. Tea tonight is Cadburys Smash instant mashed potato and Spam, with HP sauce.

It's back to the usual shift pattern tonight, with me doing two hours sleep, then coming on watch. The lightning by now is intense, zapping all around the boat, lighting up the night sky.

Thursday 20th June

It's a miserable night, with the boat stopped, unable to make any progress, and water running through the hatches. We learn our tropical storm has been upgraded to a hurricane. After no movement at all during the night we try to carry on, but it's hard work. The clouds are Stygian black, and we're doing just four knots.

Suddenly my lower back goes. It's a problem I've had before, and it's not as if I've been trying to pick up something heavy. In a great deal of pain and virtually unable to move, I manoeuvre myself gingerly onto the bunk and curl up.

Alan accuses me of whinging, and then when I hobble out to the dive platform, he shouts out: 'Shark!' I take it seriously and jump up with a start, inflicting further pain on my back. I'm not amused. He's not normally unsympathetic.

It takes a long while for me to be able to move around at all. I'm not in good shape. By early afternoon I feel well enough to write an update, and the others are dozing. When Alan wakes I suggest we might be able to go faster - the sea appears to have flattened off quite a bit. We get up to 17 knots, then as the afternoon wears on, 20 knots. I manage a shower and shave. I'm even up to reading a bit more 'Timeline'. As the late afternoon sun begins to set, we're steaming along the Guatemalan coast.

'Always a good sign when you see fishing boats out,' says Alan. 'Means they're either starving hungry or the weather's good.'

They're certainly enjoying good spoils. The water is seething with masses of shoals of fish, possibly anchovies. We arrive in Quetzal harbour after nightfall, but have trouble finding where we're supposed to go. As with many such harbours, the lighting isn't what you'd call intense. We're escorted round to the navy base in another part of the harbour, where some navy person promptly disallows us from going to the marina, maybe because he was hopeful we might take him up on his offer to tie up here for $100 for the night. I'd expect a four-star hotel for that kind of money.

So then we go off for ourselves, finding the marina, except we're not sure that's what it is at this stage. Someone comes aboard and shows us on our chart plotter where we should go, except he's actually showing us an anchorage area, since we're not supposed to enter the harbour at night. So we pootle off round there, scanning the shore with our super-powerful spotlight, but we see nothing.

We're about to tie up at a buoy when the pilot boat comes out again. We're escorted back to the marina, where this time we tie up. Alan has been doing all the line handling, given my fragile state, but the manoeuvring in here is tight, and he needs me as eyes at the back of the boat. Then he starts shouting at me because I'm not telling him anything, and we've bumped into the jetty. There's a powerful light being shone down on us, and I'm blinded by it.

We tie up, and whilst I'm still feeling sorry for myself he snaps:

'Clive, take some painkillers and go to sleep.' I'm tempted to call him a patronising git, but instead I just say I've already had some painkillers, and anyway, we've had nothing to eat. So while the marina security guard, complete with full SWAT uniform and sawn-off shotgun looks on, Steve cooks up some stew and mixed vegetables with instant potato. It's considerably livened up with one of Choy's bottles of wine from Singapore, and we end the evening feeling a good deal more relaxed.

We're not sure whether we're allowed off the boat - probably paranoia after Russia - but it's put to the test with a request to go to the toilet block. We turn in for the night - it's great to be sleeping on a bunk that's not tossing you about, although the risk of being eaten alive by the local insects is far greater.

Friday 21st June

A couple of guys turn up around 0800 - we're not sure first of all whether they're just interested onlookers, but they turn out to be marina people, ready to refuel us. We have to move the boat closer to the pump. Then a naval officer arrives, and someone from immigration. Lionel, our agent turns up. He appears to be in his sixties, and has organised everything so well we don't have to fill in any forms.

There's a note of surprise in Alan's voice when he asks: 'Is that all?' when the immigration man hands him some stamped papers.

Lionel takes Alan shopping while I remain behind with Steve. It would have been nice to go too, but he needs someone to count off 66 gallons, 250 litres, into each side tank. That needs someone standing at the pump. Interestingly, the fuel reservoirs, both petrol and diesel, are large tanks above ground. Given the extreme heat here, it seems a trifle dangerous. Most such tanks would be underground.

When Alan returns, he says the choice in the supermarket was rather limited. The people in Guatemala are poor, but they all seem to smile a lot. Not the same as the Mexicans at all. On the other hand, it is a bit more like the Wild West here. People walk the streets with firearms. Apart from last night, which I think was more down to mix-up than anything, they're a lot more efficient and not grasping at all. Lionel is almost apologetic at one point, wondering whether one particular charge is too much.

Fuelled up and re-provisioned, it's time to go. It's only 1030, so we potter out to the entrance of the harbour and have a brew up and our breakfast. It's a blistering hot day, and both Alan and Steve are bored. Their singing and raucous behaviour in close proximity is grating on my nerves. I've been on this boat too long.

I have a shower later on, memorable for the moment when Steve points out a large seagull apparently standing on the water. He's actually on a turtle which is floating along the surface. Presumably the turtle is either dead or oblivious.

The sea starts off smooth, but it turns into a head sea by the afternoon. Certainly it's uncomfortable, particularly with my back still feeling rather fragile. It's a lot better than it was yesterday, although when Alan asks how I'm feeling, I simply say I'm all right. There's not much point in saying what I really feel like if I'm going to have it thrown back at me as whinging.

Of course, we cursed the bad weather when it was cold, but it has its problems when it's hot, too. Our top hatches are open to provide some much-needed ventilation. Steve and I turn in quite early (it's dark by 1900). I'm half asleep as the conditions become more violent, and we take our first wave over the top. Suddenly I have a lapful of sea water. I register my surprise with a single word of Anglo-Saxon, and stagger up to close the hatch. I'm all fingers and thumbs, and Alan gets it down before the next deluge goes over the roof.

Steve, lying in the opposite bunk, suffers a similar soaking from above, and feels something slimy land on his bare chest. He flicks it off. When he gets up later, he sees something glowing on the cabin floor. It's a squid, about six inches long.

It is, of course, a sign. We've recently finished Michael Crichton's 'Sphere', which features, amongst other things, a giant malevolent luminous squid. Now that we're eagerly immersed into Crichton's 'Timeline', we're fully expecting quantum mechanics to transport us to another universe and another time. In fact, anywhere except here would suit me just fine.

Saturday 22nd June

By the end of my shift, we've covered very few extra miles. Then

Alan comes back on watch.

'Seen anything?'

'Not a thing,' I reply. So as I reclaim my bunk, he stretches out on the floor. Sleep isn't really possible, but he pokes his head up every now and then to make sure there's nothing coming in our direction.

I overhear the morning phone call to Bertie, who seems to be saying that we're stuck with this front, which is over 100 miles. The 'odd spots of bad weather' we'd been told to expect along the way from Quetzal to Panama appear to have ganged up on us. We go into yet another fierce tropical storm, with head seas bumping us about, and our speed reduced to three knots. It's miserable, painful, and demoralising - suddenly we're not sure any more when we're likely to arrive in Panama, although we have heard that a ship 70 miles ahead of us has reported no wind, so we know we're working our way through it, albeit slowly.

Conditions improve through the day, and our speed increases to 14 knots. We should hopefully get into Panama on Monday, so we'll still do the service lift out Monday afternoon, then spend time in Panama on Tuesday, with the big transit through the canal on Wednesday.

Sunday 23rd June

My watches during the night start later, so I get two lots of four hours sleep (sort of). During my first watch I see a few flashes of lightning in the distance, but nothing to worry about. The second one sees the sun up, but hiding behind lots of dark clouds. It's still very warm, although I do find that I need my fleece pulled over me in lieu of bedclothes, with my towel underneath and T-shirt over pillow.

We manage to increase our speed to 19 knots, and although we appear to be heading for another storm, it's nothing more than a slight spattering of rain. I have a shower and wash my shorts. The colour of the water that comes out of them is murky beyond belief. My zip-off trousers aren't much better, so will have to give them a wash when the others are dry.

It seems we will get into Panama tomorrow, and I can't wait to get ashore. I've got it fixed in my mind that the weather will be much better once we're through the canal, on the other side. It's also heartening to hear we have rooms in a posh hotel - the Caesar Park.

The most spectacular thing today is a brief encounter with dolphins, quite big ones. They rush the boat like torpedoes, some leaping high out of the water doing somersaults, and sometimes in pairs. It's the first time I've seen them that acrobatic, but they're not too keen on being filmed. By the time I get my camera out, they've vanished from sight.

The coastline of Costa Rica is dark and hilly - jungle-clad, I guess, although it's hard to tell from our position offshore. Alan and Steve take it in turns to doze during the day. I wish I had that luxury. As we get closer to the point where we turn north into the Gulf of Panama, we're not surprised to see more ships, heading towards or away from that narrow channel which takes them from one side of a continent to another.

Monday 24th June

Even the last few miles in the Gulf of Panama are unforgiving. It's as though the Pacific is fighting us every inch of the way. As we close on Panama and Balboa Port, we see lots of ships lying at anchor, presumably waiting their turn to go through the canal.

We arrive at the Flamenco Yacht Club mid-morning, and are met by Tomas Golder, director of the marina and accompanying resort. Alan and Steve sort out a few things on the boat, while I wander off and sit down to do some writing. It's nice just to get away for a while. The boat is lifted out of the water in the afternoon, and Alan and Steve change the gearbox oil. Afterwards we gravitate to a tiny outside bar which overlooks the marina, and we all get chatting to different people, which is nice.

A car arrives for us later, and we're driven into Panama City, to the Caesar Park Hotel. Panama City is a real city of contrasts, if that's not too much of a cliché. From my hotel room, I can see modern skyscraper blocks, but in between, a shanty town of buildings with tin roofs and low-rise concrete apartment blocks which don't look particularly salubrious.

Without wanting to sound callous, pondering the injustice of the inequalities of the world isn't my highest priority. We've been subjected to our own injustices and bad treatment, and this is an opportunity to escape them for a while. And here more than anywhere we're being made to feel special. The British Ambassador to Panama will be visiting us at the boat tomorrow, and then hosting a reception for us in the evening. It's star treatment, without a doubt, and we're revelling in the attention.

27
FROM ONE OCEAN TO ANOTHER

We had a wonderful time raising a glass to the arrival and then a great deal of sadness at the departure of the Spirit of Cardiff in Panama. The trip through the canal was memorable, my first since arriving in Panama in March this year. Go guys go and capture that record! You are a great credit to Cardiff.
Jim Malcolm, HM Ambassador, Panama City.

Tuesday 25th June

YOU'D THINK WITH a bed wide enough to sleep three, I might sleep well, but I don't particularly. I wake up at about four, and then don't really get back to sleep again. How can something so comfortable move about so much? I discover that my toilet is slightly blocked when I flush it, at which point it floods all over the bathroom floor. Splendid. Later I whip downstairs, stopping off at the reception desk to ask them to fix it, and then on the spur of the moment, I decide to have a haircut. The young lady hairdresser doesn't seem to speak much English, but I manage to make myself understood, and I come away with a decent grade three for just $10 - not bad for a posh hotel, and in retrospect an inspired choice when I see what happens to Alan and Steve in Jamaica.

Then we're whizzed off down to the boat, where the idea is that we refuel, do a few repairs, and get ready for the Ambassador, or the 'Ambo', as Steve calls him. This stop has been set up by Julian Johanson-Brown of Halcrow, the Swindon-based company which advises on the development of the Panama Canal ports of Balboa and Cristobal. Britain's new ambassador to Panama is interested in promoting links between Panama and Britain, and we seem to be a pretty good vehicle for that.

CONFRONTING POSEIDON

We were even going to get some breakfast in, but it doesn't quite happen like that. In fact, we don't get to see anything remotely like breakfast all day. A journalist and photographer from La Prense (Panama's main newspaper) comes along. She does quite an in-depth taped interview, sitting with us around a table in the bar, and then the photographer wants to take loads of photographs. There are plenty of ships and pleasure craft that go through the Panama Canal, but we're different. Here's something unusual, and the local media are lapping it up.

We also have to complete a lot of formalities, including immigration for Panama, and having the boat fumigated. This may seem extreme given that we have actually been taking a sea water shower every day, but the true purpose is to kill off any imported mosquitoes.

There's a lot to get ready for our transit of the canal tomorrow - it's not just a question of turning up and going through. The boat is inspected, and we're briefed on what we need to have - ropes and extra fenders which will need to be hired, and a means of signalling (Alan has bought one of those impressively loud aerosol horns). We also have to provide toilet facilities for the pilot, which, while tricky, we get around by having the bucket in the well between the forward and main cabins, with our piece of fruit-basket material from Kota Kinabalu as a curtain to provide an element of privacy. It's the best we can do, and we just have to cross our fingers that he won't be suffering from any kind of intestinal disorders.

After that it's time to refuel. This proves slightly amusing, because we run the marina's tank dry. So the boat has to go across the dock to the big boat berths, where there's an impressive large British sailing yacht. There we top up using a huge filler (80 gallons/minute), but because the pipe is so stiff, it won't bend to fit into the main and forward tank fillers inside the cabin, so we can only get fuel into the side tanks. Ironically, perhaps, we end up taking on more than necessary.

Alan had brought his evening togs with him, so when the car comes just after 1300, it's just Steve and me who zip back to the hotel to get showered and changed. I'm so hungry I raid my minibar and have a small bar of chocolate and diet Coke. It's an irony perhaps that we're staying in a luxury hotel, but can't even afford a decent meal. William, our driver takes us back via the old town centre, bustling with people. There even appears to be a pedestrian precinct. It would be nice to have more time to explore, but we have official duties to perform now.

We pass a few run-down areas before travelling along the causeway back to Flamenco Yacht Club. Not long after we arrive, British Ambassador Jim Malcolm arrives in a smart Jaguar, along with Mort Deas, Halcrow's man on the ground in Panama. Also with them is Ambassador Flavio Mendez, from Panama's Ministry of Foreign Affairs. They spend some time at the boat, getting a guided tour of the electronics - marvelling at our ability to live in such a small space, and at our tenacity for sticking it out in such horrendous conditions for so long.

Later, we head off to the Balboa Yacht Club, where a little party has been prepared for us. Here I meet Allan Baitel. Apart from being an influential businessman, Allan is president of the Panamanian Triathlon Union. He organised the first Ironman competition in the country three years ago, along with original Ironman creator John Collins, now retired in Panama. While his wife Roz has organised the party, Allan has been behind the media coverage. He's rustled up some more, so while Alan and Steve continue to press the flesh at the reception, I'm whisked back to the boat, where there's a camera crew from Channel 4 News (theirs, not ours, I'm afraid) and yet more people from La Prense.

But before I can do my media star act, I have to suffer the indignity of lugging several huge ropes and fenders off the boat. These are our 'rent-a-ropes' for use in the canal tomorrow. There are two completely filling the well in the bow, and another two on the aft deck. They're positively massive - each of them an inch and a half thick, and 150 feet long. Somewhere underneath all this blue nylon rope is our little boat, and that's what the TV crew wants to see.

Once I've done the interview, and numerous shots of my posing on the boat, doing my best to look rugged, we go back to the party, where I'm just in time to join in yet another TV interview. This one is Channel 5, and clearly on a budget, as all they have is a domestic handheld camcorder and no remote boom mike. Even so, the frenetic media activity is enough to make us think. Is this what it's going to be like when we return to Cardiff? Already people are asking when we're going to be back so they can start making arrangements. But it does beg the question - why, when we're simply passing through Panama, are we such big news here, when at the moment all we're getting is regional news coverage back in Britain, much of which is not what you'd call positive?

We finish off the evening going out to dinner quite late with Osvaldo Gonzalez, our agent, and his friend Khan. It seems Osvaldo is a bit of a lad. In his late 20s, he lives with his parents, and has four girlfriends, none of whom knows about the others. He appears to be working on number five - the waitress serving us - and I learn later that he elicits a telephone number from the girl. Unfortunately I'm really tired, and by the end of the evening, I'm very nearly asleep at the table.

Wednesday 26th June

William, our driver, is waiting for us, and we set off for Flamenco Yacht Club. Jim Malcolm and Mort Deas are already here waiting for us, a little less formally attired today, with protective sunhats. I'm dead envious of Jim's Nikon D1X digital camera. It's state of the art, but sadly with a price tag to match. One day…

The boat is going to be very cramped. Apart from our two guests, who are coming as far as Pedro Miguel Locks, we'll have a pilot and two line handlers. The ropes themselves take up masses of space. We also have a couple of large fenders.

Apart from the symbolic significance of our passing from one ocean to another, I've long been looking forward to seeing the Panama Canal, one of the greatest engineering achievements of modern times. The idea of a short cut through the isthmus which joins North and South America had existed since the 16th Century, but it was the French, fired by their success with the Suez Canal, who made the first serious efforts. But there was the world of difference between digging out vast quantities of sand from flat terrain and blasting different qualities of rock out of a jungle infested with malaria and yellow fever. Eventually, technical problems and numerous deaths due to tropical disease forced the French to give up.

It was President Roosevelt who took up the challenge to complete the project, spurred by the knowledge that an American-controlled canal would prove a vital asset to the United States' global interests.

At the start of the 20th century, Panama was a province of Columbia, and it was the promise of an American presence which gave them the impetus to declare independence. The payback from the fledgling republic was a treaty granting the USA sovereign rights in perpetuity over the 10 mile wide Canal Zone.

The Americans moved in, and the first breakthrough came in eradicating the mosquitoes responsible for the spread of disease. The technical problems were still considerable, and when the canal opened in 1914, it was an unprecedented technological feat, with the eight mile Culebra Cut through the rock and shale of the Continental Divide the most impressive. There was a complex series of locks - then the biggest concrete structures in the world - which allowed even the largest ships of the day to pass through; and the Gatun Lake, which submerged 24 towns, at the time the largest artificially enclosed body of water in the world.

By cutting off the long and dangerous voyage around Cape Horn to get from the Pacific to the Atlantic, the 50 mile (80 kilometres) Panama Canal revolutionised world shipping. It continued to be administered by the USA until 1977, when President Jimmy Carter signed a treaty agreeing to relinquish the canal after a period of transition. That ended in 1999, when Panama took full control of the canal.

There are three sets of locks - from south to north - Miraflores, with two chambers, Pedro Miguel, with one, and Gatun with three. In between Pedro Miguel and Gatun Locks are the Culebra Cut and Gatun Lake, 85 feet (26 metres) above sea level. The lock chambers are 110 feet (33.5 metres) wide, 1,000 feet (305 metres) long, and 85 feet (26 metres) deep. They're set in pairs to permit traffic either in opposite directions or both the same way, depending on the needs at any one time. And with the recent widening of the Culebra or Gaillard cut, the whole canal will permit two-way transits throughout of the biggest Panamax vessels.

Unlike the Suez Canal, we won't be setting any records this time. The US Marine hydrofoil Pegasus went through in two hours 41 minutes in 1979, which no doubt was made possible by having friends in the right places. We're just booked to do a normal transit, which should take around eight to 10 hours. All over the world, Spirit of Cardiff followers are settling down in front of their computers ready to catch their first glimpse of us on the Panama Canal live webcam. Nadia has done a good job of putting last-minute updates on our website, so people know when we're supposed to be going through.

We set off to a martialling point for the canal - a buoy within sight of the Bridge of the Americas - to wait for our pilot. We're here for a while, and then as Alan decides to move forward to the next buoy, he wonders mischievously whether he's likely to start a stampede. It's one of those situations where everyone is queued up waiting, and if one person goes everyone else will think they're likely to be left behind, and join in the throng. But there's no stampede, and shortly after we have our full complement of pilot and line handlers aboard, at which point Jim and Mort take their seats in the dress circle - or as close as we can get - up on the roof of the cabin.

We pass beneath the Bridge of the Americas, a splendid suspension bridge not dissimilar to the Tyne Bridge, high above the entrance to the canal. To the right is Ancon Hill, with its massive Panamanian flag flying proudly in the breeze. But as we draw closer to the Miraflores Locks, the first set, we can see they're still taking other ships through. We tie up alongside the Falkor, a smart 63 foot cabin cruiser. Even though we've reassured them that Spirit is surrounded by one huge fender, they're slightly concerned that we might mark their hull. So they spend some time adjusting their rented fenders - car tyres covered with bin liner and parcel tape.

The advantage of this arrangement is that the other boat's hired line handlers do the hard work, which suits me just fine. Line handling in the locks requires a certain skill in catching the weighted lines thrown down by the lock workers, and when it comes to catching thrown objects, I'm about as elegant as a duck on a skating rink. In any event, I'm now free to concentrate on shooting video and taking photographs.

We're supposed to be in the first chamber by 0900, but we don't enter until around an hour later, coming in behind a French polar research vessel called Marion Dufresne. As we pass into the first lock, the lock workers throw their thin lines, weighted at the end with 'monkey's fists'. These have to be wrapped a couple of times around the large loops at the end of Falkor's big ropes, and the monkey's fist put through the loop. With the thin line pulled tight, it can then be dragged back up for the lock workers to make secure. It's necessary for vessels to be secured in the locks, because the water moves quickly when the chambers fill and empty.

My symbolic last look back on the Pacific occupies no more than a couple of seconds. I'm glad to be rid of it. As the immense lock doors close behind us, the water comes in rapidly, with whirlpools across the surface, and about eight minutes later we're at the top of the first chamber. I can see the webcam on top of a red and white painted tower in the distance, and I wave at it. We know a special request has been made to have it trained onto us, but what we don't know at the time is that it was struck by lightning the previous weekend, and is unable to zoom in. We appear onscreen only as a tiny yellow speck, but to those of our followers tracking us on the Panama Canal live webcam website, it's better than nothing. Unfortunately, the fact that we've entered the lock an hour late means that Class 10 at Deighton Primary School in Tredegar, who've been avidly following our progress, have to abandon us to go home before they get the chance to see us on the webcam. Their teacher stays behind to capture the moment for them.

Whilst we're in the lock, Mort passes me what looks like a nice little snack, a piece of dried mango on a lolly stick. I assume the fine powder covering it is icing sugar - I'm certainly not prepared for a fiery chilli! Alan and Steve have already experienced the effects, so are looking to see my reaction. They fall about laughing as I pull a face of surprise and disgust. The irony is that Mort didn't realise he'd bought something which is more akin to what you might find in a joke shop. I'm pretty 'mort'ified myself.

Whilst we motor through the locks at slow speed, the lock workers walking our lines along the sides of the lock, larger ships are towed through by amazing locomotives - each of which cost $2.3 million - on rack and pinion railways. Really big ships may have four locomotives on each side.

The second chamber of the Miraflores Locks has us rising, star-like, to a viewing platform. Mort's wife Lyn is there waving to us, as well as a few others from last night's party, and a clutch of photographers. Once out of that lock, we motor a short distance to the next set of locks, the Pedro Miguel Locks.

After negotiating them, we cast off from Falkor in order to go and drop off Jim Malcolm and Mort Deas. It's been great having them with us, and we're sorry to see them go. Jim has also given us a contact for someone in Jamaica who might help us. We have no idea at the time just how grateful we'll be for it.

The next section is the Culebra Cut, the narrowest part, crossing the Continental Divide. They've been widening this bit, and reducing the sharpness of the bends in order to allow two-way traffic for even the largest tankers - at the moment, northbound transits start in the morning, southbounds in the afternoon.

At Gamboa, we pass an interesting piece of working industrial heritage, the Titan. Painted a mean and moody black, it's the largest floating crane in the world, built in 1941 by Nazi Germany. We don't get the chance to go ashore and see, but apparently many of the components still have swastikas moulded in them. She was appropriated as war booty and spent many years at Long Beach in California, and was then refurbished in 1996 for her new role in Panama.

From here the cut opens out into Gatun Lake, a beautiful lake surrounded by trees, where all the fresh water for Panama City and Colon comes from. There's a fair breeze blowing across the lake, so it's quite bumpy. Once again it's wildlife spotter Steve who's first to spot a Cancun alligator on one of the banks. By the time we reach the other end of the lake, it transpires we've arrived an hour early. So we moor up to a buoy and brew a cup of tea. It's so hot, I'm half tempted to have a dip, but in the end I don't.

Then Falkor arrives, and we rope together once more, and head into the Gatun Locks. We go in first this time, ahead of Marion Dufresne, so I hop on board Falkor and go up onto the flybridge to gain a better view across the lock gates, over the second chamber, and down to the port of Cristobal below.

And so we complete our transit of the Panama Canal. Eighth wonder of the world or not, it's certainly been a full and interesting day, and we all agree the experience was much better than the Suez. If there's anything that sours the occasion for us, it's talking to the people on board Falkor and learning that they paid considerably less than we did for their transit. Clearly it's a case of knowing which agent to pick.

We pull into the marina at around 1600, and Alan decides that with the wind blowing at 30 knots from the east, it's too strong for us to head straight out - our original plan. So we'll spend the night here and set off tomorrow at first light, in the hope that conditions have improved.

Alan and Steve go to the bar while I write the day's update and email it. It takes a fair while, but eventually I get my beer reward at the end. Then we're joined by Khan, Osvaldo's associate, for a meal.

Back at the boat, I rinse off my Spirit of Cardiff T-shirt in fresh water from a tap on the pontoon, and hang it up to dry from one of the rails on the roof at the back of the cabin. It's destined to remain soaking wet for nearly the next week.

28
THE ULTIMATE LOW

I have just finished work after a long day, feeling tired and brain dead. The first thing I have done is to read your report. I now have an improved perspective on my own minor grumbles!
Website posting from Gill McGowan.

Thursday 27th June

WHY DID I ever allow myself to be lulled into the ridiculous notion that everything would be fine once we were through the Panama Canal, and more or less in 'home' waters? We're up and off just after first light into unbelievably rough head seas. Supposedly it's going to die off, but I don't believe it. Alan has been telling people we're going to be back in 15 days, but I think that's taking optimism to extremes. We won't even be in Gibraltar in two weeks, let alone back home. The weather for Cable and Wireless Adventurer was obviously a hell of a lot better four years ago. We'd hoped at least to take this leg from the Adventurer - whilst our start and finish ports are slightly different, the distances are pretty much the same. They did Colon to Kingston in around 28 hours, averaging nearly 19 knots. There's absolutely no chance of that for us. We seem to be closer to nine knots.

As the wind strength increases, the character of the waves changes. We've probably been in bigger seas - these waves are mere 20 footers - but driven by what we later learn to be up to 50 knots of wind, they're angry, with white foamy crests which break free and roll across the water. The first really big breaking wave is quite beautiful, awesome. I see what I think to be a white cloud coming into view at the windscreen. It's the breaking crest of the wave, and just underneath it is enough translucence in the water to see a spectacular deep blue, the kind of intense and vivid colour you see in a glacier. Terrifying power and breath-taking beauty all in one.

But the power with which the waves hit us sends water cascading over the roof. And that means loads of drips inside the cabin, uncomfortable for me, and extremely dodgy for computer use. After one big wave goes over the top, Alan asks: 'How's the T-shirt drying going?' My shirt is hanging out the back, and is now a good deal wetter than it was after I washed it last night.

But as we ride up this, and the thousands that follow, lurching painfully from side to side, we realise that this is no 12 hour tropical storm. This is the big depression we've been following - albeit third hand - which started in Newfoundland and which has now arrived in the Caribbean. Whilst we'd hoped to arrive in Jamaica today, it seems the best we can hope for at the moment is Monday.

We ride up most of the waves, but every so often we pound straight into one, either head on, or taking it on the beam. The tube around the bow quivers up and down like an enormous jelly, sending huge vibrations pulsating right through the boat. The wind is coming at us from the east, and it's pushing us sideways at two and a half knots. So at the moment, it looks as though it will be easier to let it take us to the west end of Jamaica, and then pass along the north coast to our refuelling stop at Port Antonio.

What's most depressing is that we set off on a relatively short hop, one that should be completed in under two days, and we could end up taking five. There's nothing we can do except plod on slowly at this pitiful speed. Morale has hit rock bottom once again, as we realise that our plans to get back across the Atlantic in the next couple of weeks have once more been set back. The consolation, so we're told, is that the passage between Jamaica and Florida should be clear. But I think I'll believe that one when I see it.

By midday, we've seen lots of pieces of flotsam and jetsam. We pass yards from what looks like a snapped off piece of a varnished oar. Later we see a broken wooden spar, possibly the remains of a mast, this time upright. The way it sits in the water with the waves moving around it indicates there's a lot of weight below the surface. Could there be a submerged boat beneath it? It would be tempting to investigate, but in these conditions, we could end up damaging the boat on the wreckage. We've not heard any coastguard report of a vessel in trouble, but it looks recent, so we keep our eyes skinned for signs of a life raft.

Friday 28th June

Today sees us struggling along at four and a half knots. It's not very encouraging news from Bertie, either. This depression could be here for days. The current estimate for Port Antonio is still sometime Monday. That's instead of today. I wonder if the red carpet treatment we've been promised will still be waiting for us.

The others seem very depressed, and have spent most of the day sleeping. It does seem easier for me today, although maybe it's just because I've kept myself busy. Maybe tomorrow it'll be my turn. I've spent today sitting in the navigation seat, as it's a good place to type on my Psion without the frequent drenchings from the ceiling. All the hatches are leaking, now. The only trouble is it does get really hot here. My usual seat at the back is a lot further down and out of the direct heat.

For me there's a little pause for reflection on hearing the sad news that John Entwistle (bass player with The Who) has died. I once played bass in a rock band which nearly, very nearly, hit the big time. Entwistle's unique style certainly influenced the way I played, and, I guess still does on the odd occasions now when my trusty Gibson Thunderbird comes out of its flight case. I could perhaps also reflect that had the Sex Pistols not come along when they did and queered the pitch for every genuine musician trying to make the grade, things might just have been a little different. Being a journalist has been fun, but I do sometimes wonder what it would have been like if one of those record companies back in 1977 had actually said: 'Yes'. I wouldn't be on this boat, for a start.

By evening meal time I'm feeling so horribly sticky I have a bucket bath while the boat is stopped, sitting on the back, and pouring buckets of water over myself. During the night we shut the boat down to no more than headway speed. We discuss whether we need to do watches, but all agree we should do them, given that we've had a few encounters with ships.

Saturday 29th June

In 24 hours we've travelled just 50 miles, and the storm shows no signs of letting up. Jamaica is still 350 miles away, and if the weather doesn't calm down, we can see a time in the not too distant future when the drinking water will have to be rationed. Although we're burning it even without moving, at the moment fuel isn't a major concern, as we took on quite a bit more than we needed in Panama.

Carpets, cushions and food items in the boat are wet. The hatches - two in the cabin roof, and one in the forward compartment - have been leaking. And although the sun's out and it's hot, we can't put anything outside to dry, because the water which goes over the roof and comes through the dodgy hatches also lands on the aft deck.

Despite all of this, today we're in pretty good spirits, considering everything. We know we can't change the weather, only go with it. So we occupy our time listening to music, reading and (some of us) writing. We can't wait to try out Steve's latest culinary creation. It's a variation on his very popular Spam, Spam, beans and Spam, but this one tantalisingly with just a little less Spam.

Standing outside, the wind tears at our T-shirts, filling them with air and causing them to balloon comically. Even knowing just how much it's impeding our progress, you can't help but look at the sea with a sense of wonder. Every so often there's a rushing sound like a jet as a breaking wave comes past us. It's incredible to think that wind can turn a normally flat sea into these agitated, angry waves.

There's a certain degree of timing involved in nipping outside to use the toilet bucket. Apart from the odd rogue wave, the waves come at us in a fairly regular pattern, so the trick is to try and time one's pit-stop to fall between the waves which crash right over the roof. I misjudge one rather badly, returning to the cabin dripping wet.

Today I receive a well-meaning email message which someone has posted on the website saying: 'God has you in the palm of his hand.' I read it out to Alan.

'More like he's got us by the balls!' he replies cynically.

None of us is remotely religious, so it's interesting that so many post messages on the Spirit of Cardiff website forum with references to God. Earlier on they'd allude to speed, but now, in the midst of our brutal treatment by the weather, we have many more outpourings of sentiment. I look upon it with a degree of pride - people have clearly felt sufficiently helpless, gripped by the misery in my updates, to offer these heartfelt pleas for our safety.

On a more practical note, what Alan is considering at the moment is Plan B, basically to go with the wind to the Cayman Islands, west of Jamaica, and not attempt to get to Jamaica at all. It would mean a longer passage round the western end of Cuba rather than the east, but at least it would keep us moving, and hopefully get us to the north of this big depression. But for now, we're just keeping that as an option, and continuing to make our way north. The ultimate frustration with all this is knowing that 100 miles ahead of us the wind is just eight knots, and in Florida, there's absolutely none at all.

Sunday 30th June

We're still doing around four knots. We try to go faster, but it's no use. We have water coming through all the hatches bigtime. Sebastian Junger's excellent book 'The Perfect Storm' describes in great detail the effects of breaking waves. These are the ones that are the most dangerous, and which do the most damage. We saw a lot in the North Pacific, but not so many as we're seeing now in the Caribbean. When you see a 20 foot wall of water coming at you, you're confident the boat will simply ride up it and slam down the other side. When you see a great white foaming crest on top of it, you know it's going to hit the boat hard.

The wave hits the bow first. The big tube at the front quivers with the impact, and for a second it feels as though the boat has come to a dead stop. Everything inside that isn't anchored in some way or braced for it lurches forwards. The fact that the tube buckles inward reduces some of the energy of the impact, but in the next instant, the well in the bow between the forward cabin and the tube is full of water. Less than a second later, and the wave collides with the windscreen. Suddenly everything looks green.

We've had sufficient big bangs to bend one of the windscreen wipers. As the water hits the windscreen, it carries on over the roof, cascading in a deluge on the aft deck. Were it not for the fact that we're also enduring extreme heat, we'd have the door on, which would keep the inevitable splatters of water from outside at bay. As it is, the hatches are closed (although they still leak badly) and the cabin feels hot and clammy, like a sauna. So the water from outside splashes through the open doorway onto the carpet inside, and the wetness migrates to everything else.

We've actually become used to sleeping on damp cushions, with wet towels pulled over us to lessen the shock of the drips from above. But nothing can lessen the amount of damage this storm is doing to us. Alan has hurt ribs and collar bone from colliding with the grab rails in the cabin. I've been revisited by the lower abdominal and back pains I've been suffering on and off since the passage to Kodiak. Steve says he's OK. In truth, we're all battered, bruised, and wishing we were somewhere else.

This constant pounding means that the boat is shipping more water than we'd expect. The hatch above the front cabin is leaking the worst, and over four days has completely filled the three forward floor lockers with water. So we stop the boat, and set to rescuing what can be saved from the lockers, and ditching what can't. Then we have to bail out the lockers, forming a human chain along the boat, ferrying the water using our toilet and washing-up buckets. It takes us over an hour, and in all, we reckon to have removed around 50 gallons of water.

With nearly a quarter of a ton of weight off the front, the boat handles slightly better, and we get an extra knot and a half out of her. But the fine presentation box which housed the very nice plate presented to us by Port Said Rotary Club in Egypt is ruined, along with a pile of other things, so it all goes over the side. It's such exhausting work, and we've lost so much headway whilst drifting, we don't even have our evening meal.

It's not as though we're in any more danger, but suddenly the stress of it all is too much for me. There have been many moments throughout this trip when I've been in real pain, and I've borne it with fortitude. But here is a moment where the pain is purely psychological. I'm nearly in tears, and I obviously look glum enough for it to be noticed. Steve sits down opposite me, gives me one of his broad, beaming smiles, slaps me on the leg and says: 'Don't worry, mate. We'll look after you.'

It's not an idle gesture. Steve is as hard as nails, but he'd do anything for you. He's recognised my distress and given me some reassurance with a warmth which raises my spirits. I couldn't possibly guess that ultimately the boot might end up on the other foot.

The boat's electronics appear to be under stress as well. We're greeted by regular beeping alarms to indicate that the GPS receiver has lost its fix. The boat is set to drive on a bearing, but more noticeable is the fast rate beep which indicates the autopilot has thrown a wobbler, and the boat starts driving around in circles. Alan reckons the navigation computer needs rebooting, but this isn't really the time or place to do that.

The frequent alarms and equipment taking unpaid leave are all down to the high level of moisture in the boat. Even things which haven't come in direct contact with sea water are wet because of the lack of ventilation in the cabin. It's so bad, we've even been getting electric shocks from the sodden carpet. The boat's electrics are in serious need of a good drying out, as indeed are we.

Monday 1st July

The wind has dropped marginally, and as daylight comes, we try to add a few extra knots to our speed. But we have to be mindful of damage to the boat. Water is gushing through the front hatch. Alan and Steve try to effect a temporary repair to seal it. We have to stop the boat, which then turns beam into the sea. They're standing in the well in the bow, struggling to tape a bin liner over the hatch, which if it wasn't so vital to our survival, would be downright comical.

From inside the cabin, you see brilliant sunshine. It's only when someone goes outside that you realise the strength of the wind, clawing at clothing, filling the plastic bag with air and threatening to turn it into a hang glider. While they're doing this, we're hit by one or two extra large rogue waves. Not just the normal jet sound of a passing breaking wave, as it approaches, one of them sounds like a 747 on take-off. It's a humbling experience. One of these waves could crush us like insects.

Even with its temporary seal, bailing-out sessions are now becoming part of the daily routine. Our estimated arrival in Jamaica now is Wednesday, a full six days after leaving Panama. It's ironic to think that this leg, around half the distance of our longest around the world from Salalah in Oman to Mangalore in India, is taking twice as long. Oh, for the calm of the Indian Ocean again!

In fact, we've had to warn the people meeting us in Jamaica to be prepared for the fact that we might be a bit whiffy when they greet us ashore. Because we haven't been making the speed, our onboard shower attachment has been inoperative, and we've only dared try a bucket bath when we've had a tea stop once or twice. The problem is that when you're sitting naked on the back of the boat when a large breaking wave crashes over it, you're dangerously exposed in more than one sense of the phrase!

Tuesday 2nd July

It starts out as yet another day of torture, but as it wears on, hope grows. We're getting closer to Jamaica, and although the seas are still big, we can do better by going north and then following the coast rather than just heading for the eastern tip. Two sides of a triangle could possibly turn out to be quicker than one.

It works well, and we start to pick up speed as the wind drops. Although we're in a head sea, we're making around 16 knots. It even gets relatively comfortable when we nip in behind a ship heading for Kingston, taking shelter for a while in her wash. Then we turn the corner. The sun's starting to go down. Now we're in a following sea, and at one point, we manage to get to almost 25 knots. That's quite a change from the dismal four we've been doing for days.

We pass some impressive looking white villas along the coast just before Port Antonio, not realising that's where we're going to be staying tomorrow night. By the time we arrive at Port Antonio, it's dark, and we have trouble locating the marina. Eventually we make it in, and Tracy Prows, the American manager greets us as we stumble ashore, relieved finally to have made it. It's taken us five and a half days to do what we should have done in a day and a half. We've travelled from Panama to Jamaica at little more than walking speed. We're on our last litre of drinking water, we're suffering from various injuries through being thrown about in the cabin, and we can't even stand up straight without feeling wobbly.

We take a quick shower, change our clothes, then go into the bar for a few beers and something to eat. The people in the bar are all watching Westerns on TV. Then we take a short walk into town, winding up at a little bar where several curious locals are hitting on us, including one chap who'd earlier tried to convince us his father owned the marina. Yeah, right. Or as they say in Jamaica: 'Yeah, mon.'

29
FROM THE RIDICULOUS TO THE SUBLIME

Just want you to know that I have followed every day of your epic journey and you have added a treasured place in my life. Your courage, determination, focus and sense of humour have given me great pleasure along every leg of your adventure. While you may need to return to 'work' when you arrive home, you have given so many of us a lasting new view of the human spirit.
Website posting from Ken House.

Wednesday 3rd July
WE STRIP EVERYTHING out of the cabin, carpets included, and hang it out to dry, leaving the boat looking rather like a room waiting for the decorators. Alan and I have chopped-up swordfish with yam and banana for breakfast, while Steve does the more traditional bacon and eggs. In fact they only have two eggs, so he gets them both. The tea is absolutely brilliant, and they serve it with condensed milk. Yummy. I end up eating that which doesn't get into my tea.

Back at the boat, and I get down to some writing, while Alan and Steve carry on with the boat. The quarantine man is the first official to arrive. He ticks off Alan for not flying a Q flag (which means you are available for inspection). Then he steps aboard.

'Do you have any food?'
'No.'
'But you don't have anything on board...?'
'No.'
He leaves, utterly perplexed.

I try to phone Suzanne Levy, who manages the Trident Villas and Hotel, but she's not there. We've been promised free accommodation, which, given the boat's current state, takes on a new importance. She's away till Friday, they say, and her mobile doesn't seem to work. Maybe I've got the number wrong.

Later on Lesley Halliwell arrives with a couple of friends. Her husband Gareth works for Red Stripe brewers Guinness in Jamaica. They've brought a large Welsh flag and have some photos of us taken by local freelance everything Everard Owen. He just takes the photographs on point-and-shoot snap cameras. The local TV station uses just a Video 8 camera, but at least the microphone (with Everard doing the interviewing) has a station badge on it. Then we all retire to the relative coolness of the bar for a few Red Stripes and some lunch.

Afterwards, they take me off to the Trident Villas and Hotel, just a short drive away, where I check in to our villa. The arrangements were fine, after all. Lesley has a welcome drink with me while the others go off to get the Red Stripe supplies, enough to see us through the next evening or so.

As I'm settling in, there's a knock at the door. Earl Levy, the owner of the hotel, introduces himself. Earl is an architect by profession, and the villas and castle in the grounds here were all designed by him. It seems he's been well connected for most of his life - he was even invited to Winston Churchill's funeral.

Thursday 4th July

I'm at work all day, updating my video log. Alan and Steve are sorting out the many problems with the boat, and laying in supplies for the next leg to Fort Lauderdale. Earl has very kindly agreed to throw a small reception early evening for us, so we can meet a few of his friends and colleagues.

By 1730 Earl is wondering where everyone is. One or two turn up around half an hour later, and then along come Steve and Alan. They appear to have been attacked by a mad axeman, the haircuts they treated themselves to inflicted by someone who clearly shouldn't have been left in charge of sharp objects. The style is more mauled than close-cropped, with longer wispy bits poking through, rather like the guard hairs on some exotic fur coat. Having mine done in Panama was definitely a good move.

Later the guests start to arrive, including Pat Flynn, widow of movie legend Errol. I have quite a chat with her, and ask her about

Navy Island, the beautiful island in Port Antonio harbour where she used to live when Errol was alive. It transpires they didn't live on the island as such, but on a boat. 'The island was our garden,' she says.

Once the party winds up, we head off to a little restaurant nearby called Anna Bananas. All fishy stuff. The young waitress finds it amusing when I order steamed fish. Must be the way I say it, I suppose.

Friday 5th July

Apparently the local tourism boss went with Everard the photographer to the boat at around 0600 this morning, and there was a slight amount of consternation when we didn't turn up. But we're not sure how they decided that was when we were leaving. In a laid-back culture such as you find in Jamaica, one might expect the opposite, for people to arrive late!

After breakfast, we wander with Earl along a little winding path to the chapel, and then the castle - not a true castle, but a large house built in a vaguely manorial style, with one or two quirks, such as the moulded crocodiles guarding the doorway, made for him by the special effects man from the movie 'Jaws'. The castle was built originally as Earl's own house away from the one he has in Kingston, but these days it's part of Trident, and anyone who can afford it rents it out for a mere $6,000 a day. The rooms are all vast and elegantly furnished with antique pieces, so the place is rather like a stately home. Inside the library there's a signed photo of Tom Cruise, dating back to 1988.

Then he drives us down to the boat, signs it with a felt pen, and bids us farewell. We still have a few things to do, including formalities with customs and immigration. The tourism lady comes along and presents Alan with a cruising guide to Jamaica, making a speech and looking outward as though there are rather more people than the sole onlooker actually in attendance.

We have a spot of lunch - I play safe with a burger again, while Alan has chicken. This proves to be a mistake, as he chucks it all up later. We've had quite a few upset stomachs along the way, and it could just be that it's all too easy to have an adverse reaction to some foods having become used to the simple and restricted diet on board.

The breezes are pretty stiff, but supposed to die down mid-afternoon, so we delay departure by taking a little wander into the market, where we're accosted by everyone, all commenting on our Red Stripe T-shirts.

One chap who carves things including little pipes for smoking ganja shows us how to do a Jamaican greeting with fists - peace, love, unity, and then with thumbs, respect. Yeah, mon - it's great. The Jamaicans have a very laid-back attitude to life.

Back at the boat, there's no one to whom we can wave goodbye, so we just untie and go, past Navy Island. Once we start off properly, we get a good speed up, around 15 knots.

Saturday 6th July

It's very dark during my first watch from midnight to two. There are one or two fishing boats visible as we approach the Cuban coastline, and the sea is bumpy, but we're making around 14 knots.

About half an hour before I hand over to Steve I check the chart plotter. I remove the seat cushion which has been sitting on top of it and notice we're off course, or at least that's what I think. We're heading for land, to the left of a waypoint (a cross on the chart plotter) which I assume to be the first of several to take us around the east tip of Cuba.

I make some adjustments using the plus one button, putting on an extra 10° in all. We're not far from the next waypoint, and the way our slightly off position lines up with the next waypoint along looks fine to me.

Then when Steve takes over, he says: 'We're off course.' Alan then goes to look and says to me: 'Did you move the cursor?' I replied that I did, after which there were dark mutterings about how I shouldn't have touched it.

Having told me that he always sets the boat to run on a bearing rather than using the GPS to navigate, he's set it to navigate to the cursor position without announcing the fact. It transpires that what I thought was a waypoint we were navigating to was something we actually wanted to avoid, and that we were supposed to be heading directly for the eastern tip of Cuba.

The irony of it all is the way the boat probably went off course in the first place. At night, the light emitted by the chart plotter is blinding, and plays havoc with your night vision, so shielding it off with something is always a good idea. One of the small seat cushions covers it perfectly, resting on the grab rail just underneath. But putting a cushion over the chart plotter and then sticking his feet on it could quite likely have moved the cursor over to the left, the direction we were off course. I rest my case, m'lud.

'I can't make out these lights ahead,' says Steve later. Alan takes a look from outside, and confirms that we are in fact on a collision course with the moon. Two days of rest in Jamaica clearly wasn't enough.

My second watch from 0600 is in daylight. I've not slept well during my second four hours. The bunk on the right hand side always hurts my back, and there are the delights of Alan's phone calls to Bertie and Nadia piercing the silence, although I do at least get an idea of the forecast when I hear Alan's voice take a funereal tone. The sky is overcast to start with, which isn't bad, because it makes for a cooler start to the day.

We have a brief period of bumpy seas as we pass through a squall, which doesn't last more than around half an hour. Apparently we'll get another one in about 100 miles. In fact it doesn't come until well after dark, as we're making our way along the Great Bahama Bank.

I discover today that my bank balance is just £50 short of my £3,000 overdraft limit. Going without any income for three months after having borrowed a substantial sum and arranged a large overdraft to help fund the trip has left me in rather a financial pickle. In the meantime, Alan tells me that the Cardiff Marketing money will be available once we've arrived at Fort Lauderdale, so I'm hopeful that some of that will be going into my bank (maybe).

Tea tonight is lots of instant mash and Spam. It fills a gap, but that's about it. I end up feeling hungry later. As darkness falls we have to be a bit more on our toes, as we're now in a shipping lane.

The second squall of the day finally arrives. It's bumpy and the draught coming in through the back of the cabin is noticeably colder, and laced with spray. I end up sleeping with my arms inside my rather voluminous Red Stripe T-shirt, and my towel pulled over my head. Fortunately the storm doesn't last too long.

Sunday 7th July

My first shift from midnight to two is in darkness, with no horizon, something I always find a little off-putting. Alan has set us on a course at the very edge of the main channel between Cuba and the Bahamas, with coral reefs off to our right. So the ships that do appear, including one brightly lit cruise liner, are all around four miles off on the port side. To starboard, the clouds are doing a neon tube display, lightning flashing every so often.

There's one heart-stopping moment when something large and white appears in front. We're on top of it before I can do anything. I open my mouth as though to cry out, but nothing comes out. Fortunately, there's no large thump, so I assume we haven't run down a boatload of Cuban refugees.

When it comes to changing the course to the next marker, I move the cursor to the new position. But our course stays the same. So this time I change course manually, adding degrees 10 at a time until the line projected from the front of the boat on the chart plotter lines up with the next waypoint. We're not going off course this time!

When it's time to do my 0600 till 0800 shift, Alan tells me Steve has been shouting out during the night having nightmares. Since I didn't hear it, I can at least assume I got some sleep.

As we approach US territory once more, the entertainment is going to be whether we can get away with the visa situation. Strangely, whilst we were given a six month cruising permit, we only had 30 day visas from Kodiak, and they expired a week ago. We're just going to play dumb and show the cruising permit if asked. We certainly don't intend to fork out another $195 each for just two more short stops.

The skyscrapers of Miami appear - a long line of them along the shore. I can't say it looks particularly attractive. At least some waterfront city downtown areas look quite nice and relatively compact. This is all strung out in a long line for miles up the coast.

As we come into Fort Lauderdale, we pass Port Everglades. Tied up is the P&O Princess Cruises liner Grand Princess, one of the largest cruise ships in the world. It's rather an ugly looking brute, too, with what seems to be a large handle at the stern. I'm told this is where the night club is, accessed by a blue neon-lit stairway. It's a reminder that from Florida, cruise ships sail around the Caribbean, and it's yet another irony that we've taken such a beating from the world's most popular cruising area.

CONFRONTING POSEIDON

Fort Lauderdale has a sort of modern Venice look about it, a cliché no doubt, but that's what it is - waterways used like roads. Every house with its own waterfront, lots of expensive boats. We refuel first of all, then bring the boat around to the other side of the marina. That's when Andy Dent and his wife Tess plus four year-old son Daniel arrive. Andy's mother Norma lives in Wales, and had seen the boat in Cardiff Bay the day before we set off. Andy lives in Fort Lauderdale, so she'd emailed him and we got in touch - a fine example of the power of the internet. We head off to find some shops, then off for lunch.

Daniel seems very shy, but by the time we're near the end of the afternoon, he's a little more forthcoming. Whilst we're in Wal-Mart, Andy phones his mother, then passes the phone over to me so I can say a few words to her.

It's a shame, but once we arrive back at the boat just after six, we have to say goodbye. We've been invited to the Lauderdale Yacht Club by the Commodore, and Andy and his wife aren't invited, which seems a trifle mean. Anyway, a few of the members climb aboard, and we bring the boat round to the yacht club, spending time chatting to people on the quayside.

Then we're ushered inside, where we discover there's a table set for us, and they've printed up wodges of stuff from the website. I sit next to John Douglas, the Commodore of the club. It was through him and his Australian wife Shirley having a house in Port Antonio and knowing the Levys that the connection came about. John tells me that it was the LYC that brought the Whitbread Round the World yacht race to the USA, which must have been a real coup.

Despite the fact that we have a nice meal, and we're with people who're very interested in what we're doing, I really don't want to be here. I know that leaving earlier wouldn't make a difference, as we'll still arrive in Wilmington before the marina opens for business. But it's just one of those feelings.

Shirley Douglas fills me in on the gossip, and tells me that Pat Flynn's house in Port Antonio is in around the same unfinished state it was in when Errol died. No windows or doors. Pat now has the property up for sale, a sizeable estate, but apparently she's asking too much for it. I wonder why she didn't try and make more money earlier - a book about her life with Errol, perhaps.

We leave at around 2200, and head off out past Port Everglades. Grand Princess has gone, but there's another ship coming in. Once out of the harbour, we're under way again.

Monday 8th July

My first watch sees me nearly mowing down a sailing yacht. We're in pitch darkness, and conscious of the fact that we have no radar - it's suffering from a delayed reaction to the pounding it received in the Caribbean - my eyes are skinned for anything. I see a faint glow on the horizon. As we get closer, and it takes ages, I see a white light and a red. I assume that as it isn't coming closer to our course, he's roughly parallel, and we're simply overtaking. But we get pretty close - maybe 100 feet or less. As we go past, the red light suddenly turns green. I can't believe what's going on. Eventually I realise that it must have been a yacht at anchor, and as we went past, our wash turned him round. Must have been fun for whoever was aboard - presumably expecting a quiet night. The storm which comes afterwards is pretty intense, the thunder so loud the whole boat vibrates.

With daylight, we see there are big patches of cloud about, but most of the time it's hot and sunny. We're making a steady 18 knots today. Hopefully we should be in Wilmington in the early hours of Tuesday morning.

Poor Steve is not at all well today. He's throwing up and suffering from diarrhoea. We speculate that it's a possible reaction to the crisps and HP sauce sandwich he made earlier. I guess something must have gone off. It's surprising we haven't had more such problems given the heat and our lack of refrigeration for food items. All we can do is use it or chuck it.

Tuesday 9th July

I do a watch from 2230 to 0030. I turn in, and wake up at around 0330, when we arrive at the timing point for Wilmington. Only problem is that we can't see where to go. The safe water marker and one buoy are all we can find, which explains how Alan manages to park the boat in the mud at one point. Rather than risk running aground again, we drift offshore till daybreak.

Alan asks Steve to go on watch, but I volunteer. There's a short exchange of words between Alan and Steve. Alan says he's been on watch for six hours and Steve has been sleeping all day. Steve points out the reason for that is that he's been ill. Anyway, I end up going on watch. Alan says to wake him in an hour, but I decide to do two. You could put all this down to an apparent intolerance to other people's weaknesses on Alan's part - on the other side, we're all suffering from stress, and the fact is that trying to run the boat with a crew of two is practically impossible. It's hard enough with three.

By the time it's daylight, I crash out. I'm really tired, and I'm still asleep after we arrive in the Cape Fear Yacht Center and people start turning up to see us. I wake up and virtually immediately have to do an interview with a young lady from the local newspaper.

Supporter Neil Elam arrives, and we go off in his car to grab some breakfast. Once again I end up with my favourite comfort food - cheese omelette. Back at the boat, the next media people to arrive are Gavin Williams and Mark Simpson from WWAY Wilmington Channel 3 News. They shoot some footage, interviewing everybody. Then they ask if they can have some of our footage to add a little extra colour. It's not a problem, but we don't have the means to transfer it to Mark's camera, so I take a ride with them into Wilmington to their studios.

Unfortunately their cameras and machines aren't compatible with my camera, even though we use the same cassette (I guess because I'm shooting the European PAL format, and they use NTSC, the American TV standard). Neither do they have any firewire connectors, which would have been an easy way around the problem. In the end, they grab the footage by playing back the clips on my camcorder, and filming the LCD screen. How low-tech can you get? Before we go, I'm taken to the studio where the programme goes out - the desk where the news anchor presents the programme, and the weather corner. I get Gavin to take a photograph of me sitting at the news desk.

Back at the boat, Gavin shoots a teaser for the piece, which is going to run on their six o'clock news. They're affiliates to ABC, so the chances are it will go nationwide, but he says it will also be offered to CNN. We're headline news yet again.

Once they're gone, I get the writing out of the way, then wander off in search of a shower. I'm finished by 1530, and as I emerge from the swimming pool changing room, Neil is driving off. I say goodbye to him, and find Alan and Steve back at the boat with the refuelling under way.

We're off, taking our official departure as 1615 local. As we make our way out, I can see the problem we had coming in. The sea is boiling like a cauldron. The sand shoals shift with every tide, and it can be a real problem. On land, it looks much nicer - beautiful sand dunes, and lots of people enjoying the beach. So now we're heading off towards Canada. Hopefully we'll be there in two and a half to three days. All we need now is good weather for the next two and a half weeks...

Wednesday 10th July

We're in quite a following sea today, the flags on the roof flying forwards, the red ensign at the back hanging limply. My second watch turns into a marathon four hour shift. Not that I mind letting the others have a lie in, but I do have to concentrate on the throttle a bit more. It all goes horribly wrong at one point, though, when I don't knock it back in time, and the resulting wave goes right over the roof, cascading over Alan. Yet another rude awakening. I say I'm sorry I got it wrong, which I bet is more than Jan would have done. He probably would have made some joke about it.

The highlight of that watch is undoubtedly the school of dolphins which crosses the bow, all of them jumping right out of the water.

Our milk isn't lasting long. Apparently we couldn't get any UHT longlife milk in Wilmington, and the bottle opened this morning has lumps of cheese floating in it by this afternoon. Either it's the heat, or the constant agitation, turning it to butter.

I've hurt my back again, doing nothing more than bending over to get one of my electrical chargers out. I take a couple of painkillers, and it takes the edge off. Then I stretch out on the floor, which seems to help, too. It still hurts, but there's not the same level of weakness.

It's getting chilly, so for the first time in three weeks, I get my lightweight sleeping bag out. It feels comfortable, but by now the following sea we've had all day has gone, to be replaced by a head sea, particularly uncomfortable given the fragile state of my back.

CONFRONTING POSEIDON

Thursday 11th July

My first watch is in the dark, from midnight till 0200. My back's in a lot of pain again, so I end up standing up, then lying down in the gangway every now and then and stretching out, plus doing a yoga knee lift. It helps a little, but only inasmuch as it alleviates the pain while I'm actually doing it. I just can't find a comfortable position.

I sleep for the first two hours of my second sleep shift, more out of exhaustion, I think, as I get no sleep at all in the first. But I remember hearing Steve and Alan change over, and that's it. No more sleep after that, and the sea's very bumpy and uncomfortable.

As daylight comes, the sea flattens down, and after breakfast we're motoring along at 20 knots. We're making good progress - we'll be in Halifax tomorrow morning, and the local Raymarine dealers are primed to come and replace our radar, which packed up after the heavy onslaught of sea in the Caribbean. It really does seem like we're close to home now. Under 3,000 miles to Gibraltar once we get there.

It's definitely getting chillier. Apart from using my sleeping bag today, I end up going from 'commando' use of the shorts to underpants underneath, and zipping the legs back on. And I'm wearing my fleece jacket for the first time in ages. It seems rather smelly when I first put it on, but I became used to it fairly quickly. If nothing else, the top half of the trousers need a good wash, as they do smell a bit rancid. Tomorrow.

Steve starts feeding biscuits to some birds. They don't look like seabirds - small black and white things flitting about, just dipping their feet in the water, then flying off again. What's more scary, as a large container ship comes up behind us during our tea stop, is when he says he can hear music. When we circumnavigated the British Isles as a three-man crew in June 2000, we all suffered serious sleep deprivation, and one of the many effects of that was hallucinations, and hearing things - disembodied music coming from the VHF radio. But this time it's only Steve.

We go to bed, but I'm unable to sleep. Even in the sleeping bag it's cold, and my back is hurting.

Friday 12th July

Alan has to paddle in water swilling about the dive platform to cut off a rope which has become attached to the prop. He describes the intense cold of the water on his feet as: 'Like being burned.'

During my first watch, I get a few odd moments with lights. Why do they always head straight for me? I see white lights and a red and green heading straight for me. I bear off 10 to the right, but still it keeps coming. Steve gets up for a pee, so I ask him. He reckons it's a fishing boat - as it gets closer, he seems to bear off as well. Panic over. The next one is visible for ages before it passes, a big cruise liner, lit up like a Christmas tree. As it passes, I think of all the people on board, tucked up in their warm beds in nice cabins, and then reflect on the misery of my conditions. It's always the night watches when I get lost in my own thoughts that things seem really bad.

Today I'm preoccupied with the state of my back. I can't get comfortable with it, and the only way I can sit relatively pain-free is right on the edge of a seat facing sideways. Sitting and facing forwards is excruciating on the hard landings.

We arrive in Halifax harbour in the morning. The Royal Nova Scotia Yacht Squadron (RNSYS) is a nice yacht club, they say the oldest in North America. The boat is fuelled up, and one of the young lads there sorts out an emergency appointment for me with physiotherapist Linda Langley. I take a taxi into town, and when I arrive, I apologise in advance for if she finds me rather smelly. Linda laughs and says she's used to it herself, as she comes from a boating family. It transpires that what I'm suffering from is not a slipped disc, but it's muscular. Having caused some damage to my back, I've been overcompensating, which makes it worse.

She does a bit of massage on it, stretches me, and leaves me hooked up to some electrodes for quarter of an hour. At the end, she offers me a lift back to the boat. As we arrive, Hugh Vincent is sitting there. This is the chap that a couple we met in Panama wanted us to pass on a gift to. And it so happens that Linda knows him, as their boats are next door neighbours.

The man from the radar distributor is here with our new radar. The trouble is it's not working. Eventually they decide the wiring must be damaged. So we go off into the RNSYS for lunch. I have haddock and chips, lounging about and writing afterwards while the others go shopping for supplies for the next leg.

I wander off to rinse out my zipoff trousers and underpants, and when I get back, Alan and Steve have returned. They're having a go at rewiring the radar, so the replacement hasn't been in vain.

Later Hugh comes by to time us off - 1615 local. We leave the harbour, past a beautiful green area with a stone cross - the memorial to the Titanic victims, many of whom were brought to Halifax and buried in the cemetery. We're making good speed straight away.

Saturday 13th July

My first sleep from 2100 till 0100 isn't. Nothing to do with my back, which is feeling considerably better after treatment, but I have excruciating indigestion pains under my ribs. I try massaging my abdomen to make it go away. In the end I take a couple of painkillers. By the time I come on watch it's gone, but when Alan asks how I slept, and I tell him I've had severe indigestion, he says that both he and Steve have had it as well. The only common thing we ate at lunch in Halifax yesterday was the bread rolls.

Alan messes about with the fuel pump under the starboard rear seat. It's packed up yet again, so he ends up taking a fuel feed from one of the side tanks to keep the main tank topped up.

It's fresh up in these parts, and I'm wearing my dodgy fleece hat once more. Turned inside out, it has a serious 'wally' factor, but there's method in my madness. The seams are rather uncomfortable with the hat worn the proper way round.

The tubes around the edge of the boat are looking a bit flaccid at the moment, with that wobbly wrinkled look that balloons assume about two weeks after Christmas.

'I think we might need to pump them up before we set off tomorrow,' says Alan. Of course it's all down to the drop in air temperature. In fact we don't wait that long. We end up pumping them up straight away as we're bashing into the waves a bit. Of course, by the time we get to the Azores, we'll have to let air out again. But they are our lifeline. Without them, there are many occasions during this trip where the boat would simply have turned over and sunk.

I've also discarded my T-shirt for the thermal top which I thought I wouldn't need again. It smells decidedly musty, so I've sprayed it liberally with aerosol deodorant. Then put on my Spirit of Cardiff sweatshirt, and fleece on top. It's a bit of a mix of fabric technologies, but hopefully the net result will be sufficient warmth for the cool climes of Newfoundland.

But as we come in to St John's at around 2130 in the evening, I get the feeling that it's actually a good deal warmer. It's confirmed when our staunch supporter Egbert Walters greets us on the quayside, dressed in T-shirt, shorts and sandals.

He whisks us up to the Quality Inn so we can dump our stuff in the conference room that they've given us. Basically it was just so we can use the bathroom for a wash and brush up during our brief refuelling stop, but now we're here for the night - we can't get any fuel until the morning - we might as well doss on the floor.

Egbert drops us off in town. There are lots of lively bars and clubs. We go into an Irish bar and have some Guinness, along with a steak and kidney pie. Then we wander off to see what else there is, but it seems with a lot of them you have to pay to get in. Eventually we go into a small bar. There's a guitarist and bassist playing here, and I chat with the bass player until he asks me to do a couple of numbers. He has a Yamaha five string bass, very nice.

Sunday 14th July

It's a beautiful morning in St John's. The sun is out, and Edgar has come down to the harbour to see us off. He's delayed going away on vacation with his kayak to help sort out our belated refuelling and reprovisioning stop. He's delighted to hear we didn't get into too much trouble last night, and, after hearing the number of pints of Guinness we consumed, amazed to see that none of us is suffering from a hangover.

In fact the only item of pressing urgency comes as we're still clearing the harbour, when Steve announces he can't wait to use the bucket. He's outside sitting on it as we pass the harbour entrance, with scores of surprised and bemused tourists looking on.

As we leave St John's on the mid-ocean leg of our Atlantic crossing, the weather is a good deal more promising than it was last year, when everybody thought us insane for leaving the harbour. There was the possibility that we might have had a depression to contend with some time in the next 24 hours or so, but even that has had the good grace to move out of our way.

Now we have just one more refuelling stop - Horta, 1,200 miles away in the Azores. We should get there in around three to three and half days, and then we'll be looking at the final 1,000 miles to take us back to Gibraltar. The finish to our circumnavigation of the world is in sight.

30
THE LONGEST DAY

We don't consider it a failure but a massively courageous success in achieving what is, after all's said and done, a truly historic voyage.
Website posting from Dave 'POP' Davies.

Through your example, every student following your voyage, every armchair adventurer, every corporate sponsor, every human being can see your willingness to put friendship and loyalty above records as the essential message of your voyage. And certainly, no person should put to sea unless they are physically and emotionally ready. In a time like ours we need these examples of clear thinking, made on the basis of the heart.
Website posting from Bryan Peterson.

Monday 15th July

IT'S MID-MORNING, and we've not long had our belated breakfast stop when Steve takes the navigator's seat, then starts complaining of chest pains, tightness, and being unable to breathe. He goes outside and with an awful gurgling belch, pukes up. Then he's back in the cabin - his eyes glazed and staring, his face gripped with pain as each new wave hits him, tightening across his chest.

'I can't feel my fingers,' he says, staring at his left hand as though it has suddenly became an alien attachment to his body, and with further bouts of pain: 'Go away, you bastard.' Steve is a tough nut, and there is no way this is just another attack of indigestion. He's in serious trouble.

'Ooohh,' he gasps, 'that was a big one.' Although his face retains its colour - no ashen-ness or blue lips, the tingling numbness down his left arm is to us the give-away.

'Steve,' says Alan in a matter-of-fact way, 'I think you're having a heart attack.'

'F*** off, Al,' replies Steve through gritted teeth.

All we can do is make him comfortable. Cover him up with a sleeping bag, give him some pain killers. Put a reassuring hand on his shoulder when he's in the worst pain. I'm deeply worried for him. I'm not sure what's likely to happen, but if it was the worst, he should at least have a friendly face in front of him.

Alan gets on the satphone.

'Nadia, I need the telephone number for the Canadian Coastguard urgently.'

Her natural reaction is to ask what's going on, but Alan says he'll tell her later. The important thing is that telephone number. Within minutes she's come back with it, and Alan is talking to the Coastguard station in St John's. They patch him through to a doctor, and after describing the symptoms, Alan is left in no doubt that this is a full scale emergency. Steve's life is in danger, and he needs to be evacuated as quickly as possible. Very quickly a plan is put into action.

'I'm turning back for St John's,' Alan tells me. 'You realise what that means?'

I nod my head. I don't have to say a word. Whatever happens from now on, our fuel situation commits us to returning to St John's. Even if Steve were taken off by a passing ship in the next few hours, we would already have gone over-budget on fuel to be able to continue to Horta.

The problem for the Canadian Search and Rescue people is that 320 miles out in the Atlantic, almost a third of the way into the passage from St John's to Horta, we're too far offshore to be rescued. The C113 Labrador helicopters operated by 103 Search and Rescue Squadron at Gander can't come that far, and they don't have in-flight refuelling.

The unmoving bright light I saw throughout my first watch last night was the Hibernia oil platform. The plan is for a helicopter to come out from Gander to St John's, refuel there, fly out to the rig, refuel again and then come on to us. But we have to close the gap in the meantime. We need to make up about 100 miles. In really good conditions, we could knock that off in under five hours, but what we have is anything but. It's going to take a good six or seven, by which time it could possibly be too late.

Steve has moments when he appears not to be in pain, and is fairly calm. Then he's wracked with it again, and his eyes glaze over with a reddish mist. I can't begin to imagine what kind of nightmare this must be for him. So many times in the past when we've wished we could just snap our fingers and end the misery and discomfort. At home, we don't give a second thought to the fact that in an emergency, an ambulance is no more than 30 minutes away. But now the chips really are down. We have to get Steve out of this and into a hospital as quickly as possible. But it could still be many hours.

I haven't even thought about what it's going to be like with just Alan and me bringing the boat back in on our own. As usual in moments of crisis, Alan comes up with an amusing quip, even if the humour is as dark as you could possibly imagine.

'Steve, if you snuff it, can I have your Rolex?'

The exact reply doesn't bear repetition, but suffice to say Steve tells Alan in no uncertain terms that his watch is staying where it is. When he's not crashed out on the bunk, Steve staggers outside to use the bucket.

'I can't stop pissing,' he says. It's odd, since he's had virtually no water other than that with which to take the painkillers, and, mindful of his being carted off to hospital, and possible surgery, we've given him nothing to eat. We learn later that frequent urination is a classic symptom of heart attacks.

At 1400 we get a call from Neville at Search and Rescue to say the helicopter is on its way from Gander, refuelling at St John's and the oil platform before coming to us. They should be with us in three to four hours. In the meantime, the worst of Steve's crushing pains have receded, although his fingers still feel numb and tingly. He's been drifting in and out of consciousness, and his blood pressure must have gone down again, as his eyes are no longer glazed and bloodshot. But we have no idea what damage has been done to his heart, or whether another severe attack is imminent.

Two hours later, Neville calls again. It's still going to be another three to four hours, which means it could be cutting it fine with the daylight. Alan is driving the boat as hard as he can for the conditions - like a man possessed. We're in a nasty following sea, the kind which wrecks windscreens. Even throttled back to virtually nothing we're being tipped up at the back and pushed along at alarming speeds. I'm not sure what to worry about the most - the possibility that Steve might die, or that we all might.

The rendezvous point we're heading for is ultimately some distance out of our way as far as getting back to St John's is concerned, but I guess we have to make do with whatever cards we're dealt now. The idea is to cut the helicopter's return journey so it doesn't need to go back to the oil platform to refuel.

We get a final call at around 1800 from Neville to say the helicopter will be with us in an hour and thirty minutes.

'OK,' says Alan, 'we'll keep our eyes and ears open.'

We zip Steve into his bright yellow Gore-Tex survival suit. He's more coherent now, and even manages a quick quip - 'Does my hair look all right?' - as I film Alan putting his lifejacket on.

By the time we get our first contact from the Search and Rescue boys, it's early evening. The sea has calmed down considerably, and the sun is setting with a gloriously rosy glow. Its peaceful serenity seems a far cry from the turmoil that's brought us here. We've been spotted by Rescue Three-Two-Eight, a C130 Hercules, sent from Halifax. Their job is to locate us, guide the helicopter in, and then circle above to oversee the operation and to maintain contact with the Coastguard. In the meantime, they have some instructions which we have to follow to the letter.

'Please make the following preparations as soon as you can. Remove any possible obstructions such as mast or antennas, loose objects or equipment. Leave the patient in a warm and dry area as much as you can. When the helicopter arrives, slow to your minimum steerage speed and steer into wind. I repeat - when the helicopter arrives, slow to your minimum steerage speed and steer into wind. If you have a radar, please turn it off. Rescue technicians will be lowered to your vessel. Do not assist - I repeat - do not assist unless you're requested. All unnecessary personnel out of the way. Do not under any circumstances connect the line from the helicopter to your vessel, and ensure the patient has a passport, visa and medical records with him when he's being hoisted. How copy, over?'

'I copied all of that,' replies Alan. 'I'll wait for you to advise when to go into wind. Over.'

Before we know it, I can see the Hercules circling above us. It's strangely ironic that after a day of foul conditions, the evening has turned out so beautiful. Not that we're complaining. What happens next would be infinitely more difficult in heavy seas.

So Alan sets about removing the obstructions. Our flag-pole is unbolted from the stern, GPS antenna unscrewed, radio antenna laid flat, buckets brought inside into the front cabin. Our aft deck is going to be a pretty small target to hit for someone dangling on the end of a line, so we have to make sure he doesn't injure himself. The next voice we hear on the radio prompts a smile amongst all of us. It's in a strong French accent.

'Zis is Rescue Seven-One, the Labrador 'elicopteur.'

He instructs us to turn into the wind and reduce our speed. We can see the large yellow helicopter with twin rotors and red floats astern of us off our port beam, where he seems to be holding off for quite some time. Then gradually he moves in. I guess he's making sure he's matching our speed - about six knots - and checking our stability once we start to get pushed along by his downdraught.

Steve is obviously feeling a bit better now, and because he feels better, he has a slight pang of guilt.

'Almost seems a waste of time now, doesn't it?' he says. But we know it isn't.

The Labrador closes in on us, low enough for its powerful downdraught to flatten the waves behind us in a blizzard of spray. Closer and closer, until we're virtually looking straight up at them, deafened by the heavy beating noise of the rotors.

One man comes out on a line. He's lowered to within a few feet of the surface while the helicopter is still slightly behind and to one side of us, then the Labrador moves in, guided by hand signals from the man on the line. Before we know it he's landed somewhat inelegantly on the engine box cover. He's in a bright red one-piece survival suit, with Day-Glo yellow and orange reflective stripes on the arms, and a bone-dome helmet with darkened sun visor.

Then he's followed by another guy with a large pack of medical equipment. This is the paramedic. He comes into the cabin and takes a brief look at Steve. At this stage he thinks there's a possibility Steve may have suffered a stroke rather than a heart attack. Either way we did all the right things, and he's going to the right place now.

'See you tomorrow, mate,' says Alan as Steve is strapped to the paramedic. Before we know it, he's being hoisted off the deck and up into the Labrador. It's 1930, nine hours after the initial attack. Then the other guy is winched off, doing a rather impressive jump up in the air with arms and legs spread wide. Definitely a bit of a showman, that one. He leaves behind a light blue trip line made of Kevlar, which they've asked us to drop off at the Coastguard station when we arrive in St John's.

The helicopter keeps pace with us for a moment longer, and then as Alan gives a thumbs up, he heads away from us, the noise of the rotors fading as both Labrador and Hercules disappear over the horizon. We've been battered by the deafening noise of the helicopter for the last 15 minutes. Now suddenly it's quiet, with just the familiar hum of Spirit's diesel engine. Now suddenly Alan and I are on our own, left to ponder the enormity of what has just happened. I feel a sense of emptiness as I watch the helicopter whisk Steve across the waves. Then the emotion starts to well up inside me, but for the moment, I keep it in check.

No sooner have we re-erected the antenna, than the radio bursts into life. A ship two miles away has been conducting seismic operations involving towing a very long seismic cable behind it. The master has quietly been having kittens, hoping we weren't going to end up cutting across his expensive cable. We reassure him that we'll alter course to keep clear, and that now all we want to do is make the best possible speed back into St John's.

Then Rescue Three-Two-Eight calls us up just to sign off, adding that they managed to capture some spectacular video of the rescue from their airborne vantage point. They invite us to join them for a drink in St John's if we manage to get back tonight. We won't make that kind of speed, and they're returning to their base in Halifax in the morning, while the helicopter will be going straight back to Gander after dropping Steve off, so sadly we won't get to buy any of the guys a beer.

And then it hits us. The stress of a nightmare day has taken its toll, and with Steve now safe in expert hands, Alan and I are both hit by a wave of emotion, triggered by trying to talk about it on camera. So we do as all good Brits do in a crisis, and brew up a cup of tea, then turn the boat towards St John's. There are some phone calls to be made, including to Steve's wife Jen, and I have to think about a news release which will state what has happened, but at this stage keep our options open.

We arrive in St John's the following morning, tired and spaced out, grabbing a cab for the hospital. Steve is hooked up to a heart monitor, on a drip - there are tubes and wires everywhere. He greets us with a big smile. We, on the other hand, feel as though the trapdoor has suddenly opened, taking our last remaining reserves of strength and willpower.

Alan and I have already discussed our options, but realistically, the decision has been made for us. So many times we've stared defeat in the face and been able to drag ourselves out of it. Mechanical problems, bad weather, lack of funds, intimidation and threats, illness and injury - we've surmounted all the problems and come up fighting.

But this time it's the end. Our voyage around the world is over.

EPILOGUE

They can still feel proud that they did what they did against all the elements nature threw at them. They will still get a hero's welcome as far as I am concerned.
Lorraine Barrett, Assembly Member, National Assembly for Wales.

SPIRIT OF CARDIFF never made it back to Gibraltar. The remaining 2,300 miles of the circumnavigation - five days in good conditions - might just as well have been another 23,000 miles, the distance we'd already travelled.

Steve was lucky to be alive. That was made clear to him by the head of the Coronary Care Unit in St John's. The only thing which had saved him from dying was his excellent state of fitness. He flew back to the UK with Alan a week later, after minor surgery.

Alan and I had decided not to carry on without him. Apart from having our confidence to tackle a major ocean crossing severely dented, at that point, we were simply in no fit state to carry on. We were both physically, mentally and emotionally shattered. We found it difficult to string words together coherently, we were walking as though drunk even before the bars were open, and our muscles and insides went into painful spasms. Alan had co-ordination problems, I found my eyesight had deteriorated. Anyway, without Steve - who'd not only come with us all the way round the world, but all of the trips beforehand - it would be an empty victory. What price a world record when you can't enjoy it with the crew mate who helped make it happen?

The boat went into storage at the Royal Newfoundland Yacht Club, and Alan and I hatched a plan to come back in September with Jan to bring the boat home. In the meantime, we discovered that as far as the UIM was concerned, the clock had never stopped ticking. So provided we could bring Spirit back to Gibraltar, the under 50 feet class record would still be ours. We decided to go for it.

When Jan and I flew out to St John's on September 14th, Alan had already been there a few days. With the help of Egbert Walters, he'd put the boat back in the water, and readied her for the final ocean crossing. We arrived in St John's to the news that there was a break in the weather. The boat had been fuelled up ready to go, and we were heading off straight away. In fact it was a wind-up, a pay-back from Alan for a telephoned practical joke we'd played on him earlier in the day. Ironically, if we had set off there and then, we would have avoided the boat's final ignominious fate.

As it was, we turned up at St John's harbour the following morning to find the boat sitting much lower than normal in the water. The dive platform at the back was submerged, and when we opened the engine box, we were horrified to see it flooded. The boat had always taken on a little water when at rest and heavily laden with fuel, but the bilge pumps had never had any problems coping with it. This time, something had gone seriously wrong with the water coming in so quickly, so quickly that two of the three bilge pumps had burned out through remaining on permanently.

Apart from the engine, looking sorry with water swilling around the block, the water had penetrated throughout the boat under the deck, so storage lockers which had last been flooded in the Caribbean were flooded once more, and all the carpets in the cabin were soaked.

On the plus side, had Spirit not been a RIB with inflatable tube, she would have sunk at her mooring. The minus side was that while the city of St John's prides itself on its cleanliness, the harbour has an awful pollution problem, with raw sewage discharged into the water. So not only was the boat flooded, but everything had been tainted with effluent - survival suits, life raft, sea anchor, and many other items of equipment which would cost thousands to replace.

We knew that if the boat was playing to form, we could stop the water coming in provided we made her lighter. So the thousand pounds' worth of fuel which had gone in the day before was pumped out at further expense - diesel which was simply driven away and dumped. We pumped out the water from the engine compartment to find the starter motor unwell, and the alternator completely wrecked.

Even with everything repaired, even if we'd been able to replace the survival equipment, the last boot had already swung back ready to kick us in the teeth. We'd missed our window of opportunity to get out. Hurricane Gustav had passed by, but it was just a matter of days before Tropical Storm Hannah was due to move in. It was always going to be a gamble trying to set off across the Atlantic at the start of the hurricane season, and it hadn't paid off. The final irony was that had we got out, our weather window would have given us 10 days of near perfect conditions across to the Azores, and on to Gibraltar.

With the boat out of the water once more, it transpired that our leak wasn't due to a cracked hull, as we thought initially, but a punctured or jammed float valve - a simple plastic ball - in one of the two scuppers which drain the boat. Under way, the scuppers ride out of the water, and they sit above the water line, except when the boat is fully fuelled with three tons of diesel. Something had made the float valve stick in the open position, allowing the boat to flood.

We had indeed been scuppered, and by nothing more than a ping-pong ball worth a couple of pence. We flew home again, feeling extremely low, on September 19th. It was five months and 19 days since we had left Cardiff on Easter Sunday.

◆ ◆ ◆

Alan Priddy subsequently found himself staring personal bankruptcy in the face. Steve Lloyd moved from contract carpet laying to domestic, which is less taxing on his heart. Jan Falkowski resigned his job as consultant psychiatrist at the London Hospital. He continues to race RIBs in his spare time with great success. I went back to travel writing.

Apart from a brief message following Steve's heart attack, none of us ever heard from Alan Carter again.

As for Spirit of Cardiff - her future is uncertain. It would be too expensive to have her shipped home, so she will almost certainly be sold in Canada, possibly to do whale-watching tours, or as a supply boat to the Hibernia oil platform in the North Atlantic. Whatever happens, she has been laid up to face the extreme conditions of a Newfoundland winter.

After three and a half years of effort and expense, the dream is over. If I'm disappointed, it's only that we never received the support we should have had for a world class expedition. Having fulfilled our part of the bargain and promoted Cardiff and Wales around the world, it seems unjust that we arrived home thousands of pounds in debt. While the general public was absolutely fantastic, it always appeared to us that the business community in Cardiff failed consistently to recognise what an amazing sponsorship opportunity the project had to offer.

Having crossed the Atlantic the previous year via St John's, you could argue that we'd already been around the world. And never mind the circumnavigation record, Spirit of Cardiff still ended up with a huge tally of world records which will be almost impossible to equal, let alone beat.

Appendix I

SPIRIT OF CARDIFF'S UIM LONG DISTANCE OFFSHORE WORLD RECORDS

Around the British Isles (first ever powerboat circumnavigation), June 2000; 2,146 nautical miles, 5 days 6 hours 5 minutes
Gibraltar to Monaco, October 2000; 774 nautical miles, 1 day 21 hours 49 minutes

Transatlantic
New York to Lizard Point, May 2001; 3,544 nautical miles, 10 days 8 hours 47 minutes
New York to Horta (under 50ft class), May 2001; 2,305 nautical miles, 6 days 12 hours 19 minutes

Around the world *
Gibraltar to Valletta, April 2002; 1,010 nautical miles, 6 days 21 hours 14 minutes
Valletta to Port Said, April 2002; 978 nautical miles, 2 days 0 hours 7 minutes
Port Suez to Jeddah, April 2002; 791.8 nautical miles, 2 days 3 hours 51 minutes
Jeddah to Aden, April 2002; 758 nautical miles, 1 day 18 hours 43 minutes
Aden to Salalah, April 2002; 618.2 nautical miles, 1 day 7 hours 23 minutes
Salalah to Mangalore, April 2002; 1,251 nautical miles, 3 days 13 hours 4 minutes
Mangalore to Galle, April 2002; 618 nautical miles, 1 day 7 hours 9 minutes
Galle to Sabang, April 2002; 950 nautical miles, 1 day 23 hours 48

minutes

Sabang to Singapore, April/May 2002; 610 nautical miles, 1 day 17 hours 26 minutes

Singapore to Kota Kinabalu, May 2002; 746 nautical miles, 1 day 18 hours 10 minutes

Kota Kinabalu to Subic Bay, May 2002; 585 nautical miles, 1 day 15 hours 17 minutes

Subic Bay to Naha, May 2002; 857 nautical miles, 2 days 7 hours 27 minutes

Naha to Choshi, May 2002; 1,050 miles, 6 days 7 hours 41 minutes

Choshi to Muroran, May 2002; 421 nautical miles, 1 day 5 hours 22 minutes

Muroran to Petropavlovsk-Kamchatskiy, May 2002; 1,056 nautical miles, 3 days 8 hours 52 minutes

Petropavlovsk-Kamchatskiy to Adak Island, May 2002; 957 miles, 2 days 22 hours 43 minutes

Adak Island to Kodiak, May/June 2002, 1,057 miles, 3 days 6 hours 49 minutes

Kodiak to Telegraph Cove, June 2002; 1,057 nautical miles, 2 days 23 hours 42 minutes

Telegraph Cove to Eureka, June 2002; 780 nautical miles, 2 days 6 hours 7 minutes

Eureka to San Diego, June 2002; 760 nautical miles; 2 days 10 hours 29 minutes

San Diego to Cabo san Lucas, June 2002; 760 nautical miles, 1 day 23 hours 0 minutes

Cabo san Lucas to Acapulco, June 2002; 752 nautical miles, 1 day 16 hours 14 minutes

Acapulco to Quetzal, June 2002; 555 nautical miles, 2 days 4 hours 5 minutes

Quetzal to Panama Balboa, June 2002; 857 nautical miles, 2 days 23 hours 37 minutes

Panama Colon to Port Antonio, June/July 2002; 587 nautical miles, 5 days 13 hours 30 minutes

Port Antonio to Fort Lauderdale, July 2002; 738 nautical miles, 1 day 20 hours 47 minutes

Fort Lauderdale to Wilmington, July 2002; 498 nautical miles, 1 day 5 hours 4 minutes

Wilmington to Halifax, July 2002; 952 nautical miles, 2 days 16 hours 24 minutes

Halifax to St John's, July 2002; 501 nautical miles, 1 day 3 hours 36 minutes

Unofficial world record
Suez Canal transit from Port Said to Port Suez, April 2002; 90 nautical miles, 8 hours 15 minutes

* Still to be ratified at time of going to press.

Appendix II

SPIRIT OF CARDIFF'S AROUND THE WORLD LEGS

Gibraltar - Valletta
Time of leg: 5 days 21 hours 14 minutes
Distance covered: 1,010 nautical miles
Average speed: 7.16 knots
Total elapsed time from Gibraltar: 5 days 21 hours 14 minutes
Total elapsed time at sea: 5 days 21 hours 14 minutes
Fuel consumed: 2,222 litres
Average fuel consumption: 2.2 litres / nautical mile

Valletta - Port Said
Time of leg: 2 days 0 hours 7 minutes
Distance covered: 978 nautical miles
Average speed: 20.4 knots
Total elapsed time from Gibraltar: 5 days 21 hours 14 minutes
Total elapsed time at sea: 5 days 21 hours 14 minutes
Fuel consumed: 2,053 litres
Average fuel consumption: 2.1 litres / nautical mile

Port Said - Jeddah
Time of leg: 3 days 12 hours 6 minutes
Distance covered: 791.8 nautical miles
Average speed: 9.4 knots
Total elapsed time from Gibraltar: 11 days 7 hours 51 minutes
Total elapsed time at sea: 10 days 9 hours 27 minutes
Fuel consumed: 1427.4 litres
Average fuel consumption: 1.8 litres / nautical mile

Jeddah - Aden
Time of leg: 1 day 18 hours 43 minutes
Distance covered: 758 nautical miles
Average speed: 17.7 knots
Total elapsed time from Gibraltar: 13 days 6 hours 2 minutes
Total elapsed time at sea: 12 days 4 hours 10 minutes
Fuel consumed: 1,638 litres
Average fuel consumption: 2.16 litres / nautical mile

Aden - Salalah
Time of leg: 1 day 7 hours 23 minutes
Distance covered: 618.2 nautical miles
Average speed: 19.6 knots
Total elapsed time from Gibraltar: 14 days 17 hours 25 minutes
Total elapsed time at sea: 13 days 11 hours 33 minutes
Fuel consumed: 1,208.9 litres
Average fuel consumption: 1.95 litres / nautical mile

Salalah - Mangalore
Time of leg: 3 days 13 hours 04 minutes
Distance covered: 1,251 nautical miles
Average speed: 14.7 knots
Total elapsed time from Gibraltar: 18 days 11 hours 4 minutes
Total elapsed time at sea: 17 days 0 hours 37 minutes
Fuel consumed: 2,418 litres
Average fuel consumption: 1.93 litres / nautical mile

Mangalore - Galle
Time of leg: 1 day 7 hours 9 minutes
Distance covered: 618 nautical miles
Average speed: 19.8 knots
Total elapsed time from Gibraltar: 20 days 4 hours 16 minutes
Total elapsed time at sea: 18 days 7 hours 46 minutes
Fuel consumed: 1,293 litres
Average fuel consumption: 2.09 litres / nautical mile

Galle - Sabang
Time of leg: 1 day 23 hours 48 minutes
Distance covered: 950 nautical miles
Average speed: 19.87 knots
Total elapsed time from Gibraltar: 22 days 17 hours 18 minutes
Total elapsed time at sea: 20 days 10 hours 43 minutes
Fuel consumed: 2,029 litres
Average fuel consumption: 2.13 litres / nautical mile

Sabang - Singapore
Time of leg: 1 day 17 hours 26 minutes
Distance covered: 610 nautical miles
Average speed: 14.7 knots
Total elapsed time from Gibraltar: 24 days 12 hours 41 minutes
Total elapsed time at sea: 22 days 1 hour 5 minutes
Fuel consumed: 1,285 litres
Average fuel consumption: 2.11 litres / nautical mile

Singapore - Kota Kinabalu
Time of leg: 1 day 18 hours 10 minutes
Distance covered: 746 nautical miles
Average speed: 17.69 knots
Total elapsed time from Gibraltar: 30 days 18 hours 24 minutes
Total elapsed time at sea: 23 days 19 hours 10 minutes
Fuel consumed: 1,428.5 litres
Average fuel consumption: 1.91 litres / nautical mile

Kota Kinabalu - Subic Bay
Time of leg: 1 day 15 hours 17 minutes
Distance covered: 585 nautical miles
Average speed: 14.9 knots
Total elapsed time from Gibraltar: 32 days 14 hours 17 minutes
Total elapsed time at sea: 25 days 10 hours 27 minutes
Fuel consumed: 1,026.4 litres
Average fuel consumption: 1.75 litres / nautical mile

Subic Bay - Naha
Time of leg: 2 days 7 hours 27 minutes
Distance covered: 857 nautical miles
Average speed: 15.44 knots
Total elapsed time from Gibraltar: 35 days 1 hour 48 minutes
Total elapsed time at sea: 27 days 17 hours 54 minutes
Fuel consumed: 1,853 litres
Average fuel consumption: 2.16 litres / nautical mile

Naha - Choshi
Time of leg: 6 days 7 hours 41 minutes
Length of leg: 1,050 nautical miles
Total distance covered: 10,823 nautical miles
Distance to go: 14,220 nautical miles
Average speed over leg: 6.92 knots
Total elapsed time from Gibraltar: 41 days 22 hours 41 minutes
Total elapsed time at sea: 34 days 1 hour 35 minutes
Fuel consumed: 1,973 litres
Average fuel consumption: 1.88 litres / nautical mile

Choshi - Muroran
Time of leg: 1 day 5 hours 22 minutes
Length of leg: 421 nautical miles
Total distance covered: 11,244 nautical miles
Distance to go: 13,620 nautical miles
Average speed over leg: 14.35 knots
Total elapsed time from Gibraltar: 44 days 16 hours 57 minutes
Total elapsed time at sea: 35 days 6 hours 57 minutes
Fuel consumed: 926 litres
Average fuel consumption: 2.2 litres / nautical mile

Muroran - Petropavlovsk-Kamchatskiy
Time of leg: 3 days 8 hours 52 minutes
Length of leg: 1,056 nautical miles
Total distance covered: 12,300 nautical miles
Distance to go: 12,620 nautical miles
Average speed over leg: 13 knots
Total elapsed time from Gibraltar: 48 days 7 hours 22 minutes

Total elapsed time at sea: 38 days 15 hours 49 minutes
Fuel consumed: 2,322 litres
Average fuel consumption: 2.19 litres / nautical mile

Petropavlovsk-Kamchatskiy - Adak Island
Time of leg: 2 days 22 hours 43 minutes
Length of leg: 957 nautical miles
Total distance covered: 13,257 nautical miles
Distance to go: 11,670 nautical miles
Average speed over leg: 13.53 knots
Total elapsed time from Gibraltar: 52 days 16 hours 13 minutes
Total elapsed time at sea: 41 days 14 hours 32 minutes
Fuel consumed: 2,162 litres
Average fuel consumption: 2.26 litres / nautical mile

Adak Island - Kodiak
Time of leg: 3 days 6 hours 49 minutes
Length of leg: 1,057 nautical miles
Total distance covered: 14,314 nautical miles
Distance to go: 10,770 nautical miles
Average speed over leg: 13.42 knots
Total elapsed time from Gibraltar: 56 days 19 hours 29 minutes
Total elapsed time at sea: 44 days 21 hours 21 minutes
Fuel consumed: 2,365 litres
Average fuel consumption: 2.24 litres / nautical mile

Kodiak - Telegraph Cove
Time of leg: 2 days 23 hours 42 minutes
Length of leg: 1,057 nautical miles
Total distance covered: 15,371 nautical miles
Distance to go: 9,770 nautical miles
Average speed over leg: 14.73 knots
Total elapsed time from Gibraltar: 60 days 13 hours 42 minutes
Total elapsed time at sea: 47 days 21 hours 3 minutes
Fuel consumed: 2,119 litres
Average fuel consumption: litres / nautical mile

Telegraph Cove - Eureka
Time of leg: 2 days 6 hours 7 minutes
Length of leg: 780 nautical miles
Total distance covered: 16,151 nautical miles
Distance to go: 9,120 nautical miles
Average speed over leg: 14.4 knots
Total elapsed time from Gibraltar: 63 days 12 hours 37 minutes
Total elapsed time at sea: 50 days 3 hours 10 minutes
Fuel consumed: 1,601 litres
Average fuel consumption: 2.05 litres / nautical mile

Eureka - San Diego
Time of leg: 2 days 10 hours 29 minutes
Length of leg: 760 nautical miles
Total distance covered: 16,911 nautical miles
Distance to go: 8,470 nautical miles
Average speed over leg: 12.99 knots
Total elapsed time from Gibraltar: 67 days 15 hours 59 minutes
Total elapsed time at sea: 52 days 13 hours 39 minutes
Fuel consumed: 1,987.9 litres
Average fuel consumption: 2.61 litres / nautical mile

San Diego - Cabo san Lucas
Time of leg: 1 day 23 hours 00 minutes
Length of leg: 760 nautical miles
Total distance covered: 17,671 nautical miles
Distance to go: 7,720 nautical miles
Average speed over leg: 16.17 knots
Total elapsed time from Gibraltar: 70 days 7 hours 30 minutes
Total elapsed time at sea: 54 days 12 hours 39 minutes
Fuel consumed: 1,315 litres
Average fuel consumption: 1.73 litres / nautical miles

Cabo san Lucas - Acapulco
Time of leg: 1 day 16 hours 14 minutes
Length of leg: 752 nautical miles
Total distance covered: 18,423 nautical miles
Distance to go: 7,020 nautical miles

Average speed over leg: 18.45 knots
Total elapsed time from Gibraltar: 72 days 1 hour 44 minutes
Total elapsed time at sea: 56 days 4 hours 53 minutes
Fuel consumed: 1,266 litres
Average fuel consumption: 1.68 litres / nautical mile

Acapulco - Quetzal
Time of leg: 2 days 4 hours 5 minutes
Length of leg: 555 nautical miles
Total distance covered: 18,978 nautical miles
Distance to go: 6,470 nautical miles
Average speed over leg: 10.67 knots
Total elapsed time from Gibraltar: 74 days 15 hours 50 minutes
Total elapsed time at sea: 58 days 8 hours 58 minutes
Fuel consumed: 1,045 litres
Average fuel consumption: 1.88 litres / nautical mile

Quetzal - Panama Balboa
Time of leg: 2 days 23 hours 37 minutes
Length of leg: 857 nautical miles
Total distance covered: 19,835 nautical miles
Distance to go: 5,620 nautical miles
Average speed over leg: 11.97 knots
Total elapsed time from Gibraltar: 78 days 6 hours 8 minutes
Total elapsed time at sea: 61 days 8 hours 35 minutes
Fuel consumed: 1,829.2 litres
Average fuel consumption: 2.13 litres / nautical mile

Panama Colon - Port Antonio
Time of leg: 5 days 13 hours 30 minutes
Length of leg: 587 nautical miles
Total distance covered: 20,422 nautical miles
Distance to go: 4,960 nautical miles
Average speed over leg: 4.40 knots
Total elapsed time from Gibraltar: 86 days 14 hours 39 minutes
Total elapsed time at sea: 66 days 22 hours 5 minutes
Fuel consumed: 740 litres
Average fuel consumption: 1.26 litres / nautical mile

Port Antonio - Fort Lauderdale
Time of leg: 1 day 20 hours 47 minutes
Length of leg: 738 nautical miles
Total distance covered: 21,160 nautical miles
Distance to go: 4,280 nautical miles
Average speed over leg: 16.49 knots
Total elapsed time from Gibraltar: 91 days 6 hours 6 minutes
Total elapsed time at sea: 68 days 18 hours 52 minutes
Fuel consumed: 1,439 litres
Average fuel consumption: 1.95 litres / nautical mile

Fort Lauderdale - Wilmington
Time of leg: 1 day 5 hours 4 minutes
Length of leg: 498 nautical miles
Total distance covered: 21,658 nautical miles
Distance to go: 3,800 nautical miles
Average speed over leg: 17.17 knots
Total elapsed time from Gibraltar: 92 days 21 hours 13 minutes
Total elapsed time at sea: 69 days 23 hours 56 minutes
Fuel consumed: 947 litres
Average fuel consumption: 1.90 litres / nautical mile

Wilmington - Halifax
Time of leg: 2 days 16 hours 24 minutes
Length of leg: 952 nautical miles
Total distance covered: 22,610 nautical miles
Distance to go: 2,850 nautical miles
Average speed over leg: 14.78 knots
Total elapsed time from Gibraltar: 96 days 2 hours 39 minutes
Total elapsed time at sea: 72 days 16 hours 20 minutes
Fuel consumed: 1,944 litres
Average fuel consumption: 2.04 litres / nautical mile

Halifax - St John's
Time of leg: 1 day 3 hours 36 minutes
Length of leg: 501 nautical miles
Total distance covered: 23,111 nautical miles
Distance to go: 2,300 nautical miles

Average speed over leg: 18.15 knots
Total elapsed time from Gibraltar: 97 days 14 hours 06 minutes
Total elapsed time at sea: 73 days 20 hours 11 minutes
Fuel consumed: 1,012 litres
Average fuel consumption: 2.02 litres / nautical mile

Total distance covered: 23,111 nautical miles
Total elapsed time from Gibraltar: 97 days 14 hours 06 minutes
Average speed overall: 9.87 knots
Total elapsed time at sea: 73 days 20 hours 11 minutes
Average speed at sea: 13.04 knots
Total fuel consumed: 46,875.3 litres
Average fuel consumption: 2.03 litres / nautical mile

NB: The difference between the total elapsed and at sea times only takes account of when the clock was officially stopped between each leg. Therefore delays such as the three days in Malta, and another three days ashore between Naha and Choshi have been counted as at sea.

Spirit of Cardiff
  Length: 33 feet (10 metres)
  Beam: 10 feet 6 inches (3.2 metres)
  Dry weight: 2.75 tons
  Fully laden weight: 6 tons
  Top speed: 35 knots
  Cruising speed: 20-25 knots